Fuelling the War

FUELLING THE WAR

Revealing an Oil Company's Role in Vietnam

Louis Wesseling

I.B.Tauris *Publishers*
LONDON • NEW YORK

Published in 2000 by I.B.Tauris & Co Ltd
Victoria House, Bloomsbury Square, London WC1B 4DZ
175 Fifth Avenue, New York NY 10010
Website: http://www.ibtauris.com

In the United States and Canada distributed by St. Martin's Press
175 Fifth Avenue, New York NY 10010

ISBN 1 86064 457 0

A full CIP record for this book is available from the British Library
A full CIP record for this book is available from the Library of Congress

Library of Congress catalog card: available

Typeset in Stone Serif by Dexter Haven, London
Printed and bound in Great Britain

CONTENTS

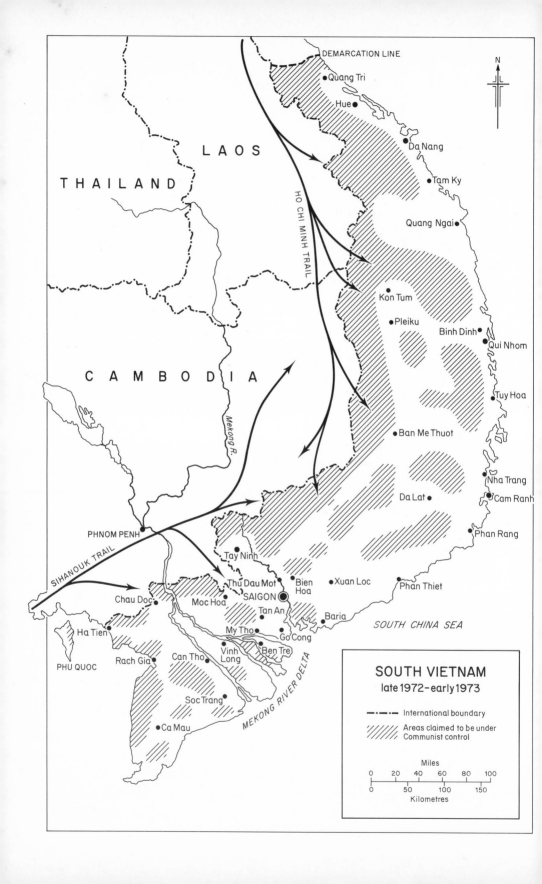

DEMARCATION LINE

Quang Tri

Hue

Da Nang

Tam Ky

Quang Ngai

L A O S

T H A I L A N D

HO CHI MINH TRAIL

Kon Tum

Pleiku

Binh Dinh
Qui Nhom

C A M B O D I A

Mekong R.

Ban Me Thuot

Tuy Hoa

Nha Trang
Cam Ranh

Da Lat

Phan Rang

PHNOM PENH

SIHANOUK TRAIL

Tay Ninh

Thu Dau Mot
Bien Hoa
Xuan Loc
Phan Thiet

Chau Doc

Moc Hoa

SAIGON

Tan An

Baria

Ha Tien

My Tho

Go Cong

SOUTH CHINA SEA

PHU QUOC

Rach Gia

Can Tho

Vinh Long

Ben Tre

MEKONG RIVER DELTA

Soc Trang

Ca Mau

SOUTH VIETNAM
late 1972–early 1973

—·—·— International boundary

/////// Areas claimed to be under
Communist control

Miles
0   20   40   60   80   100
0   50   100   150
Kilometres

Foreword

Vietnam and its war are like a virus in the soul – they never quite leave you. This is a personal story of the end of that war.

When I left Saigon on a bleak April day in 1975 on one of the last commercial flights out of the city, I was already committed to the next stage of my life. I had spent three years of that life running Vietnam's largest and strategically most important oil supply network and in the process had become sucked into what appeared to be one of the world's most intractable conflicts. Though I battled day-to-day to overcome the military, political, bureaucratic problems relating to supplying fuel to a war, I failed to realise how deeply I was becoming affected by the country. For all the corruption, degeneracy, destructiveness and death associated with the closing stages of the war, nothing could hide or suppress the spirit and ingenuity of its people, their warmth and their doggedness (even when it became infuriating stubbornness).

On that fateful April day leaving Saigon, before it became Ho Chi Minh city, I did not realise how impossible it would be to wash away the experience of those years. This book is in part the reflection of a need to come to terms with that period.

In part, the book also has a less self-indulgent purpose. Rarely can a business executive have had a better view of the interaction between conflict and commerce, between business and war. Shell in Vietnam was not a belligerent, nor indeed were its shareholders, directors or senior management participants in the war. Shell was a multinational corporation, founded as an Anglo-Dutch enterprise and now with a worldwide shareholding, engaged in the business of oil. As such, we considered ourselves beyond the fray, a normal commercial enterprise servicing clients, who happened to include the American and South Vietnamese military.

But oil is never beyond any fray. It is a commodity central to war. Vietnam was no exception. What gave Vietnam a new dimension was that Shell, the principal oil supplier to the anti-Communist war effort, also saw its oil going to Communist forces. The supply was – of course – not direct, but Shell's vast network of distributors, retailers and customers, including the military, provided ample opportunity for supplies to find their way into 'leakages'. By my estimate, some 7 percent of Shell's oil-flow into Vietnam ended up in Communist hands. Given the low-tech nature of the Communist war-effort (they used no vast fleets of jet fighters, bombers and helicopters), this probably meant that we ended up satisfying a large percentage of the Vietcong and

North Vietnamese oil needs in South Vietnam. The leaked oil helped to make possible their much-vaunted military mobility. It would be wrong to say that we as managers looked the other way. But as managers we also had the responsibility to produce profits and to make decisions. So we decided to stay the course, rather than withdraw, the only sure means to prevent our oil from reaching the Communists.

For Shell's top management in London and the Hague, the company's activities in Vietnam were loaded with contradictions and ambiguities. On the one hand, we were making a useful contribution to Shell's overall profits. And yet, our presence in Vietnam was regarded by many as distasteful, awkward and full of potential for adverse publicity. But then, Shell's vast presence in the United States was a crucial factor in our overall business interests, and had Shell pulled out of Vietnam, it would have dealt a body-blow to the American effort to sustain South Vietnam – hardly conducive to good relations with the all-important American administration.

Within this complicated framework of conflicting priorities, the company's top management did not want to face additional problems in operations – including the issue of oil leaking into 'enemy' hands. Part of the process that rationalised Shell's continuing presence in Vietnam was the acknowledgement that some things could not be acknowledged. From the perspective of Shell's top management, the company had a competent local manager whose brief was to spare the Shell name any embarrassment in Vietnam. I believe I succeeded in that purpose.

*   *   *

Many experts, of different nationalities, and friends have commented on drafts of my book, or have made helpful suggestions over the internet. Without naming them, I confess myself deeply indebted to all their contributions. Any possible remaining misconceptions are my own.

To my ex-colleagues in Shell, my apologies for synthesising their views and criticising with the benefit of hindsight our collective actions during the 1973 'oil crisis', which turned out to have such a dire effect on the South Vietnamese defence.

To my Dutch compatriots, finally, apologies for not writing in our own language, and for allowing a lifelong tinkering with English as a working language – and an English wife! – to take the upper hand.

L.W.

PART I

Year of the Mouse

1

Keepers of
the Grail

Shell Centre

I flew in from Brazzaville, a sleepless night-flight full of stops and fitful conversations with African politicians, world bankers and other fellow travellers of the economic circuit. London's wet and hearty welcome on that blowy morning in the spring of 1972 slapped me into a positive frame of mind, however. A smiling company driver picked me up from the Heathrow arrivals hall and delivered me in my crumpled light-weight suit, still reeking of liberally applied airline aftershave, directly to the Central Offices.

Shell Centre consists of a few concrete buildings around a squat tower on the South bank of the Thames. Its thousands of inmates and dozens of senior managers rarely take the time to enjoy the grand view over the Houses of Parliament on the other side, or to study the phases of the river as it rises twice a day from a muddy presence to a mighty stream in full flow. This is because 500 operating companies, from all around the world, keep throwing money and hot information at the Centre non-stop, while at the same time trying to prise out from it funds for reinvestment. And it is no mean feat to service all these demands. The result is an army of analysts, managers and directors, whose job it is to shuffle investments and international staff, like me, around the globe.

The infallible Personnel System had tossed my name on top of a list of candidates to head the Shell operating company in Vietnam. I felt lucky to be chosen, considering where I came from. The Director in charge of the Far East, A.E. Vizard, 'Vee' to his colleagues, had never set eyes on me and yet, on the strength of the System alone, we were already on first-name terms, chatting as if we had known each other a

3

lifetime. As my eye shifted to the familiar London panorama behind him, from Westminster Bridge, down to Battersea Power Station in the middle distance, past Chelsea and beyond, I wondered what my new life would hold in store for me.

The evening before, on the tarmac of the hot and humid airport of Brazzaville, in equatorial Africa, I had bid an emotional farewell to French and Congolese colleagues, with whom I had run an essential capitalist service under the unstable Marxist bureaucracies of Central Africa. Together we had hauled oil over the dirt tracks, along swollen rivers and decrepit railroads, from the mouth of the river Congo to the immense deserts of Chad. This had of course been a commercial enterprise, but it was also good to know that we had played our part in encouraging some measure of economic development despite the rapacious meddlings of the 'revolutionary' armed forces and their gun-toting soldiers, who never failed to arouse the contempt of even our humblest local crew members. Even last night these thugs had tried to impress, studying my exit visa in painful ignorance before passing it to their Cuban commander.

Opposite me, Vee settled back on the settee to hear my personal gloss on a career which he already knew from the System's staff reports. These gave a dry picture of life, its above-the-belt aspects, so to speak. I merely filled in the details, of how once upon a time, after learning Arabic at the British Foreign Office school in Lebanon, I had been sent to manage my first company on the barren peninsula of Qatar in the Persian Gulf, chosen for its excellent air and camel communications. Without much fixed investment, we were soon profitably buying and selling oil and chemicals throughout the Middle East and out-performing rivals with embarrassing ease, racking up 30 percent annual increases while building firm relations with the local and Palestinian élites who ran that part of the world. As a reward, Shell had promoted me back into the Centre, into a highly-regarded 'maturing' job, a well-meant compliment, but also the start of trouble. Here, Vee pricked up his sensitive ears. Having spent his whole working life in the London hierarchy, he had a habit of peering down over his glasses at junior overseas company managers. The way his mouth kept involuntarily opening and closing from sheer concentration made me smile.

I described what I had found in the Centre. Back in the sixties, when everyone else seemed engaged in singing and dancing and free love, the world's straight-laced technology-driven major oil companies kept transferring their own produce, anything but freely – indeed under tight control – from source to market within their own systems. These integrated companies, being producers of expensive crude oil in the US, Africa and Latin America (in the 'upstream' part of the oil business), were making sure that upstart independent producers of cheaper

Libyan crude would knock in vain at the door of the European market (part of the 'downstream'), which was to remain closed to them. (Occidental's Dr Hammer, without European refineries or market outlets, was foremost amongst these Independents.)

This meant, amongst other things, that the refining and marketing affiliates of the integrated multinational companies, such as I had managed in Africa and the Middle East, often paid higher prices for their crude than could be obtained from the independents. A glaring conflict of interest existed therefore inside the integrated multinationals between their 'downstream' affiliates, manufacturing and selling refined products to outside customers on the free market at the very end of the chain (from which I hailed) and their 'upstream' affiliates, who were responsible for extraction and production often at a cost significantly higher than oil produced by the Independents.

The highly sophisticated Exploration and Production Department, into which I had been promoted, was not only the heart of the 'upstream', but the dominant power within Shell. It lay safely ensconced inside the Centre, and took captive customers and ever-increasing prices for granted. For its investment proposals, it had a knack of replacing ruling market prices, almost by sleight of hand, by higher 'future planning values' to justify hundred million dollar investments bearing fruit perhaps in ten years. As guardians of the company's future, they pretended to see things more clearly than the mere marketers. Its lawyers, moreover, set great store by precise long-term profit-sharing agreements with developing countries, which, as I well knew, had no intention of observing legal niceties.

I simply could not adjust to the rarefied atmosphere of this capital-devouring ivory tower, which considered itself above the facts of supply and demand. Between the abundance of Libyan oil on offer at low prices, which our marketing affiliates and refineries were not allowed to buy, and the higher planning values used by the Exploration Department to justify technological achievements by its affiliates in ever more remote and inaccessible places all over the globe, yawned a credibility gap. Even managing directors and the board dared not risk their fingers in it. In any case, I never saw them turn down an investment proposal from the Exploration Department, these Guardians of the Holy Grail, no matter how far-fetched it seemed from a marketing perspective.

Where angels feared to tread, however, I jumped in with both feet. As I naively saw it, Exploration's need to field-test all the latest technologies in ventures dressed up as business opportunities wasted money which had been earned by people like me in the real market. Everyone knew that Middle East and Libyan oil were cheaper and more abundant than anything we could possibly produce elsewhere in the foreseeable future. It therefore annoyed me seeing optimistic geological and cost parameters routinely fed into the Centre's computers by highly qualified but disaffected minions to produce bogus 'economic' justifications for more exploration. In the long term, higher crude prices were essential to explore for oil and gas, for instance in the strategically important North Sea. But if the whole process could have been recognised for the problem of timing it really was, gambling with leading-edge technology and advanced mathematics on future price rises, economic results would have been far better. Against the use of multiple layers of management to produce merely obfuscation, I had recommended laying the roots clean by sharply reducing senior staff numbers.

This did not, however, suit one of the managing directors who told me to manipulate the existing manpower figures instead. Obviously, I had blotted my copy-book and been banned to Africa for my troubles.

Vee now began to smile thinly: a waiter in wine-red jacket meanwhile placed jugs and cups with Shell emblems on the table, and the Director ceremoniously poured out the insipid corporate coffee. What had attracted me to Vietnam, he inquired kindly. I mumbled something about Vietnam's fatal attraction to 'The Best and the Brightest', referring to the ironic title of David Halberstam's book which was a searing attack on the architects of the American military involvement in Vietnam, and we had our first good laugh together. But our laughter did not deny a basic truth which we both knew: Shell fundamentally supported the American intervention and considered the mistakes revealed by Halberstam as the inevitable fumbling of any large-scale enterprise. In fact, Vee's reputation rested in no uncertain fashion on his achievements in the British Army during the last war. Some said he had been a brigadier; others insisted he had never been in uniform at all. His language in any case was larded with military expressions like mission briefings, attack schemes, D-days, blitzes etc. Obviously he took great pride in assisting the American armed forces effort in Vietnam, although noticeably less so in supplying the South Vietnamese. He certainly lamented the untimely withdrawal of the American forces, whom he considered worthy customers.

The oil thirst of the American war had indeed been spectacular. The resulting increase in world oil consumption can only be grasped if seen as the sudden appearance of a new medium-sized industrialised nation on the map, like a massive island arising out of the ocean by geological accident. Tan Son Nhut, the sleepy South Vietnamese airport, became for a few years the busiest in the world in terms of take-offs and landings. The air war's fuel requirements exceeded by far that of major airlines. The US Navy's battleship and carrier fleets consumed oil like major city power-plants, and the ground war's thirst was simply insatiable. Moreover, the construction of modern war facilities resulted in the largest fuel contracts in the world, and Shell's fuel installation at Nha Be was the world's largest. Vee knew first-hand how profitable fuelling a war could be to the few who were able to supply on this scale. After weapons and ammunition, oil supplies constituted the US military's largest on-going cost item.

The terms under which all these supplies flowed were negotiated each year by Shell, Exxon and Caltex in Washington with the US Government Procurement Office. An American affiliate signed for Shell, but the actual transport and delivery of fuel and other products from refineries in Singapore was carried out by operating companies in Singapore and Vietnam. Vee took executive overall responsibility. Lately, the war had slowed its pace and our sales had somewhat decreased. Shell Vietnam's results now mainly depended on the oil consumed by the tanks, ships and aircraft of the South Vietnamese forces. Although American naval and air power was still a factor, the poor Vietnamese clearly had to fight a less energy-intensive war, and Vee rather doubted their staying power, especially after the last foreign troops had left Vietnamese soil. To me – though I kept quiet – that transition was the key to my interest in Vietnam and in taking the job.

I hardly listened to the Director describing the financial package, the luxuries of a Saigon lifestyle and his explaining with relish that our executives in Saigon had the highest risk allowances and death benefits in the Shell group of companies. Their spouses apparently enjoyed a dazzling staff compound with swarms of servants and English and French schooling for their children. The company itself was so predominant that any of its top Vietnamese executives could become government ministers any time they wished, if they did not mind exchanging Shell benefits for a meagre ministerial salary. We seemed to be on intimate terms with all the key members of the government. Moreover, the leader of the parliamentary opposition, Vu Van Mau, was also our company lawyer.

But there was a sting in the tail. Vee threw me a sharp glance before referring casually to the existence of malicious rumour and persistent British and French press reports – not substantiated – which claimed that our products sometimes crossed the fighting lines to fuel the communist war effort. Of course we denied any involvement. It was not our business to know where our products were disposed of once we had made delivery to a legitimate client. It was well known also that the North Vietnamese ran thousands of miles of pipelines into the South from their coastal harbours. Could it be perhaps, these reports asked in the same vein, that the North Vietnamese received tankers supplied from the same refinery sources as ourselves? Could it be that the smudgy little tankers under Chinese flags were carrying oil from Singapore over the high seas, right under the guns of Admiral Zumwalt's gleaming warships, right into North Vietnamese harbours? Vee did not know, and did not want to know. If any unsavoury or embarrassing dealings ever came to light, however, he would truthfully deny any knowledge of them. I alone would be answerable for my company's actions. Obviously, London would not hesitate to fire me if I violated their 'trust', and I thought that entirely reasonable. We laughed and went to lunch.

In the corporate dining room, two dozen individuals converged on the table at the sound of a gong. They were directors and key executives of different nationalities, colour and age who happened to be passing through. The family resemblance was striking nevertheless. We wore dark two-piece suits and spoke in clipped tones as from a shared data-bank. All of us had conducted negotiations with governments and businesses at the highest levels, and could make lucid presentations at the drop of a hat, but we would have been hard pressed to make our own airline bookings.

Pre-lunch drinks had softened the edges, and I was the object of much leg-pulling and mock condolences for my new appointment in Vietnam. Indeed, I had enjoyed more prestige before, as a junior in the Exploration and Production Department. My current standing as General Manager of a far-away operating company was hardly impressive. Vietnam, that central issue of our generation, was a fringe interest to this select club, whose members' standing was determined by their proximity to the strategic core of the world oil business alone. Proximity was the word, because claiming actual individual influence over such a vast international industry would be ludicrous.

The executives around the table probably had the rising international oil worries reflected in their blood pressures. Oil had come of age. We saw ourselves no longer as the swashbuckling profiteers of the bad old days, when local gluts were allowed to alternate freely with scarcities and low prices with rollicking high ones. Instead, we prided ourselves on being the conscientious intermediaries of the world's most explosive and largest traded commodity. The Organisation of Oil Producing Countries (OPEC) having established a producer cartel in 1960, we saw ourselves above all as careful negotiators with them on everything from prices to volumes, always – of course high-mindedly – on behalf of the consumers. We particularly prided ourselves on the conclusion of the 1971 Teheran Agreement stabilising the world price of oil for the foreseeable future. Since then, however, OPEC had found its stride, engaging in hostile rhetoric and imposing punitive taxes and outright nationalisations. Instead of freeing up markets by welcoming US independents and French or Italian or even Soviet newcomers into the supply line, we had allowed ourselves to be pushed into a lobby which was prepared to play OPEC's price-fixing game. While struggling valiantly to negotiate and exert control over prices, there was a nagging doubt, however, that we were fighting the wrong strategic battle. The one sure thing in our minds was the near and violent demise of the current world oil trading system as we knew it.

Over smoked salmon, one raconteur entertained us with his own latest OPEC experiences, travelling with the white-robed Arab ministers from Baghdad back to London. Not only did these Muslims insist on drinking their whisky from teacups, but on arrival changed into Savile Row suits to sample the illicit pleasures of London without the handicap of their flowing national dress.

Then, over beef and burgundy (the calorie warning on the menu was there to be ignored), an oil trader bemoaned the Arab obsession with Israel and OPEC Resolution 120, which kept increasing the stakes from one ministerial confrontation to the next. He still put his faith, however, in Saudi princes to keep us supplied in case of conflict. But had he listened to the news in Arabic, he would have realised that behind the super-rich Saudis, Kuwaitis and other Gulf emirs within their arbitrary borders, stood the demands of 80 million have-not Arabs. We had stone-walled those claims for too long. Now we had passed the point at which any Saudi prince, or Shah of Iran, could halt the slide towards confrontation. Someone suggested military action to hold the line against the Gaddafis of the Arab world, odd though it seemed that we should abdicate our own responsibility and talk of war as a remedy. And what could be the aim? The roll-back of Arab domination over territories conquered under the banner of Islam twelve centuries ago? The liberation of the Berbers and the other autochtones of Northern Africa? Nobody had thought that through. But it surely would put the Vietnam war in the shade.

Meanwhile, as I listened bemused to the idle chatter of some of the world's top oil men, I noticed, looking from the high window, that the Thames had shrunk back to a sliver, hardly flowing at all between the brown pebbles of low tide. After spending the rest of the afternoon in briefings with financial and marketing experts up and down the tower, I had more than enough of Central Office overviews. I took a colleague to a pub in the shadow of Shell Centre, built into the blackened brick vaults of a Victorian railway bridge, to toast with her my dreadful Vietnam assignment.

2

Who Are these Vietnamese?

A Historical Point of View

Vietnam: what forces had shaped the exceptional character of its people? The first impression of the new arrival in the countryside in 1972 in the middle of one of the most brutal, modern high-technology wars of the twentieth century was that the country had experienced no visible change at all over the last thousand years. The languid river delta itself was clearly eternal. The women under their conical hats worked the fields exactly as in antique drawings, dressed identically too. Their tools for cutting or husking the rice had never developed. Not even the wheel had caught on for other uses than the ox-cart. The barefoot peasants had not adopted it wholeheartedly, and were still fashioning it out of straight planks, despising the Europeans, who had to cling to highways in servitude to the wheel. Right under the landing approaches of the jumbo jets to the modern airports, impenetrable bamboo hedges still shielded the secretive hamlets and their councils of elders against all outsiders, be they the Emperor's robed mandarins of old, French officials, American soldiers, the grasping bureaucrats of President Thieu, or the fierce tax-collectors of the Vietcong.

It was not the infinity of the delta, but rather the bamboo hedge which symbolised the mindset of the poor in a world that had given them nothing. The cities abounded with young superficially open-minded intellectuals, but the peasants, 80 percent of the total population, simply gazed at outsiders through blank eyes, like their buffaloes standing nostril-deep in the pools and irrigation ditches. According to them, Heaven alone ordains the rice-growing cycle, and with it the miserable lives of man and beast. And everywhere, shrines for the ancestors occupied the best land. Superstition reigned, and

10

mystic leaders could found new creeds with millions of devoted followers in a few decades. Thus, Ngo Van Chieu created the Cao Dai religious sect in 1919, with saints like Buddha, Victor Hugo and Sun Yat Sen, complete with a main temple in Tay Ninh and a powerful private army. The peasants' keen practical intelligence only truly shone when fighting for their lives, or for the freedom to improve their lot, as the Americans would discover to their cost.

What, then, made this people of contrasts, which seemed so slow in social and economic progress, so invincible in war? Reviewing Vietnam's history of geographic expansion, one reason stands out. The impossibility of feeding the chronic population surplus in the region has always made the conquest of arable land to the south a survival condition. It turned the peasant into a hardy warrior. Losses of life in war were not only acceptable, but part of the solution for a surplus population. Peasants, however, cannot write history books, and the tiny élite of city *literati* never cared to dwell on such facts. They much preferred to describe the noble causes and the *beaux gestes* of emperors and courtiers. But the reality sings through loud and clear. Land hunger, caused by famine, pushed the Vietnamese tribes, from their first incursion into the northern Red River delta 1500 years ago, into all the rich ground towards the southern ocean. They carved out the nation and shaped the national character of extreme attachment to the land and of unlimited endurance to hardship.

The unfettered simplicity of the Vietnamese peasant community, even the backwardness, was a weapon. The Viets carry no unnecessary social or cultural burdens into battle. They were, and still are, no inventors, builders of great monuments, or traders. As early as the fifth century, after covering the Red River delta with family-sized rice plots, a deprived but armed peasant family had no choice but to advance southwards to forage for itself, or had to allow warlords and other powerful foragers on the drive into the south (sometimes several at a time) to recruit their sons. Sated sedentary opponents – like the indigenous Cham, who had lived in what is now central Vietnam since neolithic times – though culturally and economically more developed, could not sustain the centuries-long gradual onslaught from the northern Viets. Their complicated centralised government structures broke down towards the end of the fifteenth century. Their intricate temples and large-scale irrigation channels were destroyed by the Viets, who planted rice over their graves. 'Barbarian' and less developed nomadic tribes from within the region were simply pushed out of the way, up into the mountain ranges, unsuitable for rice culture, where they still survive today on 'slash and burn' agriculture and hunting. The Khmer kingdom, containing what is now Cambodia and South Vietnam, became the next victim. In the late seventeenth century their capital city, later renamed Saigon, was conquered by the Viets, and Cambodia itself could only be saved from them by the French declaring it a protectorate in 1863.

The history of Vietnam as the Vietnamese would tell it in those days, with a twentieth century gloss, was a very different one from the story of a war-like peasant population expanding southwards in search of fertile land and food. For the Vietnamese historians, their glorious past consisted of a string of brilliant military victories and the occasional heroic defeat against the Chinese Emperor. The country's intelligentsia had no interest in the peasant origins of their culture. The most common pejorative amongst city dwellers was 'nha que', 'peasant'. Embarrassed by their land-grabbing past and their later easy submission to the French, and by a conspicuous lack of home-grown economic and scientific development, Vietnamese intellectuals needed a glorious national identity to anchor their self-respect. They therefore created a romantic past, pitting themselves against China as a powerful and stern father-figure from whom they constantly struggled to break loose. Only the Chinese were an opponent worthy of the Vietnamese. Out went the historical facts of their own humble beginnings as a Chinese tribe in search of food. In came the glorious myth of the noble natives, true descendants of the Dragon King, defending their country against the Celestial Empire. The mythical Vietnamese victories and the rousing speeches of legendary leaders, like the warrior Trung Sisters and Lady Trien Au fighting in golden armour on elephant-back, were learnt by heart in every school. The Vietnamese acceptance among the educated classes of wholesale indoctrination was not something that came to the country for the first time with Ho Chi Minh.

In fact, the Vietnamese were a tribe of Chinese origin which gained a foothold beyond the southern borders of the Heavenly Empire. An 'independent' Vietnamese Empire was established only in 967, but it seems to have lapsed often, and strings of victories were needed to restore it. Still, according to Vietnamese court accounts, throughout these struggles, the 'victorious' Vietnamese Emperors kept paying tribute to their Chinese overlord in the Middle Kingdom, like any other vassal. Their capitals in Hue and Hanoi were small-scale copies of Beijing, complete with concentric walls, forbidden cities within and artisans' quarters outside, while Vietnamese rulers wrote in Chinese ideographs and applied the same Confucian moral principles relating to family and justice. In perspective, therefore, the wars with China seem more like family quarrels, compared with the bloody day-to-day business of the ongoing southern conquest. War or no war, Chinese from Yunan continued to run the Vietnamese copper, zinc and silver mines and most of its trade, as they have done in modern times.

For as long as the peasants were allowed to expand southwards, they maintained a superficial allegiance to the various dynasties of rulers in Hue, who must have seemed as far away from them as heaven from earth. In the middle of the sixteenth century, however, European trade and influence began to encroach directly on the population. The court, until then mainly involved in ceremonies, scholastic mandarin education and taxation, was intrigued by the new weapons, and allowed the Portuguese to work for them as founders of artillery pieces. After Portugal's decline in the seventeenth century, it allowed the Dutch, after many gifts to court mandarins, to introduce their florins as the official currency and to manage the export of all local products – wood, tusks, lacquer and silk from factories on the coast – in direct collaboration with the population. The court, however, feared the power of direct commerce, and began to obstruct the foreign merchants.

A century of imperial decline later, the French entered the scene with missionaries and mercenaries. They helped Gia Long defeat his rivals to the throne and establish a new dynasty. In 1802, the court allowed French Jesuit missionaries to transcribe the traditional Chinese ideographs into the more accessible Roman script for the Vietnamese language. Conceived and used as a basis for the spread of popular education, the script known as *Quoc Ngu* is still in universal use. For the first time, the mandarins no longer held the monopoly over the written word. The peasants, with new markets for their produce, were overjoyed. In the course of the nineteenth century, however, emperor Gia Long's xenophobic successors, Minh Mang and Thieu Tri, reneged on the treaty with France and, fearing loss of control over the population, began to strangle the barbarian intrusions in red tape, and to kill some foreigners. Under these conditions, trade seemed pointless, but French missionaries and colonialists hung on nevertheless.

A despondent French missionary wrote in 1878, 'Only through greater freedom for commerce and individual initiative in the choice of cultures and products can the richness of this country develop. As long as the Imperial government regulates everything, orders certain cultures, prohibits others and creates monopolies of the State, it is impossible for agriculture to develop.' Those words still apply. Foreign trade and new ideas had been bypassing the inhospitable Vietnamese coasts for a long time. It comes as no surprise therefore that the increasingly isolated and backward court, powerless to oppose French encroachment in the south, could be casually overthrown by a few hundred French adventurers on their way back from China. In 1873, the Hanoi citadel was taken, under the eyes of a peasant population totally indifferent to the fate of their rulers. Thus the French domination of

Vietnam became officially complete in 1887 when emperor Dong Khanh was forced to accept French colonial status for his country.

This event could have marked the start of democratic institutions. The new French Governor, like colonials elsewhere, however, found it easier to use the existing imperial court for the ratification of his decrees. Henceforth, Emperors were to be selected by the Governor and educated in France, their decrees written by the new élite of French and Vietnamese graduates from modern schools, rather than by unworldly mandarins. Even after the fall of the Chinese Empire in 1911, the French kept propping up the Vietnamese imperial facade, while transforming the economy with a flood of technical innovations. New drainage works doubled the rice acreage, and for the first time conquest was no longer the only alternative to starvation. But once again, only the city élite were favoured with education. If they adopted the French language, rapid advancement was assured. The new harbours and railroads, and the plantations of rubber and sugar mainly benefited them and the big landowners, while 95 percent of the rice-growing population were left as exploited and ignorant as before, and equally disaffected. In fact, the new taxes on salt, opium and alcohol pressed harder on them than on the townspeople with their three times higher income. The traditional peasant lethargy therefore came to be punctuated by angry revolts, which flashed like brush fire and died just as quickly without leading to change. Peasants had numerous grievances, but as yet no unifying ideology. They were the tinder box waiting for a match, as Mao had already observed in China.

In 1930, when the system was reeling from a worldwide recession and a catastrophic fall in rubber, rice and sugar prices which bankrupted French and Vietnamese plantations, a peasant revolt with a difference broke out in the over-populated Ha Tinh and Nghe Anh provinces. Farm labour unemployment and hunger were the immediate cause, but this time there was a vital difference: a Communist leadership, which had managed to acquire real influence.

The Indo-Chinese Communist Party, founded a few years before, originally held that in the 'correct' scheme of things only the Party, representing the 'urban proletariat', could initiate revolutions, whereas the peasant revolt had been spontaneous. 'Urban Proletariat' was an imported figure of speech. It did not yet exist in Vietnam. All Party members were French-speaking journalists, teachers, students, sons of mandarins, without a labourer amongst them, as elitist as all governments or aspiring governments of Vietnam had ever been. But of all opposition groups, they were the only ones to recognise (after agonising reappraisal) that in Vietnam power lay not with the intelligentsia, the police or the army, but with the overwhelming rural majority. They succeeded in capturing control over the peasant leadership and propagated themselves as the 'Soviets of Nghe Anh'. In 1931, the French, with barely 20,000 local troops in a country of 20 million, restored order easily. But in those few months, the legend was created, linking French authority forever with the shedding of Vietnamese blood.

In other respects, not much had changed. Colonial rule, under Governor Georges Decoux, set a perfectly acceptable standard to the majority of educated city Vietnamese. They did not mind that he supported the Vichy government in France against de Gaulle during World War II. In particular, they admired his skill at keeping Vietnam out of the war, even if at the price of collaboration with Japan. The prospects for a peaceful post-war decolonisation seemed reasonable.

If one Western statesman can be called responsible for destroying those prospects and for plunging that fair and fairly peaceful Vietnam into a 30-year war against France and America, and finally against itself, it has to be General de Gaulle. Convinced that only a French feat of arms could earn a seat for him at the forthcoming Allied Summit on Asia, he – all on his own and behind Governor Decoux's back – issued the fatal order directly to the French forces to eliminate the Japanese forces. The Japanese general, upon interception of the order, attacked pre-emptively, destroyed the French forces and locked survivors up in the Hanoi citadel to die of hunger. That led to catastrophe. By early 1945, Hanoi was a city clean of rats, which had been eaten as good protein by the population. A million, perhaps two million, somnambulant living skeletons died of hunger all over North Vietnam. The famine was due directly to the breakdown of the colonial infrastructure. Northern peasants had been forced to grow cotton for Japanese uniforms instead of rice for themselves. Normally they could count on the abundant rice stocks in the south, but with the French civilians, on whom transport and railroads depended, in concentration camps, the fragile supply and government structure, and all communications, collapsed. Burials in Hanoi became hurried mass affairs, not at all proper for a people who revere the dead. Nobody knows the number of these dead, but the physical and moral degradation of the survivors made a peaceful transfer of power totally illusory.

The bomb on Hiroshima ended the war in 1945 and pushed the demoralised Japanese back into their barracks. It also created a power vacuum in Vietnam. The old national political parties were debilitated. The French were out of action, and only a few thousand Communist guerrillas in the mountains on the Chinese border, fed, armed and supported by the Chinese – and, ironically, the Japanese and US representatives, both fearful of chaos – remained capable of action. Their charismatic, Moscow-trained leader, Ho Chi Minh, also an able opportunist, risked little and had everything to gain from marching his troops into the enfeebled capital of Hanoi itself. He seized his chance.

His male and female shock troops, in shorts or black trousers, hurried in before the Allied armies' arrival. Other Vietnamese nationalists, ravaged by hunger, tried to counter with popular rallies, but found themselves hijacked at the point of a gun, their places usurped by Red Brigades who taught the eager crowds to raise clenched fists and chant revolutionary slogans. The population was fed with the remaining rice stock as well as the relief food hastily shipped in by the Allies, for all of which Ho Chi Minh took the credit, to the acclaim of the genuinely grateful people. Even the Emperor Bao Dai, in his lonely palace in Hue, who only knew his people from their backs as they prostrated themselves before him, now terrorised by the Communist murder of his viceroys, abdicated in favour of the republic proclaimed by Ho Chi Minh. The Party history books call it the 'Glorious August Revolution'. It would keep the tiny élite of Communist leaders, in their thirties at the time, in power until their deaths from old age in Hanoi, far beyond the failure of their political ideas.

The country was now split in two, following a decision taken a few months before at the Potsdam conference in 1945, where the Allies had allocated the occupation of the North to the Chinese and of the South to British forces. Historical precedent for the split existed: several times in the past the South and the North had fought each other, under different dynasties of warlords. In the seventeenth century, the South had beaten the combined forces of the North and their allies the Dutch fleet, by the innovative use of rowed galleons. In the disorganised South of 1945 however, the Communists were just one group amongst many competing nationalist, religious and warlord groupings, and had been unable to establish ascendancy. The British Gurkhas restored order and, on their heels, the French had repossessed that part of their colony. The South thereby retained the old regime.

In the northern capital Hanoi, however, the US representatives, anxious to dismantle and displace the colonialism of Europe, together with the remnants of the Japanese army, and keen to please their victorious people, prevented the return of the French. The result was that revolutionary chaos reigned everywhere. Slogans splashed on every wall, and on the hides of buffaloes, shouted 'Down with taxes!', 'Down with colonialism', 'Down with the Bank of Indo-China!' Ho's own comrades thrived on adversity, but of peacetime management they knew nothing. They organised Hanoi schoolgirls in white *ao dai*s to march past his palace singing, 'We love you, Uncle Ho', just as the same delicate creatures had been organised to sing, 'We love you, Marshall Petain' a few months before. Ho grandiosely abolished gambling, banks and prostitution, along with all taxes. These last were now called 'voluntary contributions' and extracted twice as ruthlessly. During 'Gold Week' women were forced publicly to throw wedding rings and ornaments into melting pots, a terrible predicament for families whose gold was the only shield against bad times. Moreover, it went straight into the pockets of the Chinese and the Japanese in return for weapons for the Red Guards. But when, in accordance with the Potsdam Agreement, a ragtag Chinese occupation army began to swarm in from the north, like locusts, in torn yellow uniforms, looting their way through Vietnam, cold reality set in.

Ho himself called back the French, the old colonial masters, to restore order, and not a moment too soon. They alone had the administrative know-how to take practical measures, like abolishing the 500 piastre note, which the Chinese had counterfeited and given to their troops, and realigning the currency to stop the sell-out of Vietnam to the Chinese. They alone were able to negotiate the withdrawal of the Chinese, by the surrender of all French territorial claims on China. For a brief period, and for the sake of appearances, Ho tolerated a coalition government, but ministerial titles meant little. Communist Party members retained control of the army and of all other vital institutions, reporting to the ministers in theory only. With his economic base and territorial integrity assured by the French, Ho had his hands free to negotiate amiably throughout the summer and into the autumn of 1946 with successive French governments in Fontainebleau about degrees of independence. Meanwhile, his militia at home systematically eliminated his Vietnamese opponents.

This last chance for a negotiated transfer of sovereignty, however, came to naught because the weak French governments of the Fourth Republic could not bring themselves to cut their losses and let go of their colonies, like the British and Dutch, for whom colonies had always been more of an economic than an ideological issue. But one has to respect French political rectitude: Ho was a Communist, and his access to power would have meant the speedy elimination of any democratic freedom in Vietnam, Cambodia and Laos, and perhaps elsewhere. In the wake of Mao's victory in China over Chiang Kai Chek in 1949, and the North Korean attack a year later, the Communist advance in Asia might well have become unstoppable. The line against Communist ambitions had to be drawn somewhere, and the French, to their honour, recognised that.

So, inevitably the French expeditionary army began to clash with the Communist forces in North Vietnam, giving Ho Chi Minh the opportunity to withdraw his troops to the mountain bases on the Chinese border, to regain the single-mindedness needed for the long war of liberation with which he hoped to emulate Mao's Long March. Many families sent their sons to serve with him, to balance other sons' service with the French, because self-interest comes first with a Vietnamese family and it always hedges its bets. A medical doctor, brother of the anti-Communist Governor of Hanoi, was transported with his family and belongings to Ho's mountain base, where he became the communist Minister of Health, in charge of war hospitals and the teaching of basic hygiene in the jungle.

The French political tactics to re-impose themselves in Vietnam were, to put it mildly, not well judged. They put the discredited ex-Emperor Bao Dai back on the throne and imposed the 'Union Française' on Vietnam. Instead of insisting on a prime ministership for a reformist national party leader, such as Hanoi Governor Nguyen Huu Tri, endorsed by General de Lattre and by the American advisers, they allowed Bao Dai to promote old cronies and stifle political development. Without political freedom, the regime of Bao Dai turned amazingly quickly from initial benevolence to suppression. But then the Vietnamese had never tasted the luxury of freedom.

Perhaps more influential than politics was the choice of military options. There were two wars: the conventional military one and the primitive one of the villages. Whoever controlled the watery rice fields with the majority of the population, denying food and recruitment sources to the adversary, was bound to prevail. Foreigners might win conventional battles, but they could not win the village war. Governor Tri of Hanoi therefore had armed the peasants and encouraged them to organise themselves into self-supporting villages. The experiment showed that control of the rice fields, the real issue of the war, could indeed be achieved by local forces. This in turn would draw the Communist main force out of their mountain hideouts into the open delta, where they would be at a disadvantage.

The French, however, wavered in their support for Vietnamese troops, and the American generals, used to bankrolling the French expeditionary force to the tune of $700 million a year, could not even think in terms of cheap popular welfare, obsessed as they were by the possible recurrence of the Korean nightmare: the appearance of millions of heavily-armed Chinese 'volunteers' on the border. The crusty American generals, speaking neither French nor Vietnamese, wanted heavy divisions under Western commanders to fight the Korean war all over again. They did not care for training and outfitting lightly-armed Vietnamese militia to fight lightly-armed Communists in their own way, as even Bao Dai had implored them to do.

And yet, even in their pitifully neglected state, those same mobile militias of Vietnamese and Laotian highlanders were undeniably doing most of the fighting and taking over half the battle casualties. At Phat Diem, Nam Truc, Nghia Lo, Mao Khe and Dien Bien Phu, Vietnamese and Meo soldiers held firm after the French regular forces had given up the battle. On their own, they harassed and frustrated superior communist divisions in the field, while the French locked themselves up inside their fixed fortifications. History books have concentrated on the French action, because their generals wrote the memoirs. But Vietnamese have claimed ever since that a fraction of the billions of dollars spent on the slow-moving French mercenaries would have sufficed to establish a strong Vietnamese force for a different outcome.

The French and American strategy finally collapsed when 15,000 of the French Expeditionary Corps, by all accounts badly prepared and led, provoked a senseless conventional battle at the remote hill-fortress of Dien Bien Phu, far from any strategic objective. There, General Giap, assisted by Chinese generals and a Chinese supply line, defeated them in the spring of 1954. The aftermath was a very Asian affair, often glossed over. Of the 12,000 captives, 9000 would not survive the hunger, disease, punishment and brainwashing of the prison camps. For every soldier fallen in battle, three died in the camps. President Eisenhower went on record with glowing praise for the defence of Dien Bien Phu, describing it as a 'gallant outpost of France', urging France 'to continue the war, true to the honour and glory of its heroic past' but quite ominously not honouring the valiant Vietnamese fighters with a single word. Half the 'French' casualties had been Vietnamese. In spite of these encouraging words, the French withdrew in accordance with a Geneva peace agreement brokered by Chinese diplomats (the same individuals who would later help Nixon extricate himself from Vietnam). The French had to surrender all territories north of the seventeenth parallel because they were truly beaten.

By the time I arrived in Saigon, 18 years later, in 1972, the Americans had come close to being beaten themselves by repeating the French mistakes to a staggering extent.

3

Handover in Saigon

First Warnings

As my Air France Boeing 747 was beginning its descent to Saigon, down in that city the man I was coming to replace climbed into his car for the drive to Tan Son Nhut International Airport to meet me. The Shell Mercedes, with the chauffeur in starched white uniform, shot out from the pillared office entrance, swung into the fast lane of the Thong Nat boulevard and sped past the US Embassy and the presidential palace. The only other white Mercedes of the same old vintage belonged to the occupant of that palace, and in the driver's view both of them had automatic preference over all other traffic. In the Hai Ba Trung boulevard, however, overloaded scooters, hand-drawn carts and Renault taxis held together by string, inevitably slowed him down to a snail's pace. The driver cocked an apologetic eyebrow in the rear mirror at his soon-to-be-ex-boss, Mike Corrie, whose lower jaw was sticking out like a barracuda's. The golden Shell clasp with three diamonds on his tie was his badge of honour for 25 years of international service to the Shell empire.

The last three of those he had spent dominating the Vietnamese operating company, Cong Ty Shell Vietnam. It had come into being casually in 1911, when Henri Deterding, a founding father of Shell, had arrived for a tiger hunt in the Vietnamese highlands. Here was a region which provided an ideal outlet for lamp-oil from Deterding's production in the Dutch East Indies, and right from the start the market had exceeded even his high expectations. From the French administration, Shell had unashamedly obtained a colonial decree, giving it the lion's share of the civil market in Vietnam, Laos and Cambodia, as well as the exclusive right to supply the army. After the French defeat in 1954, it had abandoned its properties in North Vietnam to the communists and had retreated with most of its loyal North Vietnamese executives to a new neo-colonial baroque office in Saigon, where it proved equally adept at working the South Vietnamese free market. Flexibility is the hallmark of a good company. English-speaking staff were hired to replace the French, to cater to the growing American influence. Meanwhile, the old Shell storage tanks left behind in the North became the number one item on the US airforce bombing targets list. Their eventual destruction, however, never choked off the oil supplies to the communists, as I was soon to discover.

Following the retreat, Shell's southern installations, but particularly the main one at Nha Be, outside Saigon, had to be quickly extended to handle the vast flow of oil products to the American forces there. It had grown by leaps and bounds, into one of the world's largest oil storage facilities without much thought of vulnerability to attack from the outside.

Mike thought in fact that the main threat to his business came from within, from his own Vietnamese staff. He was proved wrong much later, when it became known that they had not been infiltrated by communists at all. But Mike had powerful psychological reasons for distrusting local staff, having, in a previous existence, been part of the local staff of Shell's old Egyptian operations. His attitude was still shaped by Shell's setback in Egypt. The nationalisation, without compensation, of Shell's oil installations by President Nasser, together with the subsequent Suez Canal nationalisation, was to Mike, then a young and idealistic Egyptian executive, akin to a betrayal by his countrymen of his beloved employer Shell. He severely criticised his Egyptian Shell colleagues for allowing themselves to be bought to run the nationalised oil industry, the Suez canal itself and a host of other state enterprises. For him there was no choice but to leave Egypt. Mike changed his surname from Khoury to Corrie, joined the Shell international staff and never looked back.

Now, in Vietnam, he had compulsively put international staff, dependent on him for promotion, over long-serving outstanding Vietnamese. Moreover, by restricting the flow of information and limiting subordinate managers to narrow spheres of competence, he both provoked and enjoyed the resulting boundary disputes and the in-fighting which landed him the role of pivotal arbiter. If such problems arose, he alone could solve them, and if he did so successfully few would question why they had arisen in the first place. On the old French experts, who instinctively distrusted him because he did not understand their language, he turned the tables by changing the written company language to English. He worked hard, checking every detail, but in the end he wore himself out, as his outlook on life soured and his touch became less certain.

On my final descent to Tan Son Nhut airport, meanwhile, I had my first look at Vietnam. The green mountains had given way to flooded rice fields, criss-crossed by roads. Rays of slanting sunlight picked out crowded market stalls and the ant-like stream of human beings with crates and vegetable baskets. As our 747 swung over the airport perimeter, the idyllic picture of Vietnam gave way to the one which the world media had made more familiar: barbed wire, watch towers and the burnt-out carcasses of aircraft. We taxied past empty aircraft dispersal points to the ramshackle Saigon terminal, where passengers were asked to descend by old-fashioned stairs onto the steamy heat off the tarmac.

From afar, Mike stretched his barracuda jaw into a broad smile. We had never met, but recognised each other instantly of course. By flashing his security clearance, we strode past the officials. The company's travel agent, a war widow, took care of the rest, and we entered the cool Mercedes limousine with its drawn curtains less than five minutes after the plane's touchdown.

While Mike was bantering, I observed, through the window of the air-conditioned car, the knotted leg muscles of coolies powering the ubiquitous taxi tricycles. No consumers of oil, they. The uninviting bars along the Hai Ba Trung still had their windows protected by chicken wire against hand grenades, although Mike told me that security was no longer a problem after the departure of the American customers. He seemed vaguely disparaging even of such small improvements, because it was all part of the 'Vietnamisation' of the conflict. Besides making the war messier, the Americans' sudden departure had decreased profits on his military contracts by millions of dollars. The South Vietnamese could not even afford a properly mechanised war and Mike disliked them for having to fight a poor man's war, which diminished the value of his company. True, Cong Ty Shell was still by far the largest business in Vietnam, but that was meagre consolation for Mike, who once had revelled in the conspiratorial air around the military supply contracts and in the personal friendships in high circles in Washington to which they had led. Yes, he had even enjoyed his acrimonious run-ins with Senator Proxmire. It tickled his fancy to defend the stream of private money against the audits of the most powerful bureaucracy in the world. Only a handful of executives understood the ramifications of our contracts with the US military, and of those, he was the best. But now, he was anxious to hand over the torch, before it burned his fingers.

Half listening, my jet-lagged first impressions seemed to gain extraordinary force from being so different from the dreadful TV images that had conditioned my mind over the years. With disbelief I stared at the healthy bustle outside. Everything was humming industriously. Every man, woman and child seemed busy selling chickens, pots and wood carvings on the sidewalks. The afternoon sunshine created a harmony from the contrasts and wounds that made up Saigon. New buildings under construction and traditional wooden houses with curved roofs under old trees comfortably coexisted with each other. War cripples and Buddhist *bonzes* walked together on the banks of putrid streams, from which glittering fish were caught by naked children. Out of the roar of a thousand combustion engines, you could pick out the sound of a single gong. So it seemed to me in my hyped-up state. People ate from their soup bowls on the sidewalks, oblivious of city pollution. Women moved sensuously through the throng, while juvenile soldiers guarding high bridges with M16s on the hip stared aimlessly at the passing crowds.

The villas of our residential quarter lay sheltered behind high stone walls. Our street, Phan Dinh Phung, was named after a high-minded leader of the 1885 mandarin revolt against the French protectorate in Vietnam, whose resistance had been utterly futile but whose famous exhortations against foreign domination were still taught reverently in the primary schools. On our approach, the garden gate swung open, just in time, so as not to slow us down (the job of the invisible guard and his family). Tall traveller palms fanned out over a pond, at the far end of which stood our villa. Its high ivy-covered walls and those of our two weighty neighbours, the Archbishop of Saigon and the President of the Banque de L'Indo-Chine, gave a vertically enclosed feel to the place, like looking up from the bottom of a green well – a secret pleasure garden, where the trees raised mossy arms with culti-vated orchids to the sky. The swimming pool reflected dwarf trees in earthenware pots, with odd fleshy flowers. And on the steps to the door the inevitable reception committee awaited us: Beb, the cook, with a cigarette sticking to his lip and a smiling rotund wife at his side; first servant Sao, bow-legged, white uniformed, with a big smile of gold and rubber teeth, with his shadow, impeccable second servant Hao, and assorted guards, gardeners and children in their Sunday best. Up to 20 people stood there, people living on the same property as we, but living unseen and unheard in shacks in the shadow of the main house.

Flushed by their smiles and greetings, I was blissfully unaware of the critical attention they paid to my physique: my long nose, a blemish common to all foreigners, my face too angular for their liking, my lack of belly betraying signs of insecurity, all vital indicators on the correct interpretation of which their future happiness depended. At the Chinese imperial court, the first priority was to re-measure all distances of the realm into the specific arm-lengths of the new Emperor. And what went for the Ancient Empire still held true for my good Confucian household in 1972.

For my first evening in town, Mike, wasting little time, had arranged what he called a small dinner party for 50 people to introduce me to Saigon society. An hour before the arrival of the guests, I found Mike ready for action, black hair combed back, glossy shoes creaking on the marble, surveying the dazzling long dining table with a hawk's eye. Practically every weekend, he entertained the Saigon establishment at the swimming pool, with a game of badminton and a famous dinner, often followed by a preview of the latest Hollywood movie, borrowed from one of our tankers. I would follow this tradition, which automatically conferred on me the status of a Saigon insider. Calligraphed name cards on the table read like the *Who's Who* of South Vietnam.

Outside, two burly civilians, walkie-talkies in hand, were already examining the bushes in the garden, the normal security check before the arrival of eighty-three-year-old US Ambassador Elsworth Bunker. As Mike distributed the cards, he commented on the peculiarities of his guests. The US Ambassador had an elephantine memory for facts and an unshakeable loyalty to 'his' people. However, once he included you as a true friend, onto his own invitation list, the whole American establishment would fall in line and shower you with attention, not a negligible achievement for an outsider like Mike, considering also that our competitors, America's greatest corporations, would normally have the inside track.

But perhaps the most interesting name on the table was that of CIA station chief Tom Polgar. Mike had got on better with his hair-shirt predecessor, William Colby, who always struggled with moral doubts about the dirty war he had to run. Tom, with his instinctive Eastern European acceptance of the need to fight the enemy on his own level, seemed to stay looser from his terrible responsibilities. The 'Phoenix' elimination programme, a police operation inherited from his predecessor, which he supervised, was effectively wiping out the Vietcong infrastructure in large areas. Later the Vietcong would admit that they feared one good Phoenix agent more than a battalion of regular troops. Tom easily accepted that the vicious programme was sometimes misused and often illegal, but still he judged it more selective than any military assault could hope to be. The Vietcong could hardly object: it was only an improved sanitised version of the Tru Gian programme of the Vietcong themselves, which had since 1957 killed a thousand village chiefs, youth leaders, police officers and other pillars of the southern government each year rather more indiscriminately.

For strictly business purposes, however, no one could be more important than Economic Minister Pham Kim Ngoc, called Mr Ten

Percent for taking the government cut on all imports, from rice to Japanese Hondas. He showed clever judgement, however, by leaving oil, the only law-abiding sector of the economy, completely untouched by such well-known shenanigans. The serious and incorruptible President of the Central Bank, Le Quang Uyen, would also be there with his beautiful wife, who was much involved in Catholic social work. Amazingly, President Thieu treated such powerful civilians as mere technicians, somewhat below the standing of his generals.

Two star US general John E. Murray was a very quiet presence at these gatherings. He was invited to smooth Shell's relations with the American military bureacracy because he supervised our military contracts. Unfortunately, he left far too much detail to corrupt American civilian employees who extorted money from sub-contractors, and he appeared deaf to our repeated warnings. The British, Australian, New Zealand and Korean Ambassadors, some of them with military forces in the field, came as solid personal friends. In any country where Shell has an interest, the British Ambassador in particular usually becomes a trusted friend to the local manager, with whom he can exchange security, economic, political and commercial information. Saigon was no exception, and Mike had taken special care to cultivate Brooks Richards.

Mike's criterion for inviting single Vietnamese women seemed to be that they had to be of independent means. Of course wives, from the President's down, practically ran the whole economy, supplementing the official salaries of their husbands by influence-peddling and business deals, serving as intermediaries with the big Chinese money-men. Women were also our best dealers, but single women, mostly war widows, were, it had to be admitted, a super-class apart. They controlled whole swaths of economic and intellectual life and the government subsidies that went with it. Moreover, they all looked twenty-five, until they themselves decided otherwise, and it was always notoriously difficult to tell mother from daughter.

Perhaps I had expected too much, but so soon after reading about these personalities in the press and seeing their faces on TV, actually meeting the top Americans in my own house fell short of my fantasies of a super-power's 'Best and Brightest'. Their conversation was that of middle-ranking officials anywhere. Not imaginative, as the table-talk in Shell Centre, nor brilliantly amusing, as in any French embassy even in the middle of Africa. They just spoke with dull restraint and some despair about the war's progress, in correct commonplace phrases so as not to give handles for attack. The war was something to be endured with quiet determination, and they seemed to have no passion left. Only later I came to appreciate that with me as a newcomer they had to take caution to extremes and hide behind the grey language of responsibility which differed from the colourful, sometimes obscene, but at least human language they too used in private.

The ambassadors arrived in reverse pecking order, the smiling inconsequential Indonesian first, the ramrod-stiff Elsworth Bunker last, as befitted his vice-regal status. After greeting Mike with genuine affection, a dry martini was put in his hand by the experienced Sao, followed quickly by a second. It was known that he would take no more until dinner. For my benefit, given my Dutch background, the flinty eyes behind the lenses flickering, he began to regale us with a personal recollection of how he had forced the Dutch, ten years before, to transfer sovereignty over the formerly Dutch part of New Guinea to Indonesia, rather than to the independent Papuan republic on the eastern part of New Guinea. He had forced the deal through at the request of President Kennedy, to keep President Sukarno on board as an ally of the United States, against the legitimate wishes of the poor Papuans, who clamoured for independence. Even though he now realised that the artificial allocation to Indonesia might still unravel itself in bloodshed one day, and even though he might admit that it never really influenced the volatile Sukarno, Bunker nevertheless took immense pride in having carried out the presidential instructions to the letter. It had undoubtedly helped in his promotion to the current Vietnam assignment. The Indonesian Ambassador himself, in a flowery shirt and with the disarming open smile of his people, wondered aloud about Sukarno's value as an American ally and reminded Bunker politely that Sukarno had had to be removed shortly afterwards, in 1968, by his own military for his communist leanings. But it made no difference at all to Bunker. First impressions do count. When we got to know each other better, I could never find in him a prime mover of events, but ever the proud and utterly faithful implementer.

The other before-dinner performance I remember came from a Vietnamese gentleman with gold spectacles and a heavily made up wife with a prominent bosom. He was a high court judge and former minister of justice, of rare honesty, whose teenage daughter had inexplicably turned to prostitution. He kept bending our ears with the latest corruption scandals in Saigon, with names of principals, bank account numbers and sizes of kick-backs, with his wife looking on proudly at her husband venting his anger on cases he would never be allowed to hear in court. However, the evening really seemed to start with the late arrival of a lady in green velvet *ao dhai*, the tight-fitting national dress worn by most women, who rushed up to the terrace, smiling apologetically. She was President of the nebulous but influential War Widows Association, and was either unaware of, or used to, the effect of her entry. Mike bounded forward, Tom Polgar insisted on a handkiss, and Bunker hugged her and took her to sit on his right at the table.

Over dinner, Minister Ngoc, clever as a rat, kept telling me that Shell should invest heavily, now that the enemy had been fought to a standstill. It was a familiar wish, voiced by all governments in desperate circumstances. He knew full well that foreign investments do not normally precede formal peace. But, as a patriot, he wanted outside investment to strengthen the economy, for the 'continuation of war by other means'. In his view, the economy had long ago replaced diplomacy as a means to obtain what cannot be had by war.

Polgar joined in enthusiastically. I studied the intelligence chief keenly, looking for tell-tale sinister signs. But I could find nothing sinister or mysterious in the small bald man with the warm voice and melodramatic eyes, and could only envy how the ladies fawned conspicuously over him. Polgar too agreed that South Vietnam's best chance was to beat the system of the North economically, joking that if Ngoc was too successful the communists might need a Berlin wall to prevent their people from joining the prosperous South. Sensing support from Polgar, and missing the irony in his words, Ngoc insisted that we should act right now, while those at the peace talks in Paris were still bickering about the shape of the conference table. He meant us to invest heavily, build a refinery and explore for oil immediately to make the desirable impression of a South Vietnamese economic renaissance right now. Never mind that I had been sent to do just the opposite.

The walls had ears, and through the swing doors to the kitchen I could see Beb, the cook, listening to the talk and wondered what he made of it. After dinner, Mike, waving his big hands, announced that he had not been able to borrow a pre-release movie from a tanker in port, but that coffee and cognac were served on the terrace. We trooped out behind him. A few minutes before curfew, the guests began to leave, Bunker first with his guards, Minister Ngoc last, in his beaten-up little car, a pistol bulging in his back. In the distance, the artillery firing made an almost unreal sound.

With the guests gone, the reception room was free to reveal its plain naked awkwardness. Outside, coloured spotlights pierced the dark of the tropical night; the shrill of cicadas almost perforated the eardrums. Inside, the house was obviously square company accommodation, home only to wanderers like us. While Sao drew down the metal screens over the windows, Mike produced a cognac and suddenly handed me a large-calibre pistol. Once he had thrown expensive porcelain vases to scare off an intruder, but then an embassy guard had lectured him on the equal uselessness of vases and of elegant small-calibre firearms, and sold him on the old-fashioned concept that only large bullets could knock down drugged attackers. So the theory went amongst professional body guards. Mike joked, however, that it kicked like a mule and that he could not hit a target at ten paces anyway. At the same time, he began to talk compulsively about misgivings he had shared with nobody yet.

Although in total sympathy with the American cause in Vietnam, he had to admit that the US military invasion, especially the disproportionate violence dispensed by the American armed forces, had made no sense whatever. The essential war of the villages, the war fought among the Vietnamese themselves, had been as ill understood and under-funded financially as in the days of the French war. The US Airforce bombing alone cost many times more per year than the $1.6 billion GDP of the whole of North Vietnam. This could not make sense, except to suppliers of fuel and munitions. Moreover, because the air attacks against the few authorised targets were fairly predictable, and therefore the targets well defended, they had been taking heavier losses than necessary.

But then, the US Navy, whose Admiral Elmo R. Zumwalt was a great friend of his, as well as a great customer, outdid even the Airforce. It maintained no less than five aircraft carriers, escorted by a screen of protection and service vessels, steaming up and down the coast, under orders from Washington to allow all enemy supply ships, even oil tankers and those with Russian missiles plainly on deck, to enter and offload at Haiphong harbour unmolested. This had formed part of President Johnson's policy of pulling his punches and of sending diplomatic smoke signals to the enemy. The North Vietnamese interpreted his restraint only as weakness. To the unfortunate navy pilots fell the task thereafter of risking their lives to destroy these same supplies entering the South over the Ho Chi Minh trail, by the light of flares, seeking trucks under double-canopy jungle, zooming between mountains at 400 miles per hour.

But when all was said and done, the Army took the crown for sheer cinematographic lunacy. General Westmoreland's priority was not to go out and learn about the nature of the conflict, but to draw loosely with a grease pencil on the map of Vietnam $4 billion worth of facilities, eight harbours, umpteen airfields, six-lane highways, huge military camps and a smaller version of the Pentagon for his command. The protection alone for these fine new structures against rag-tag saboteurs guaranteed the immobilisation of a full third of American military manpower. With another third engaged in rear echelon tasks, only a third was left to fight. Numerous civilian contractors, like Brown & Root and ourselves, lapped up the spending spree and could hardly believe the riches so lavishly thrown our way.

The decisive daylight battles, for which these structures formed the underpinning, never materialised. The huge search and destroy movements, supported by unlimited firepower, failed miserably. While the pincers closed over empty terrain, however, they did manage to chase four million peasants off the land. Over half of Americans listed as killed in action fell to transportation accidents, friendly fire and booby traps. And to make sure that the soldiers on the spot could not learn from hard experience, ten-month tours of duty were the norm, reduced to six, or even three, for men on the line. Any business with such a rapid turnaround system would have collapsed, and even war correspondents had a longer service time.

No wonder that by the late sixties President Johnson's peculiar conduct of the war had exhausted the patience of the American people. From the day of his inauguration, in January 1969, the new president, Nixon, proved himself a more subtle warrior. He began to isolate the North Vietnamese from their supporters through negotiations with China, carried out in secrecy by resourceful diplomats. And he began at last to support and field the South Vietnamese forces seriously. As a result, the American troops could be withdrawn, and the much-maligned South Vietnamese Army had proved itself a much better force than expected. Even Mike had to recognise this.

However, all this reduction in scale had a negative side. As long as the war was an opulent $30-billion-a-year American affair, a little black-marketing on the side between American officers and Vietnamese dealers could be ignored. But with the war, shrivelling ever-faster under Nixon, spurred on by the Watergate scandal, to a $1 billion military assistance affair in 1972, the petroleum trade began to stand out very large indeed. Every Vietnamese tried to lay his hands on the remaining black gold, and Shell was marked out by people in high places as their key to fortune.

Mike knew very well that when a valuable commodity flows through an impoverished country corruption was unavoidable. Usually it took the simple form of duly authorised government or army officials signing the company invoice for correct receipt of the goods into their storage, but instead diverting part or all of those goods to dealers on the black market and splitting the profit with them; or of aircraft crew taking less kerosene than they signed for and selling the rest as lampoil. The resulting shortfalls in customer storage could be easily masked by recording phoney military operations never carried out in reality which used them up. Because these practices required minimal organisation and small payoffs to others, they were much favoured by American supply officers. The American authorities, however, were not keen to investigate, to say the least, understandably so, because they had a large war on their hands, and an unwilling conscript army. In Shell's case, the company itself was not defrauded, since Shell received payment on invoice. The company's books were in good order, with no loss suffered. So there was no incentive to investigate all the rumours and pursue too closely where Shell's products were ending up.

As for fuel being delivered to the enemy through Vietnamese army and civilian channels, we knew that trading of hard wood or rice with the North Vietnamese or Vietcong was a common occurrence, given the intermingling of the two opponents. Oil was no exception. The exchanges between the two sides helped keep the parties in some form of contact, obviating the need to kill for supplies. It would evidently have been a very grave matter, however, for our own Shell red-and-yellow trucks to be seen inside the Vietcong enclaves. We knew the North Vietnamese were so desperate for oil that they were prepared to pay South Vietnamese colonels double the normal price. We also knew that our oil frequently landed in Vietcong and North Vietnamese hands. Oil is like ammunition or hard currency in war, so it was not surprising that the other side's desperation for fuel often resulted in 'seepages' of our product. We kept ourselves out of this process, but were willing to accept it as a reality. Of course both in Mike's time and in mine, if we had hard information about, say, a truck driver engaged in what appeared to be petty thieving or conspiring with the black market to deliver supplies which might end up on the other side, we fired him. But we were unwilling to engage in investigations that would have been fruitless. Mike, and later I, certainly would not have reported such matters upwards to London. While we did discuss local corruption at top management level in Saigon, we would never have wanted to trouble London with it. Vee had pointedly praised Mike for his discretion when giving him a salary rise. What was important for Vee and top management in London was that subsidiaries like Saigon deliver their profits without involving them in our local traumas. Trading with the enemy was certainly not part of the corporate strategy. So long as I delivered profits and kept the company's nose clean, the corporate bosses in London were happy. If anything untoward was brought to light, Mike and I realised that our heads would roll.

Down to the smallest wheels, Vietnam was lubricated by oil. Irregularities, and even crimes, were less reported in Vietnamese society than elsewhere. Vietnamese combatants on both sides kept the facts of life routinely away from their Russian and American patrons. Oriental armies prefer business deals to fighting, and when necessary turn a blind eye to each other's patrols. In the circumstances, Mike's advice was simple. Trust nobody: not the President of the country, not your own staff, not the banks. Keep a daily, repeat daily, check on your cashflow. And increase prices with inflation, or you are dead. Rotate

Vietnamese staff often, always through the Vietnamese personnel manager to avoid personal blame. Keep London off your back by first setting your own targets and then over-performing, without ever spelling out the facts of life. Protect the hub of Shell's supply system and the largest oil products depot in the world, the great Nha Be installation, like the crown jewels. And give up any hope of a quiet life. 'You are Dante entering Inferno', said Mike as he bid me good-night at the end of my first day.

4

War Risks

The Northern Military Region
and the Rung Sat Swamps

In the last months of 1972, as the failure of the Communist offensive became evident, Saigon presented an almost unbelievable facade of peace. I at least had difficulty taking it at face value. The war in the cities seemed to be over, and the town people exuded confidence and civil pride. Some said that the whole war was already over, and an amazing number of citizens claimed never to have witnessed any war action at all. Previously unsecured motorways were now regularly choked with holiday crowds on their way to the beaches, father, mother and five children on a Honda scooter, or packed in an old American car. At a remaining American camp, I saw what must have been the last perimeter patrol of American marines, big men employing Vietnamese girls to carry their guns. They had taken no part in the recent fighting, and they too must have believed it was virtually peace, but were they right?

One good reason for optimism was the blocking of the North Vietnamese military supply line through Hai Phong harbour, by order of President Nixon in concert, this time, with the Russians and the Chinese, who all shared an economic interest in lowering the heat and sidelining the Vietnamese conflict. The North Vietnamese Politburo had reason indeed to feel isolated, but with reunification their lifelong objective and their economy in shambles, they would never accept peaceful coexistence with their prosperous Southern brothers. The mere suspicion that their Russian and Chinese patrons would force them sooner rather than later into peace negotiations had been the main reason behind their last roll of the dice, the 'Nguyen Hue offensive' (named after the twelfth-century emperor who fought the

Chinese). It had been a very close-run thing, and only failed because US bombing helped the Southern army to stand its ground. Nevertheless, it had been quite a shock to fail against that 'puppet' army without American support on the ground. The Hanoi leadership was obviously not going to accept the latest status quo quietly.

If there was a vantage point from which to observe the military balance of forces, the Northern region provided it. There, both armies had massed their élite divisions on each side of the demarcation line between North and South Vietnam, where most of the recent heavy fighting had been. Apart from doctors, nurses and aid people, few non-military foreigners went there. It was amongst these, and numerous Vietnamese families, that I took my first field trip to the Northern region to familiarise myself with the working of Shell in Vietnam. Flying by friendly Air Vietnam, it was easy to be charmed and perhaps fooled by the peaceful tapestry of rice fields below, the dizzy mountain spines, the spectacular waterfalls, the close-cropped jungle, occasionally scarred by aerial bombing, and the whitest widest beaches on earth, with idyllic islands and innocent fishing boats bobbing on a turquoise sea. For raw tourist potential, Vietnam was unrivalled.

At lower altitudes, however, travelling closer to that glorious scenery by borrowed military helicopter, to isolated dealerships, it was the strict survival rules observed by the pilots when over-flying safe and hostile zones which left their mark. They would pull up, abruptly, out of range of potential small-arms fire from a few bushes near a river bend. 'Safe' villages, you learned, had the national flag painted on their tin roofs, for security. Other villages seemed to look sullen and aggressive, even from the air. In the deep countryside, apparently, neither party had relaxed or disarmed. The company's local gasoline dealers and contract transporters, and the district officials we visited, would casually indicate no-go areas on maps, with the names and numbers of enemy military units residing in particular villages, able to tell you exactly whether the villages were hostile, friendly, or no-man's land. They were intimately aware of the morale problems of the government and of the enemy troops. And they could not know all this without some covert links with the enemy, convinced anti-Communists though they might be. Many interlocking interests were at stake for these people. I sensed that here was an example of a time to rein in my natural curiosity. Here, so soon after my arrival in Vietnam, I was face-to-face with smiling individuals with links to the other side. It was uncomfortable.

The heaviest fighting of the Nguyen Hue offensive had taken place on the demarcation line, near the Han river. On my first visit to the region, I landed in Danang, headquarters of the Northern military region and also the location of our own branch office, a dramatic site, with green mountains to the north, offshore islands to the east, and a curved sweep of beach of breathtaking beauty, offset, however, by swollen refugee camps, derelict American service establishments, laundries, brothels and bars. My host and guide on this trip was one of our more forceful branch managers and undisputed master on his own terrain. He stood waiting on the airfield, a solid man with a solid neck and a square head, with a hairline starting just above the eye-brows. As often with powerfully-built men, the eyes could look curiously helpless at times. Ex-Colonel Le Van Phuoc had a fearsome and well-deserved reputation as the top policeman of former Head of State Ngo Dinh Diem. Amongst other military achievements, he was credited with the eviction of the militant Buddhists from the Saigon pagodas in 1963. The brutality of the action, recorded on TV, had raised world-wide indignation and contributed to the American approval of a military coup, which led to the downfall of the regime and eventually to the murder of his boss, President Diem.

Well before that chain of events, as chief of a fiercely-contested province, he had already shown his inclination to settle security matters by military action, with little compunction about killing innocents along with suspects. It certainly subdued the province, but – to say the least – made him unpopular in the process. After his hurried departure from the army under Diem's successors, Shell, for reasons I still found hard to understand, had saved his livelihood by employing him, and Phuoc had served us unstintingly in return, espe-cially through the use of his network of contacts with old military friends. His installations were often attacked, but never successfully. Gratefully making use of his extraordinary achievements in the field of security, I wondered nevertheless what future a sophisticated company could offer a man whose main qualities seemed to be loyalty, discipline and military ruthlessness. But I soon came to appreciate his fox-like cunning too.

On my first meeting, Phuoc took me to see the commander of the region, Lieutenant General Ngo Quang Truong, now a national celebrity for stopping and rolling back the Nguyen Hue offensive a few months before. The tiny general was wearing starched American battle fatigues which seemed sizes too big for him, receiving us in the old American headquarters, which seemed far too large for his modest staff. Solely on Phuoc's say-so, he took me completely into confidence, drawing the curtain away from a top-secret wall map with the order of battle of his own and his enemy's units and answering my questions without apparent reserve. To a layman, his position seemed shockingly inadequate. Even including the country's élite mobile reserves, which could be called away at a moments notice, his troops were decisively outnumbered by the enemy. And those particular enemy troops were the most feared divisions of the whole Communist army. Yet, like most Vietnamese, when confronted with an obvious contradiction, the general smilingly denied the existence of a problem, professing total confidence in his position. Such bluff can have its uses, and in any case the disparity of forces was not of his making, and the implications were not for him to consider, but for Headquarters in Saigon. However much I had to admire his courage, I could not fail to worry about the extreme temptation for the enemy to take advantage of its numerical superiority.

In its enthusiasm to make General Truong a national hero, the American embassy had also built him up as an example of personal incorruptibility. It was this overblown reputation that Phuoc had cleverly manipulated to his advantage. In Phuoc's relations with civilian authorities, 'gifts' for small favours, as he called them, were a way of life. Province chiefs collected them as a sort of business tax. Most were modest petty-cash payments for expediting the clearance of documents and of allowances which were due anyway. A big man like Phuoc needed to dispense a certain amount of largesse around him.

Relations with the military were much more sensitive. The oil Phuoc routinely delivered was worth a fortune to anybody, and certainly to the officers who signed for receipt. Officer salaries were steadily eroded by inflation, and not sufficient to support a family, while the oil under their control constituted a fortune in an appreciating easily convertible currency. So tank exercises would be planned, scheduled and even reported in the press, but not executed. This all of a sudden liberated tons of product for the black market. Phuoc, though not personally involved, knew how to take advantage of these goings on. One day he marched up to the incorruptible Truong and privately handed him a slip of Shell stationery with all the detailed proof of his staff officers' involvement in fuel trafficking, asking him what he was going to do about it. They had looked at each other in silence for a long time. Clearly, not even Truong – certainly not in his precarious military position – could afford to act against his own officers on any large scale. On the other hand, Phuoc had counted on these facts of life to give him a stranglehold over Truong, should the general ever think of lifting a finger against Shell. And in sharing this information with me in a light-hearted way, he made me an accomplice too. Perhaps Phuoc, with his deviousness, was the right man in the right place after all. It seemed part of an elaborate game: everybody needed to gain a hold on everyone else in Vietnam. It was part of the system.

The road to the northern provincial capital, Quang Tri, was still lined with the debris of recent fighting, carcasses of tanks and spent ammunition, not yet looted. Phuoc took me there to see the remains of our modern service stations. Quang Tri itself was 100 percent destroyed, pulverised and ground down by tank tracks. We scraped our boots on the surface of one of our flattened service stations, whose operator had been killed or abducted. Four North Vietnamese divisions had been pushed back by Truong's marines beyond the Han river. They now held only the citadel south of the river. It felt almost obscene that our little group could drive in perfect safety through scenes of such recent carnage. On either side of the small stream, an unofficial live-and-let-live truce prevailed between the worn-out troops. We did not need to take cover within small arms range of the enemy, and could observe them at leisure through field glasses. On the other side, the flag with the red star floated like an *ao dhai* in a Sunday breeze. An enemy trooper, washing clothes in the stream, waved at us. Both sides washed in the stream. There was no official ceasefire, but any shooting, by either side, would be suicidal under the machine-gun vigil of the other. All this was unofficial local accommodation.

I asked the accompanying commander where the famously contested citadel was. He pointed to some earthen hills quite nearby. The former stone walls had been reduced to gently undulating sand and rubble. The moat had been filled in, leaving only a shallow depression, giving easy access to a shallow rectangular heap in which no life could be observed. Still, the remnants of two enemy battalions somehow survived underneath the rubble. Once in a while, our commander would run his tanks right over the top, dropping explosives in holes, not so much to dislodge them as to remind them it was time to go. Each attack caused more unnecessary casualties. No military purpose was served either by holding the fort or by attacking it. According to our commander, one night, the North Vietnamese would surely have to withdraw over the river by themselves. With the contempt of the military professional, he joked bitterly about politicians crazy enough to order him to fight over the ruins of the citadel for its symbolic value at the forthcoming peace negotiations.

Back in Saigon the day after my first field trip, two porcelain vases arrived with a note in French: 'Madame Phuoc joins me in asking you to accept, in memory of your visit, these Ming vases, which have been in my family for centuries'. If they had any real value, I could obviously not keep them. So I took them for valuation by an eminent collector of antique porcelain in Saigon. The old scholar was resting on a wooden bed, with his fragile skull on a polished wooden headrest amidst dusty shelves full of cups, plates and vases of antique porcelain and celadon. His fingertips reluctantly stroked the surface of my vases, his eyes showing his distaste: 'Imitation Ming vases, recently made in the Peoples Republic of China'. He laughed noiselessly through bluish lips. 'They use the same clay, the same colours and techniques of their forefathers, but the magic has gone. Compare them with my vases, touch them and you will see what I mean.' I thanked Phuoc curtly for his generous gift, and felt that we understood each other well enough to work together.

The Northern region was obviously stable for Shell while Phuoc kept a firm grip on the security situation. But the next blow to our business hardware, as everyone already seemed to know, was planned right under our noses in the South. No more than 30 kilometres north west of Saigon, covered by the forests of Hau Nghia province, was the temporary base of the Command of Communist Forces in South Vietnam (COSVN) under General Tran Van Tra, himself a Southerner. From the air, his staff rooms might look like ordinary thatched cattle pens, but they were filled with the paraphernalia of military office, radios, maps, tables and telephones. Concealed trap doors led to an underground maze of tunnels, air raid shelters, hospitals, store rooms and camouflaged firing positions. Meals for his troops came from kitchens whose smoke was dispatched through separate channels to avoid detection from the air.

In this strange war, the Americans had rarely plucked up the determination to go after the enemy nerve-centre, as it moved backwards and forwards over the Cambodian border, and the army of the Republic of South Vietnam (ARVN) was simply forbidden to cross the border, and tried to live with the consequences. Thus the Vietcong and North Vietnamese staff officers, over the years, had clung to life in the slimy underground, while the Americans and the South Vietnamese enjoyed the fat cities. And from there, General Tra had sent the élite sapper units to their deaths in the opening raid on the American Embassy during the great 1968 Tet offensive. That offensive, ordered by the Politburo and portrayed as a Communist victory in the Western media, had in fact been a military defeat for Tra's Southern Command, one which he still resented bitterly. A whole generation of experienced Southern Communist cadres had been sacrificed. It had marked the end of guerrilla warfare as a possible route to victory, and had eroded southern support for the Communist cause. But arguably, and more importantly, it had also fatally weakened US resolve.

Now, after the failure of his latest conventional military offensive, General Tra had to play the waiting game once more, until his troops could be re-supplied and reinforced by young recruits from the North. Meanwhile, he wanted to create maximum discomfort for South Vietnam by escalating limited blows against its most obvious strength: the economy. It so happened that the chosen instrument for this action, an élite North Vietnamese sapper group, was already travelling southwards. Their main objective was the Southern petroleum supply system, at the heart of which stood Shell's Nha Be installation on the Saigon river, opposite to the infamous Rung Sat swamps. How did we know this?

By piecing together incidents, a lot of rumours and some hard intelligence from the CIA, including information gained from the interrogation of captives and from intercepted messages from Tra's headquarters.

The Rung Sat, or 'Assassins' Forest', opposite the Nha Be installation was one of the most impenetrable parts of the Mekong delta, a vast expanse of mangrove marshland, strategically situated between the capital and the ocean and laced with water arteries. The largest of these was the Long Tan river, along which had to pass all the heavy and vital supplies from overseas that kept Saigon alive. Much of the 400-square-mile area consists of islands, tightly packed with vegetation, separated by waist-deep mud. During the eight-foot high tide however, loaded sampans can travel anywhere. Under Bao Dai's reign, already it was a preferred rear base, well outside the range of justice, of 10,000 members of the Saigon criminal gang the Binh Xuyen.

When the Vietcong arrived, they found it a convenient shelter against the mechanised American way of war. The swamps were not truly land that could be used by the motorised US Army, nor were they suitable for conventional action by the Navy. The Navy had obvious high-seas capabilities, but no 'brown water' experience and no doctrine, as yet, on amphibious river operations. As a consequence, the US marines stayed well away, and were exclusively deployed on dry land in central Vietnam. A hastily formed US coastal surveillance force therefore had to improvise and experiment with none-too-successful earlier French practices. It made one half-hearted attempt, in 'Operation Game Warden' in 1967, to sweep the area in utterly predictable fashion, starting with the construction of cemented artillery positions supplied by air, giving ample warning of things to come (later these would be replaced by artillery barges). After heavy bombardment of the general area, they introduced troops by air and by motorised launches for daylight fighting: severe disappointment. Progress overland was only a mile a day, because of the mud, the tangled mangrove and tightly-packed nipa palms, giving the enemy plenty of time to disperse. According to the medics, foot rot (immersion foot) disabled the American soldiers within 24 hours, boat crews refused to work for more than two weeks on the murky brown water, and the attack bogged down even before contact with the enemy. In view of the hostile environment for expatriate troops, the operation had to be proclaimed a victory, before it had properly started. One empty guerrilla base destroyed by massive aerial bombing and a dubious enemy body count of 50 were the trumped-up results, and little was achieved, as the hard-won experience remained un-analysed. Thereafter, the responsibility for the Rung Sat reverted to the Vietnamese Navy, which based a somewhat leisurely river assault group (RAG 22) in Nha Be to cope with any eventualities.

By 1970, these Vietnamese forces, with the usual competent Australian advisers, had brought the Rung Sat under some sort of control, by concentrating patiently on the supply lines leading into and out of the zone. Fortunately for Shell, the hunted Vietcong operating from the Rung Sat had their hands full with their own survival, and were not in top form either. They had shot and rocketed the installation for so long, so incompetently and with such negligible results, that we had grown complacent. Just after my arrival in August 1972 I used to cross the river in the morning after a night attack with installation staff to look at the improvised bamboo launchers they left behind, and laugh at their primitive efforts.

By the end of that year, however, new information from the CIA indicated that élite sappers, seriously trained in North Vietnam with scale models of our installations, were being transported by truck to General Tra's headquarters in preparation for their move into the Rung Sat. They would be an entirely different enemy. We guessed that they would first try to sink one of our 30,000 ton tankers which, unlike the sampans, had to take the one available deep channel. Moreover, the tankers increased their vulnerability by arriving with clockwork regularity at the mouth of the delta, and never varied their routine. With the reversal of the tide in the Long Tao river arm, they would start the dangerous 60-kilometre dash through the Rung Sat to the Nha Be installation under full power, presenting a fast moving but good target all the way. The risk to attackers was minimal, since the South Vietnamese could not afford the helicopter gunship protection which the Americans had lavished on our tanker escorts before.

5

The Red Files

Hidden Truths

Oil supplies to the South Vietnamese occurred by the grace of the American taxpayer. The US Procurement Office in Washington bought supplies for its own and for the South Vietnamese armed forces through a massive supply contract, negotiated and solemnly signed each year with Shell, Esso and Caltex. Habitually, Shell had the lion's share in Vietnam because of its deeper implantation and better ability to deliver up-country. For Shell, London orchestrated the contractual supply-line of affiliates, purchasing Arabian crude, manufacturing products in Singapore refineries and shipping them by tanker to Nha Be and to coastal depots at Nha Trang, Da Nang and Qui Nhon etc. In Saigon, we had a young American executive dedicated to business relations with the US and Vietnamese armed forces, and few Vietnamese executives or indeed any others had access to the military contractual details.

Civilian supplies were sold by us directly to Vietnamese wholesale distributors and dealers against payment in piastres, but US Aid guaranteed the dollar costs of supplies to Shell, and to some extent the convertibility of piastres into dollars. I dealt with the US Aid administrator, but the Vietnamese government also had considerable power. We had to negotiate the price of import with the Vietnamese government as well as the posted retail prices for each product in the market. In the hyper-inflationary environment, we had to be very quick in obtaining approval from the economic minister to adjust prices, and be adept at sensing when the Central Bank would be making one of its frequent devaluations, which they always tried to time just before one of our big transfers.

Some days the office resembled a beehive. Up-country dealers and Saigon retailers liked to come in person to deal with us and meet each other. The toothless old police guard had to push the monumental doors hard against the flesh of customers already inside to force us in. The solemn entrance hall looked a street market, with Chinese and Vietnamese dealers shouting at our salesmen and each other, supporting arguments by clacking and hitting their wooden abacuses. A marble barrier contained them, behind which our uniformed clerks passed documents against cash, through openings in the bullet-proof glass. The smiling girls might operate the latest Japanese calculators with fluttering fingers, but could never work as fast as the rowdy dealers with their abacuses and their rude gestures. I would have to elbow my way through. A word here and there, but no special courtesy shown on either side. All in all, our relations with the Saigon petrol dealers were as blunt as they were durable. Due to their cheerfully admitted lack of creditworthiness, we required them to pay cash before delivery.

On the first floor, through the swing doors sprawled the accounts section, an awe-inspiring sight. Hundreds of low-salary clerks, most of them women in white *ao dhais* over black silk trousers, working on ledgers in longhand in stunning silence. My scalp itched when walking up the central aisle. At the end, in an old-fashioned glass office, sat their supervisor, a young flaxen-haired Dutch accountant, and next to him, in a similar glass cage, his grizzled deputy, Tao, who had been producing the monthly financial statements to London by the same old manual system all his life, taking the blame if things went wrong while his boss took the credit for innovations. But it was the Dutchman who had become frustrated and embittered within a year, while Tao had kept his cool.

The division of responsibilities was unfair on both of them. I was eager to promote proven Vietnamese as soon as they could be held responsible for management and innovation at the same time. Already we had too many expatriate advisers, and too many of them had made the mistake of dreaming up Western systems, only to fail in their hand-over to the Vietnamese. In future, expatriates would have to accept successful hand-over as the main test of their own work. Tao would be put in charge of the production of accounts and the Dutchman put up for transfer to greener pastures.

The latter was sharp in his reactions, however, and made the radical proposal to replace the clerks with a computer after his departure, which would have meant sacking half of them in the name of progress. But in a country of cheap labour, the clever proposal had a negligible cost advantage. In the unsettled times, I preferred to live with the old system and with Tao for a little longer.

Also on the first floor lived a former Egyptian banker from Cairo, in an office without glass walls, who claimed to supervise Tao too. An old friend of Mike's, a Christian Copt who took his role terribly seriously, he delighted in playing the 'observer'. But we already had a surfeit of supervision. The Swiss expatriate finance manager nominally supervised this gentleman and, somehow, I was supposed to follow them all with my eagle eye. In truth, the polished and distrustful ex-banker had only been employed to keep an independent check on the bank balances each day, on the payments and receipts in the pipeline for the next week, and on any bad debts or financial disasters on the monthly horizon. Mike trusted nobody in the Finance Department, convinced as he was that they were only interested in ensuring that the arithmetic all added up correctly. When the ex-banker apologetically presented me with his total daily output – a single sheet, with yesterday's bank balances, today's estimated deposits and expenditures, and tomorrow's cash position forecast – I could only wonder what paranoia had caused the wild growth of checks and balances. I had already decided to trust the finance manager instead. With his finely-tuned sensitivity the worthy old gentleman avoided embarrassment by suggesting that he would leave as soon as I had arranged a dignified official reason to dispense with his services. I was grateful. At least he needed no replacement.

In the carpeted hall outside my third-floor office, a holding area had been created for the many people supposed to be queuing up to see me, lined with a row of fake leather seats under a bronze plaque of founding father Deterding's gloomy features. But nobody ever waited outside as far as I knew, because they all preferred to chat – or better flirt – with my secretary in her office. Nguyen Thi Nhung was glamorous, with a pouting expression, usually seated at her desk between the potted palms, but she would, on occasion, rise slowly in her silk *ao dhai* to command instant respect, like a stingray undulating upward from an underwater cave. To me, she was essential, given her total discretion in hand-coding my telexes with London. Telephones were tapped regularly, but we assumed at the time that our company code was almost unbreakable. My Vietnamese-style hold over her was, typically, through her minor vice of gambling. Once a year, she would confess her mah jong losses, weeping copiously, in the knowledge that I would have to bail her out to keep my business secrets within the family.

The office was a rectangle in gold and yellow, with wooden furniture, local artists' paintings on the walls and an immense glass-topped desk with black telephones, whose plastic cables snaked over the silk carpets. Like the classic Chinese palace, it had to have three doors, one from Nhung's office, a second off the waiting hall, used by department heads, and an escape exit for me through the telex rooms.

Stacked high on the desk lay the red files containing restricted telexes in the 'personal' channel, between previous holders of the job and Vee, which were considered as private letters, outside the scope of official company communications. Legally, they did not exist, but without them, no true record of the company's activities could be construed. I read them avidly, before anything else. Official accounts register past performance, plans and capital budgets are the formal blueprints of the future, but only the red files gave the true picture in unvarnished language, including grammatical errors made in haste, of how things happened in the minds of the principal actors. They contained personal reasons for sending back staff, and blunt political appraisals at variance with official pronouncements. One theme spun out over the years concerned our public promise to the South Vietnamese government to build a refinery with Exxon and Caltex somewhere on the coast, 'when conditions were right'. In spite of constant blandishments from the government, we were stringing them along with public reassurances while privately scheming how to get out of our refinery commitment. Amongst the various unflattering references to proposed staff, I read with interest one from Mike in which he said that the last place to look for his successor would be Africa! These were the gossip, the speculation and discarded options which take 90 percent of management time. In these red files I read how predecessors had shadow-boxed over the years with threats like the nationalisation of our company. I became engrossed in the intuitive judgements, the failed initiatives and personal prejudices whose productive and candid expression was only made possible by the absolute trust between the two correspondents, their shared commitment, and by the security of Nhung's coding. One thing I did not find was any reference to corruption, or to Shell's oil ending up as part of the enemy's supplies. Even the sacred red files remained silent on these sensitive issues.

The danger of keeping such private information, however, and its possible use in subpoenas and as legal evidence against us, was very real. Although only the president of the Vietnam company originated and had access to all red file subjects, it was clear that sometimes he had received help from senior department heads when their responsibilities were involved. I discussed my worries with our marketing manager.

Eric Precious was one of those enviable human beings with a high class English drawl, an Oxford degree and obvious erudition, who wear their handsome faces comfortably and authoritatively wherever they go in the world. Only the Personnel System's reports could have the temerity to question his incisiveness, his readiness to sacrifice enough for his career, his slight eccentricity and his many time-consuming outside interests. Suffice it to say that at thirty-five, he was no longer in the Shell fast track. He had provided much of the controversial material discussed in the red channel, in particular in a telex bearing his imprint which mentioned that, in retrospect, we had overstated our real costs in the official price build-up in a previous US defence contract. As a result, Uncle Sam had unwittingly paid above the agreed norm. I asked if perhaps we should have informed the Defence Department afterwards of our mistaken estimation?

To a smooth executive like Precious there was no question of that. Firstly, he pointed out that the contract had been signed by our sister company in New York, and was their formal responsibility. Secondly, he saw no wrong in estimating on the high side to build up a reserve against war risks. Thirdly, fluctuations in soft currencies made local costs impossible to predict in hard dollars anyway. And finally, our price had proved itself competitive in the bidding process, had it not? (Long live the free market, with *caveat emptor* and all that). When I inquired how he would react to a demand for a US government audit on our price build-up, he replied simply that he would refuse them entry to the premises, as was his right as a free contractor in a foreign country. Quite the rapid-fire reaction to be expected from an executive of Precious's class. But suppose now, I asked, that the Vietnamese Finance Minister, who bought 16 million barrels of oil a year under the civilian assistance programme, sent an auditor, as was his right, to discover that the ex-Singapore price to civilians was higher than to the military, in spite of his most-favoured-customer clauses? Could he not claim a rebate? Again, Precious stressed that prices to different classes of customers were negotiated competitively and separately. At the time, our price offer had been accepted as the lowest, and our cost indications had been given in good faith, without the benefit of hindsight. He was right of course. A deal is a deal, and free markets are hit-and-miss affairs, with swings and roundabouts.

I was worried, however, by the false impression that could be created in the outside world if unscrupulous people gained access to our internal deliberations. This was the stuff of easy distortions by hired lawyers. Some action groups were so eager to blame multinational companies for all ills that they would not hesitate to break into our files and put their own spin on our private communications. In Tokyo, the Economic Police had already raided the Shell President's office and impounded the red files in an anti-corruption chase with anti-foreign overtones. The same could easily happen in publicity-hungry Saigon. As we had no obligation to keep a record of this personal channel, I decided reluctantly to shred our red files and keep no copies in future.

Amazingly, our Vietnamese and foreign executives had never faced each other openly in the past. The American military contract manager, the English operations manager, and the Swiss finance manager had seldom met together around the boardroom table, and they all held back details from each other and from the Vietnamese as a matter of course. I now hastened to bring them together in the bright board-room on the third floor, next to my office, with overhead projectors, screens, flip charts, lime juice and coffee, to test the waters of more open communication.

The Swiss finance manager, Hans Haerry, made a start by reporting the monthly results in piastres, which of course exceeded the forecast to London by a wide margin, due to our habitual under-estimation of Vietnam's galloping inflation. It never ceased to amaze me that we, as an affiliate of a foreign company, judged ourselves by local, not share-holders', currency standards, and even more that our own shareholders in the London Centre allowed us to report our results in piastres, which was a slippery currency at best. Hard currency dividends were seen merely as the icing on the cake. But in my view, such real divi-dends were the only standard we had for evaluating our performance, and the Centre was far too lax in demanding them from its marketing affiliates all over the world. It was the old preoccupation with inte-grated profit by maximising our own crude production. The bigger the marketing 'outlets', the more crude oil they 'bought' at the high prices prevailing within our system, the less significant their individual returns needed to be, it seemed. Even losses were tolerated. The large European affiliates paid negligible dividends, Japan and Brazil none at all. Only small fry like ourselves paid up. On the whole, the Centre's ambitions seemed concentrated on collecting its bill for crude oil or products they sold to us at artificially high prices. This of course pro-tected the profitability of crude-oil production, but at the expense of marketing efficiency and accountability.

As soon as a young Vietnamese from the marketing department asked the obvious question, about translating our results into dollars, the cat was among the pigeons. Haerry began to stonewall from force of habit. The ways we channelled money to London and the amounts involved had always been considered off-limits to local staff. Our most senior Vietnamese executive, however, leaped to the aid of his young colleague, perhaps to test the limits of the new openness.

In every way, personnel manager Tran Ngoc Giu in action was a fascinating sight; velvet eyes in a maliciously refined Asian face; every-thing about him slight and elegant; a silk necktie covering his whole chest, he nevertheless seemed able to strike fear into the largest oppo-nents by lifting a manicured finger. Younger Vietnamese graduates, educated with Western concepts, all deferred to him. But Giu was of a different and older breed. He spoke his languages fluently, and had mastered all the modernities of Shell management in Vietnam and overseas without the slightest concession of the inner mind, as had the Japanese, adopting Western material progress after the Meiji restoration while holding fast to their traditional beliefs. Giu and his family, proud descendants of a long line of court mandarins, had left Hanoi in 1954 because they could not live under Communism, but he despised the vulgar democracy of the Southern government almost as much. Always he acted as the archetype mandarin, a great though unpredictable friend, and a powerful force for Vietnamese interests.

Giu started quietly by admitting foreign shareholders' rights to a good return in dollars; piastres were valueless, he agreed. But then, suddenly, he raised the tone of his voice a little, and with one of his high-pitched, chilling laughs began to spit out his real venom at the unjust discrimination in pay between groups of personnel. Western expatriates, barely out of business school, received fantastic dollar salaries, he said, Vietnamese executives only piastres. Expatriates retired on comfortable pensions, Vietnamese were left with a handful of paper money. We set aside part of our cashflow for our own dollar/ sterling pension funds, but we did not make similar arrangements for Vietnamese executives. Giu admitted that the problem was not of our making. In a country sinking ever deeper into poverty, you could not survive without taking advantage of local wages. Everyone, and above all the state, did so. Soldiers' wages too had dropped to their lowest real level in 30 years, and army wives had to work and prostitute themselves to support families. The army maintained farms just to feed the soldiers' families. Our own labour force had to be paid partly in rice and children's education, because wages could not buy all these essentials. And if we did not provide, we knew the Communists would recruit them. Giu's statement, delivered with Mandarin refinement, but barely concealing his anger, certainly exploded the superficial good-will generated by my openness experiment in the bright boardroom.

Precious, however, in his usual good-natured manner, took the sting out of the situation by freely admitting that Giu's point was all too true and familiar: the world was patently unequal, and moreover bucked all attempts at equality. Without exploitation of those 'unfair' differences, there would be no economic development for poorer countries. He joked that he himself had come to Vietnam only because it paid better than staying at home. In the same breath, he confessed a jealousy towards his military sales assistant, who made more money than he himself simply because he was a Yank, who had to be enticed away from the even higher home salaries while Eric himself was only a poor Englishman. His words broke the tension somehow, and we moved more easily into other subjects.

Diem, a sturdy sales executive from the North not even afraid of Giu, brought up another sensitive issue. Over time, Cong Ty Shell distributed a remarkably stable volume of oil in Vietnam, when military and civilian sectors were taken together. The two sectors often seemed to relate like two communicating vessels through the mechanism of the black market. If one rose, the level of the other dropped. In times of heavy military action, the South Vietnamese army could justify larger purchases, and its illegal sales to our dealers, at lower than our own prices, would rise. The army used more oil and its officers made more money in war than in times of ceasefire, when the economic revival pushed up civilian sales instead. Lately, however, military activity had been reducing and military off-take declining, but civilian sales had failed to rise in proportion, not only because of rising prices, but also because of Communist attacks against the rural economy, which reduced peasant activity and demand. Amidst signs of all-round poverty, the great equaliser, the black market, had taken a turn for the worse. The military badly needed to supplement wages, and our dealers needed to obtain the cheaper oil they had become used to. But with declining availability, the fight became more vicious.

Of course we knew of our retail dealers' illegal black-market involvement. Comparing the totaliser meters on the pumps at their gas stations, which registered their total sales, with our total deliveries, we knew exactly the size by which their black-market purchases exceeded our legal deliveries to them. But they would rather smash the meters than let us use them as proof of breach of contract. The police and the courts were of course useless. The black market was invincible, and both the government and the Vietcong were using it in everything from operating rice storages to munitions dumps to oil. When Prime Minister General Nguyen Cao Ky ordered the execution of a Chinese businessman for black-marketeering, he knew he changed nothing. From the President down, high officials kept depending on Chinese intermediaries. We might not like being drawn in, nor even admit it, but it went on regardless.

The subject seemed one of posturing and empty threats. I wondered if the government or the CIA had ever gone deeper, and studied the dependence on our oil and other commodities of Vietcong forces inside the South Vietnamese no-go areas, the so called 'leopard spots', which were all over the map of South Vietnam. The entire Vietcong military and political structure depended on the workings of the South Vietnamese economy. In the matter of rice production in the Southern delta, at harvest time large-scale military action was promptly undertaken by both sides to obtain the maximum amount by force from the peasants. In the matter of hardwood production from the Vietcong-held jungles, an arrangement was tolerated. Chinese middlemen were 'allowed' to buy the wood at negotiated prices and to export through South Vietnamese ports, bribing the officials. In oil I knew that it made sense for the Vietcong to pay almost double South Vietnamese prices, in dollars, rather than import it the hard way, by railway, truck or on the back of coolies over 1000 miles. But these deals with the Vietcong were the shadowy province of the South Vietnamese military. Of course we knew that some of our oil would end up in Vietcong and north Vietnames stores in Cambodia where no Southern soldiers could follow them.

We could not put a stop to trading on the black market, or prevent supplies reaching the enemy. What we did do every six months or so was sack symbolically the more outrageous dealers who simply went too far. But even that was not simple. We had the sorry example of our Swiss aviation manager to ponder. Recently arrived, and not tuned in to the ways of Vietnam, he had personally tried to prevent the diversion of a lorry load destined for the airport into the black market. The next thing he knew, an attempt on his life was made. The severely shaken man had taken the first flight back to Zurich, and only from the safety of Switzerland had he explained the true reason for his sudden departure. The event was of course glossed over in our dealings with London. From long exposure to war and revolutions elsewhere, they fully realised that operating in Vietnam had risky and unsavoury aspects without the details being spelled out.

Diem had reported developments objectively, not in the hope of finding answers but almost as if he expected things to get worse. Expatriates, however, feel acutely uncomfortable with such open discussion of what is unacceptable and hardly mentionable in their own countries. None of them would profit personally, and they looked to me for the traditional forthright condemnation of the corruption that went on under our noses. I duly obliged. I swore to fire any corrupt employee who benefited from malpractice, whatever the temptation, knowing that the issue would come back to haunt me.

Phuong, another Northerner, wore a black band around his left arm, in the old French manner, for a younger brother recently fallen at Quang Tri. A sniper, overlooked in the rubble, had got him. As he was the second brother to fall in action, Phuong was now responsible for three families. His clothes were cheap and mended. Speaking softly about the security threat to Nha Be, he made a plea that the navy and army officers and men allocated to our installation's defence be treated as part of the Shell family by improving their rations and accommodation as incentives to defend our installation.

The subject of inland transportation brought some welcome light relief. The recent extension of safe areas had opened up hundreds of kilometres of previously inaccessible roads. Cong Ty Shell's bulk lorries, however, designed for American super-highways, were too heavy for the neglected French roads of the thirties, and their excessive back axle loads broke up the old bitumen surfaces. Instead of half-filling the lorries, as the authorities had suggested, a brilliant young graduate, named Trung, had the idea of fitting additional back axles, purchased from US supply dumps, to spread the load. It was not the first time that I heard Trung's name linked to original innovations. He already ran a larger part of the operation department than its expatriate manager cared to admit.

I thought the meeting a success, but Precious spoilt it for me, remarking casually that he, for one, found it a total waste of time. Why bother with togetherness and the raising of consciousness when all the sales boys wanted was faster sampans, the operations experts new back axles, and the finance wizards better computers? Why could I not dish out these toys to them separately and keep them ticking over nicely in the dark, in ignorance of the overall picture, as Mike had done? In a burst of naive candour, I started to explain that we needed their informed points of view for the new Corporate Plan. Precious's laugh was infectious. Both of us accepted that in Shell a well-reasoned well-executed long-term plan, more than attractive immediate results, made all the difference between an ordinary plodding company and a high-flying one, especially for its chief executive, looking forward to the next rung on the international ladder. High annual profits only had meaning if all alternative courses of action, carefully considered and rejected in the context of the plan, inexorably led to poorer results. The interest of a company therefore came partly from the local President's pop-art presentation of potential and alternative courses of action to London directors, who were suckers for imaginative ideas and local colour.

Precious knew this, but had lost the taste for the additional work involved. He advised me to climb down, not to try to dazzle with sparkling presentations. In his view, Shell in Vietnam was better served by making good money in the same old way as before. Shell in Vietnam had no future, and unwarranted displays of brilliance could only attract attention to our precarious existence on the periphery of the Shell Group. Shell loved our profits and hated our existence, with all its public relations risks. Besides, the Centre had other things on its plate right now, like the creaking international trading structure, OPEC, and the end of our indulgent Western lifestyle based on inexhaustible oil. They did not need executives from an awkward part of the periphery holding out improbable business opportunities. But, in my enthusiasm, I happened to disagree. Less than two years before, the abandonment by the US of the gold standard had benefited those who had taken the trouble to prepare for the eventuality. The Oil Standard might be the next to go. Moreover, if peace was achieved in Paris, might Vietnam not suddenly convert itself from an ugly duckling into a swan, or an Asian tiger, with promising vistas for exploration and refining? To prepare for such eventualities, all staff had to believe in a future in order to contribute their thoughts. To Precious, however, company wisdom meant surviving, simply drifting with the stream, staving off disaster by making small adjustments. A haphazardly constructed raft, with its criss-cross planks, suited his ideas of comfortable survival much better than my idea of a stream-lined plan.

I found my Exxon colleague, Bob Ketchum, having to toe Eric's cautious line. But in fact, he was just following directives from his home base. The Exxon board had even ordered him to offer their assets in Cambodia to Shell for one symbolic dollar, so anxious were they to strike a public relations liability off their books. We declined the kind offer.

Returning from the Esso office, I came upon Giu and Eric Precious having an argument. Apparently, Giu had authorised the annual cere-mony for the 'wandering souls' to take place in company time and in the company parking space. He felt it proper to endorse officially the widespread custom of honouring the souls of those deceased without proper burial. He even made it part of a drive to avoid industrial acci-dents amongst Vietnamese personnel, who generally believe that the wandering souls harass the living and cause all kinds of accidents if not duly placated. He had urged Eric to attend, but Eric did not believe in the supernatural, and found pretending against his taste; he had, of course, every right to refuse.

To my mind, however, the reconciliation of phantom souls seemed wholly respectable, and I offered to join Giu. In the courtyard, an altar had been improvised next to a fire hydrant. Two *bonze*s in orange robes officiated. From a kneeling position, they handed joss-sticks to hundreds of employees passing before them in a long queue. Giu and I proceeded undemocratically to the head of it. One impassive *bonze* hit the gong and offered a burning joss-stick to Giu, who took it between outstretched fingers, raised it to his forehead, bowing deeply to the altar. He handed it back to the *bonze* who placed it unceremo-niously next to the others in a heap of sand. Giu threw a few coins into a receptacle and waited for me to do the same. Another gong, and an expressionless bare-shouldered *bonze* held a joss-stick up for me. I imitated the movements, and after a quick muttering of prayer, my stick joined the others.

6

Saigon Hostess

Saigon's night-life was hectic, but severely shortened by the midnight curfew. A string of invitations for official receptions, parties, cocktails and dinners kept coming to me as a result of my weekend pool-side entertainment. The town's most envied invitations, however, came from Mme Do Kim Chi, President of the Vietnamese War Widows' Association, she whose charms had smitten both the American Ambassador and the CIA station chief at that first dinner hosted by Mike Corrie. Saigonese of all walks of life would pick up the lively boulevard press for her latest reported remarks, or for pictures of her recent appearances.

Vietnamese women were endlessly interested in physical detail, and always tried to conform to some or other 'norm'. In the past, ladies of the Song Dynasty bound their daughters' feet at the age of five, to create the deformed stumps on which they could not walk. This then became their 'norm'. Even in today's world, young sophisticated Vietnamese women would gladly suffer similar indignities to conform to the modern norm. They would hide their legs in silk trousers forever if they found them a fraction too muscular. They would use plastic surgery on their beautiful slanting eyelids to turn them into crudely rounded ones. And not only society women believed in the norm. Even the poorest, lowliest female work-gang members wore broad-brimmed hats and full-length gloves in the midday sun to protect skin whiteness, in emulation of the admired Hong Kong movie stars. Kim Chi just seemed to have the self-confidence to make others believe that her individual features were the norm.

Before going to my first dinner at her house, I decided to spend some moments on the roof terrace of the Caravelle Hotel, which served as a meeting point and information exchange for foreigners and journalists reporting the war in comfort. We males also paid obeisance to the fashionable norm, but less physically, mainly in our dress code. I wore a dark blue rough-silk suit of exaggerated cut by the French tailor of Tu Do Street with a loud tie and, I shudder to remember, crocodile leather shoes with large metal buckles. On that terrace, however, such attire was unremarkable. The roly-poly French businessmen and Corsican Mafiosi, escorting scantily-clad ladies, all went to the same tailor. They comfortably hung their bellies over the modishly tight flared trousers. The Caravelle roof garden was our very own grandstand view of the war. In total safety, we marvelled there whenever the horizon lit up with tracer ammunition fired from 'Puff the Magic Dragon' planes, or when a rocket cut a trail across the night sky. To us, those deadly shows on the edge of our city were visual displays of history in the making, like watching the making of a war film on set. We even criticised the scenario and suggested alterations to the script.

From the Caravelle, my driver Tao took me, through the garden gate, past two alsations on chains and a sandbagged bunker, to the entrance of Kim Chi's house, where I joined the others in a long reception hall. Of the hostess there was no sign yet, but her imprint was everywhere in the interior decoration. I was intrigued by the uninhibited passion for artful effects, and by the free spirit of extravagance. Standing aside in a corner, I watched a fresh water stream gliding over mossy rocks, then gurgling into a marble pond. Cushions had been laid on the side for those wishing to study the goldfish at ease. There was a grand piano nearby. Black lacquered sofas inlaid with mother of pearl and white raw silk upholstery lined the wall. Antique rosewood chairs polished by age, around low tables on curved legs, displayed images of birds and flowers between thick layers of lacquer. One length of wall was taken up by a mural painting of a rice harvest, in cinema poster style, somewhat marred by a vertical stain caused by a leaking roof. And looking up to the blue-domed ceiling, I saw a stuffed eagle with outspread wings slowly turning in the slipstream of the ceiling fans.

The far end was dominated by a life-sized, rough-grained, press photograph of battle tanks moving through jungle grass, the guns hung with baskets and bananas, and, in the centre foreground, Mme Do's late lamented husband. Ah, the brief joys of military life and the long-lasting sorrows of the widow! The General, with the shaven bullet-head of a Buddhist monk and the happy sunlit eyes of a child, was exchanging jokes with his officers. Everyone knew that his only education had been at Saint Cyr's Military Academy, and that his only true family were the paratroopers. With them, as a colonel, he had legitimised the rule, and perhaps saved the life, of President Ngo Dinh

Diem, by beating the Binh Xuyen gangsters, back in 1955, for the control of Saigon, and with them he had later forced the same President, by surrounding the palace, to release an imprisoned brother paratrooper. Because he was one of the real generals with real troops near the capital, no coup d'etat could succeed without his previous telephoned approval. But politics never held his interest, because at heart he was just a professional soldier. For this reason, the Americans had chosen him to command the last offensive of the South Vietnamese Army, the Cambodia incursion of January 1971, but they were astonished when nothing moved on the appointed day. The President of the United States wanted explanations, Ambassador Bunker and General Abrams were livid, but no one dared to tell these important figures the publicly-known reason: his wife's astrologer's insistence on a 24-hour delay. He always respected her wishes, and when he did attack, he overran the Communist headquarters and their supply caches the same day, critically weakening the preparations for the communist offensive of the next year.

Lights came on in the upper gallery. Kim Chi descended the stairs in an aluminium sheath which offset her brown skin, her confident face framed in curls. We almost applauded, as for an actress's entrance, although she was quick to laugh away the impression she made on her guests. Amongst them were serious Vietnamese officers, whose troops at this moment patrolled the fields. The commander of the Navy, Tran Van Chon, was using the occasion to apologise to me for the inadequate protection of our tankers on the Saigon River. What did such men seek in her company, I wondered? Confirmation that they still counted in the real world? I saw old lions of the past exchanging harmless gossip, but also General Quang, very much in charge of current psychological warfare, retailing his misinformation to some female guests as if his belief in himself depended on his achievement in these circles. Had they gathered around one woman, on the flimsy excuse of exchanging serious information, or in need of entertainment? After all, the management of a 20-year war finally became a boring nine-to-five job like mine. We all needed entertainment.

I picked up a photo album from a low table. The first glossy picture showed an immense funeral cortege in white, with barely-controlled crowds trying to touch the General's coffin, followed by picture upon picture of famous men, some of whom were now in the room, laying wreaths for the fallen warrior. And there was a last riveting frame, of the guard of honour at the grave-side being jostled aside by grieving women in formless white robes of mourning. My eyes fell on one prominent face, partially covered by a triangular cape, hiding hair and eyes but leaving a strong chin exposed, flowing with tears. With a physical shock of recognition I looked into that wide open thick-lipped mouth, with rows of even strong teeth, in total surrender to grief. A far cry from the controlled expression she wore tonight.

A servant held a board with the seating arrangements in Gothic letters. The highest in rank took their places in the middle around Kim Chi, the others, in order of diminishing importance, towards the ends. As a businessman, I sat at the bottom, next to other minor personalities like the wretched Admiral of the Navy, whose obsolete ships inspired fear only in his own fishermen. A few ex-ministers and a buxom lady politician joined us, and on the whole they were lively and enjoyable company. As the mood mellowed, the older diplomats at the centre began making toasts to themselves, commemorating various events. Touching the long-stemmed glasses with a silver spoon for silence, they would launch into faltering speech. Bunker loved presiding over such Vietnamese occasions. Finally, he touched his glass to command silence for our hostess, and I was surprised at the change that came over her as she rose. Face-to-face, she made good common sense, but with all eyes on her, a cascade of frivolities poured out, delivered in a childish voice, sustained by peals of laughter, in which people joined without knowing why. The double meanings of her jokes went heavily underscored by winks and flashes of the eyes. Ripples of applause carried forward her solo performance, and she could easily have ended in mid-sentence, by just raising her glass. Instead she wandered on, drawn by adoration, stringing together happy phrases like pearls. When she finally stopped, there was an ovation. Almost immediately, however, the officials had to leave because of the curfew, and they filed out in a hurry to where the drivers waited in the official black limousines, with the curtained windows and the loaded guns clipped to the backs of the front seats.

The reality behind Kim Chi's performance of celebrated hostess, as very few of her admirers knew, was totally different. Her society position rested entirely on make-believe, which made the government 'forget' the rent on her house as long as she served to let its ministers meet the heads of the American establishment privately, and it made the CIA pay an exaggerated rent on her own villa in Dalat for the same privilege in reverse. Tonight's performance had cost more than a widow's monthly pension, and she had an extended family and retinue to take care of. It required whole blocks of freshly-printed bank notes just to maintain her status. And those banknotes were largely generated by Kim Chi's farm.

Normally she rose at dawn, ready for work, without make-up, her hair held back with a traditional clasp, a linen shirt tucked into black peasant pants and her feet in clogs. In that attire, none of her nightly dinner guests would have given her a second glance. In her Volkswagen bus, her driver would place a wicker chair, next to sacks of cement, so that the servant girl could sit on the metal floor at her feet, and via the back streets they would head towards the farm, while the city was still asleep.

Well before Bien Hoa, the VW bus would jump off the asphalt onto the low wasteland, which was stone-hard and dusty in the dry season and muddy in the wet, the tracks changing all the time. It was anonymous terrain, neither field nor village, pasture nor workshop. Poor people scraped a living there in shacks between roadside eating-places and junk-yards. But these haphazard communities, with their ducks and dogs, were her shield and network of protection. So the bus would stop often for a chat with an owner, or to distribute sweets to the children. Her earthy remarks split dark peasant faces into wide grins. These were no diplomatic pleasantries. Beyond those shacks, the terrain sloped down to a stream and rose up on the other side towards no-mans-land, at the jungle's edge. There stood the farm, with its long modern pig-sheds built in the shadow of eucalyptus trees, its manioc fields planted in straight lines. A bridge gave access to a house with an aluminium roof, tall radio antennae and helicopter pad, the latter in disuse since the General's death. Boys in army greens, deserters working in exchange for a safe refuge, would unload the bus.

Hers was the largest pig farm in Vietnam, yet it existed largely outside the law. It supported not only her family, but also surrounding villages and sub-contractors, supplying Saigon with low-priced meat. It was protected from government harassment only by her name. She had bought the land cheaply, when no-one else dared invest, because it lay in a contested zone. The corrugated iron roofs, scrounged from US surplus stock, rested on pillars made of spent artillery cartridges, filled with concrete filched from the Public Works Department. But the layout of the farm, its feeding systems and its administration came from the latest Danish agricultural pamphlets, which she was the first to apply in Vietnam. Neighbouring market farmers sold her the green offal they had previously thrown away. The labour-force grew its own food, and only the foreman received a salary. She and her neighbours obtained relative security through mutual accommodation.

When the foreman made a disastrous mistake, such as when newly-bought pigs were mixed with the existing herd, she would have to pitch in like an ordinary labourer. On one occasion, a disease from a new animal had spread to a few hundred other pigs and a score had already died. An epidemic of this order could wipe her out within days. She could not wait for a vet from Saigon, and after the segregation of the sick animals, she had to do the injections of antibiotics herself, in rubber boots, jumping astride each animal while it was held by two men, inserting the needle between the shoulder blades while another man dabbed it with purple and chased it into a different shed. Thus she would stagger on until late afternoon, and only if the animals lived would she too survive. But she was not one to dwell on the negative side.

As she left the farm in the bus, loaded with eggs for the Saigon market, she would lift her eyes to the high ground near the stream and dream of the two-storey colonial house which she planned to build there.

7

A Vietnamese Labour Dispute and a Skeleton in the Closet at Nha Be

For nearly a year, Giu kept playing a game of tortuous negotiations with the Petroleum Workers' Union, of which all the labourers in our industry were paid-up members. As it was the biggest union in the Vietnamese Confederation of Labour Unions, the talks had a nation-wide impact. Traditionally, when Cong Ty Shell agreed a new two-year labour contract, the rest of the industry immediately followed its terms. In retrospect, I may have allowed him to drag out the nego-tiations for a little too long, but at the time there seemed to be no urgency. Despite the lapsed contract, our workers remained normally at work without threats or complaints.

After a while, however, Giu's strange disregard for concrete results made me wonder if he was dragging out the negotiations for their own sake. Many times I had been willing to settle on reasonable enough terms: an increase in wages below the rate of inflation and the usual benefits of free meals, housing and schooling. Giu, however, always found some last-moment minor reason to block the signature, and appeared to enjoy the labourers matching him tit-for-tat. To him, the talks seemed good sport, and the match more important than the result. As long as the labour representatives kept talking to him like sons to their father, as he saw it, the family relationship would leave no room for a strike, and holding the talks in itself would strengthen those family ties more than a mere signature on a contract. I prayed that Dr Kissinger and his all-American diplomatic crew at the Paris peace talks knew better than I how to cope with such Vietnamese games. My own instinct, meanwhile, was prodding me that work con-ditions should not be left indefinitely to personnel managers and union representatives, and that I should perhaps take them directly to the rank-and-file myself, rather than blaming Giu for his leisurely approach.

In the outside world, meanwhile, the fears of labour strife resulting from our delays were mounting. I must have been over-confident, or temporarily deaf to the warnings. Not only my colleagues in the oil industry were nervous at the delay. Two ministers warned me simultaneously that they had inside information of an imminent petroleum workers' strike against Shell which, spreading throughout South Vietnam, could undermine the government's position at the Paris peace talks. This sort of warning – if you had learnt to read the signs – could only come from President Thieu himself. Potential trouble amongst the industrial working class rated as highly in his suspicious mind as in the minds of the Politburo.

A phone call from Tom Polgar clinched the matter. He invited me to come and see him in his own lair in the bunker-like American embassy. My car and driver had to stay outside the gates, of course. Only I was allowed entry by the starched Marine guards, and that only after lengthy telephone checks. Cameras from different angles, meanwhile, were conspicuously following me with their glass eyes to deter me from blowing up the gate. Thereafter, I was marched to the front entrance door of bullet-proof glass, and like a package handed to another marine. Inside, more checks, signed forms and discreet electronic surveillance, but at long last a civilian human being, a blue-haired motherly secretary to accompany me to the lift to the top-security CIA floor. The offices had little to distinguish them from the normal deep-carpeted American business environment, except perhaps that middle-aged women executives seemed to be more prevalent, and have more self-assurance than I was used to. Beside them, the tough young men wandering in and out of closed rooms looked like postgraduate students. None of these was armed, but broken noses seemed to be in fashion. I had met some of them outside Saigon, and they seemed to have no reserve in talking to me in confidence as a friend of the boss. I never inquired if they had established a security clearance for me to consort so regularly with the top brass, here and at their own parties. None of the doors along the corridor had numbers or name-tags, but each had a buzzer. When we got to Polgar's nondescript, door my chaperone buzzed twice and the door clicked open. Polgar beckoned me into his office.

Apparently, his patience was also wearing thin with our negotiation, with what they insisted was the Communist-infiltrated Petroleum Workers Union. Years later, the CIA were proved wrong in their accusation, but at the time I could only say that I personally had detected no ideological infiltration, and that I still fully trusted the common sense of our own labour force to come to an agreement. Polgar abruptly brushed my objections aside. This was now his business, and his 'advice' to me personally was to seek guidance directly from Tran Quoc Buu, the 'reliable' President of the overall Confederation of all Vietnamese Labour Unions, who also happened to be on the CIA payroll. All my previous experience made me suspect that Buu, as a politicised labour bureaucrat, might be further removed from the realities of the work situation than me. But under the circumstances, I was left no other choice than to settle for a secret late-night meeting alone with the famous man, at my house.

Buu arrived driving his own car. From the moment he entered the room in a crab-like manner, with his head to one side as if fearing blows to it, his intelligent eyes kept scouting restlessly behind the thick lenses, and never stopped measuring me. I had expected to feel antipathy, but to my surprise the old man's demeanour almost disarmed me. I could only feel sorry for his wretched state, and by making full allowance for it we got on reasonably well. His proposition was as simple as it was brutal, however. According to him, the allegedly Communist chairman of the Petroleum Workers Union, a labourer of Shell at Nhabe, kept putting forward unacceptable demands with the sole purpose of provoking a general country-wide strike, from which only the Communists would profit. If we let that happen, the Petroleum Workers chairman would then leverage his prominence into challenging Buu himself for the top job at the Confederation. This was his real concern.

I fetched him a double whisky. Clearly the old man's priority was to eliminate a rival, rather than to help us towards a negotiated solution. Years of secret CIA grooming as the political voice of labour, and even as a possible substitute to President Thieu, had taken their toll of his self-respect and sense of reality. He had become their all-too-eager stooge. In my firm belief, not even a Communist chairman could induce our stubborn men to strike if they felt that our terms were right, but taking Buu's concern at face value I offered to conclude the agreement within the next few days. I hoped that this would take away the spectre of the dreaded strike.

But the prospect of a peaceful end to the negotiations without his help seemed to agitate Buu more than anything else. He began to shout that the purchasing power of government employees and soldiers had halved since the departure of the Americans, that a third of the labour-force was without a job and that a 'soft' agreement with the already-favoured petroleum workers, negotiated with a known Communist, could only worsen the injustices of the whole system. These were fair points, though nothing we could do much about. Having voiced his objections loudly, he became menacingly calm.

This was Vietnam, he explained grimly, and he was in the best position to advise us just how to deal with local agitators. The right solution was for us to refuse any further negotiations at all, and thus to provoke the chairman into calling a strike. Before he would be able to follow through, however – Buu sliced his fingers delicately across his throat – Buu would have him silenced forever, to teach our labour-force a lesson and make them conform without arguments in the future. Obviously there was no common ground between us, and we parted politely as opponents.

To pre-empt such dire solutions, I called the workers together for a final meeting with Giu, in the basement cafeteria the very next morning. As we entered, the ten representatives and their reputedly Communist chairman rose formally, and serious handshakes were exchanged. These men had been rolling red and yellow Shell drums by hand since before I could have found Vietnam on a map, and although they now operated fork-lift trucks and intricate machinery, they did not forget that the company had taught them to read and write and that their children too were being taught at the Shell school. They knew the valves and pipelines of the installation better than their bosses, and the weathered faces above the spotless white shirts looked entirely self-confident and yet respectful. Their positive attitude strengthened my conviction that no Communist could tell them how to vote. But, while they did behave in accordance with the solemnity of the occasion, their attitude was only one of impersonal respect for Giu and myself. They knew too well that we as individual managers had to make the expedient trade-offs which sometimes rewarded the quick above the poor and honest. Their true loyalty went to the institution, which had picked them from the streets and the rice fields, and which clearly rose above all our human frailties. Giu and I were mere representatives of that venerable entity. On the physical level, my tall-ness suited their ideas of hierarchy, they being small and wiry, but a boss also needed to show by little details such as manicured hands that he was above menial work, and there I disappointed them. There was no way my appearance could satisfy them: according to Chinese concepts, I was born with a fire-type face – the forehead broader than cheekbone and jaws – which stamped me as being disposed to change, while they put stability above all else.

Advisedly, I did not try to assume any ill-fitting mantles, and I did not try to raise expectations, but merely went over the course of nego-tiations, describing the remaining differences between us objectively, sticking to our guns and explaining why. During Giu's unhurried translation, I watched the lined faces assimilate the new formulation of the old arguments, while trying to remain expressionless. But I began to like those straight faces, and soon I felt a positive response in return. After finishing on the reminder that it was time to shake hands on a deal, there was sober applause. When, after the recess, the chairman started his reply, I saw that he too was trying hard to establish the proper atmosphere for a final agreement, so much so that I wondered fleetingly if word had got to him somehow that his own life hung by the single thread of a successful conclusion. We had no way of knowing if he was a Communist, but he certainly proved himself worth more to us alive than dead. Next day, he delivered the signed agreement, and as far as I know he never angled for Buu's job.

To celebrate the signature, a 'family' day at Nha Be was organised for all employees from high executives to drum-washers. Expatriate executives, mildly ironical about such egalitarian shows, accepted them nevertheless as part of the worldwide Shell family culture, which was nowhere more emphatic than in Vietnam, where the family always counted for more than the individual. They played their role in the games good-naturedly. The huge and ugly installation had been swept clean and decked out with bunting, and transformed into a playground for workers' families in their Sunday best. Underneath the cosmetics, however, she could not hide her true age and the ravages of half a century of wild growth. Only the older workers were fully familiar with the inefficiencies and hideous complications of the complex. The earth underneath was so saturated by leakage that the bitumen installation looked worse than a derelict Venezuelan oilfield. However, above it all rose a rollicking welcome song from the junior school children, arranged in ranks and waving their paper flags with military precision. I gave the starting shot in a teenagers' contest and lost a sack-race against the union leaders. Then I wisely went to inspect the schoolroom, where the mothers had deposited their offspring so that the labour and their guests could ravage the open air buffet without inhibitions. I observed with amazement a young teacher order the toddlers to take a siesta. At a clap of her hands, the children obediently hit the wooden floor, put their heads on their arms, closed their eyes and slept on command. Try that with European toddlers, I thought.

During the celebrations, Vien, as I will call him, the first-ever Vietnamese manager of the installation, whose appointment I had approved, was leading us around. He personified the new generation of executives, university-educated, sensitive, rational without edges, speaking good English and therefore the automatic darling of expatriates. In discussions, he liked to pose as a trendy leftist intellectual. His reports were always lucid and reassuring. If they did contain rather a lot of suggestions for improvements in his own accommodation, it had to be remembered that the old expatriate installation managers had been rough-living Scots. But tiny grains of doubt about his effectiveness remained. When asked about excessive product losses, Vien never took responsibility, producing statistics 'to put them in perspective' and blaming under-deliveries by the tankers from Singapore. The decision to appoint the talented Vien had indeed been contested by few. Only Giu had preferred another candidate, ex-colonel Phuoc, the Da Nang branch manager who had impressed me on my visit North as the most basic of executives, whose strong suits were discipline and insistence on detail, whose educational certificates were military recommendations and who spoke English in army command fashion. Only his French-educated wife somewhat softened his image. Giu might have different local criteria, but I had initially felt a warm glow putting the installation in the hands of the suave and talented Vien.

When, at dusk, the security lighting came on, the crowd assembled in a clearing near the river, where the fire brigade had lit a bonfire next to a steel watch tower. The soldiers left their guns on top and were allowed to join in. A smell of roast pig wafted across the field; usually sober men indulged in a lot of drinking, and girls laughed immodestly. Games became sillier. In one, acting the fool, blindfolded, I had to pin a tail on the backside of a donkey drawn on a notice board. An attractive local girl sang Vietnamese and Western ballads on a dais, writhing in the spotlight.

Afterwards, Giu and I were sitting relaxed on the grass among the crowd with our rice bowls and beer cans when young Trung happened to saunter by, looking ever so slight and innocently friendly. We knew that he was not in the habit of doing anything without a purpose. Everyone also knew that, though only a junior executive, he ran most of the operations department. His bright ideas had often cropped up in management meetings, and he had a self-assurance that was practically an insult in someone his age: a younger version of Giu and twice as talented, which guaranteed, of course, that the two would never get along.

Trung now regaled us with his most casual smile and just seemed to pause for an innocent remark on the product losses, which he had accidentally heard Vien explain so exhaustively to me. Surely, he remarked-off hand, I knew them to be theft, pure and simple? While he kept smiling, I saw Giu wince, and I had no choice but to ask him to justify such a serious accusation. Trung pleasantly complied, pointing to the suspicious regularity of the recorded surpluses, which seemed to accumulate in the tanks over a period of several weeks and then change overnight into a single barge-sized loss. His expression in the light of the campfire was now dead-pan, a true poker-face.

On such nights, he continued leisurely, only one junior employee, like a stock clerk, would be on duty – with a few watchmen – in the whole of the installation. They would be very much awake, however, straining their ears for the expected sound of an engine approaching over the river. In the early hours of the morning, an unmarked military barge would duly enter the floodlit circle around the jetties, the lights reflecting on the helmets and guns of half a dozen regular soldiers on board. Hoses would be connected on orders from the stock clerk, pumps switched on, and half an hour later the barge would leave Nha Be, filled to the brim with our product. Instead of duly making an invoice, however, our clerk would simply reseal the valves and enter the delivery as an unexplained loss in the books. Theft was therefore the main reason for our excessive losses. Giu reacted sharply: why had he not made his accusation through the hierarchy to Vien? Because Vien himself was in on the act, perhaps blackmailed by his own clerks, Trung dryly explained. But Trung's reporting all this directly to me, neglecting seniority and the chain of command, seemed a bigger crime to mandarin Giu than the theft itself.

Firecrackers zoomed through the air; a pop-eyed dragon appeared on rickety legs, but I no longer saw them, reflecting on the implications of what I had just heard. I suddenly felt cold. From Trung's cool, reasonable tone I knew he was telling the truth, and Giu's strange reaction proved that he, too, had been substantially aware of the facts but had kept them away from me. My predecessor had never hinted at theft on this scale in our own installation. Even our respected internal audit, through naiveté or corruption, had never even investigated the possibility of theft by the army, abetted by our very own personnel. The labour-force around us would certainly be in the know, and would be awaiting my reaction with interest.

A chasm opened at my feet. Where could the barge go? Would it perhaps go along the myriad of channels of the Mekong delta and drift into Vietcong territory? Was I to sack Vien and replace him with someone like Phuoc? But we had no legal proof, Giu warned. Trung, however, had an answer for everything: proof could be obtained the hard way, by setting a police ambush at the appropriate time to arrest the culprits *in flagrante*. The risk of a shoot-out between the police and the army, perhaps easily acceptable to a twenty-four-year-old graduate, represented a big escalation which could go dreadfully wrong. Giu insisted that the time-honoured way to deal with the problem was for me to appoint a special committee to look into any 'abnormal' losses. Their report would vaguely confirm our 'suspicions', sufficiently for us to impede but not to stop the thefts, by installing more security equipment and rotating suspected staff without prejudice: the time-honoured mandarin's way of problem solving without making waves.

But I, with my hard-line Western principles, felt in a cleft stick. Having been brought face-to-face with a serious accusation, I felt I had to act, on penalty of losing all the respect of my staff. Morally challenged, I opted for direct action and police intervention, bypassing the now suspect Vien and the established line of command, and entrusting young Trung with organising the trap with the police on the earliest possible occasion, which is what I told him to do. I authorised the trap in spite of Giu's misgivings.

8

Peace Negotiations
in Paris

Economic Warfare
in Vietnam

Much larger developments began to overtake us. The monsoon had brought cooler autumn weather to Saigon, and with it a whiff of hope that the Paris talks might move beyond 'form of the table' squabbles (on the possible admission of more than the US and North Vietnamese participants) to the drafting of a definitive peace proposal. As soon as the details of the secret deal between Henry Kissinger and North Vietnam's Le Duc Tho oozed out onto the Saigon social circuit, talk of the negotiations became unending. One night, President Thieu's insufferable thirty-year-old nephew, Hoang Duc Nha, swirling cognac in an outsized glass after dinner, managed to shock even a circle of hardened ambassadors by the casual claim that he had personally rejected on behalf of his uncle the proposals, approved by Kissinger and Tho and carried by General Haig to Saigon for acceptance. Communications between Thieu and the Americans were obviously at their lowest point. Nha's impudent baby-face, long hairs dangling from the warts on his chin to ward off bad luck, was positively beaming with boyish pride. To show his contempt, he was bragging that he found exchanging phone numbers of call-girls with Kissinger more rewarding than trying to improve a bad deal. These were ominous signs.

Although Thieu had, in May, already accepted a draft of the 'bad deal', whereby each belligerent would be left in control of the area they held in South Vietnam, the fact remained that Thieu, as traumatised by the prospect of peace as Hanoi, was now summoning all his ingenuity in trying to torpedo it. Instead of throwing his weight behind a peace proposal, which would improve living conditions throughout South Vietnam, including Communist areas, and stop further bloodshed, he kept dreaming of a purely military solution, disregarding his inferiority in numbers and material support. Just one year of peace could have created a rice surplus for export, two could have seen South Vietnam on its way to an economic miracle and tentative democracy, in sharp contrast to the shrivelled economy and institutions of the North. He should have publicly discarded the military option. This was his chance to nail his colours of peace to the mast and improve the political and economic condition of his people. God knows, oil companies were anxious enough to explore the South China Sea basin and help pull the country up to Taiwan's economic levels.

The question amongst his friends was: why did Ambassador Bunker display so little personal initiative, when he should have been pushing nephew Nha aside and shaking Thieu awake to his last chance at this crucial stage? Why did Bunker stand aside, letting the blame fall on poor isolated Thieu for his lack of understanding? True, Thieu invented maddening pretexts for not receiving Bunker, or for letting Kissinger cool his heels for days in Saigon, before granting an audience, in the most infuriating tradition of the old Vietnamese court, exactly as Ngo Dinh Diem had behaved with Ambassador Henry Cabot Lodge before. Two successive American ambassadors seemed incapable of getting through to the Vietnamese mind, while the State Department had never even felt the need to have a Vietnamese in its top negotiating team, nor for taking any high-level Vietnamese into their private confidence. They dealt directly with the enemy and submitted texts, once negotiated, in English to Thieu only for his views on dots and commas. On the hapless CIA, with its large budget for spying on South Vietnamese intentions, fell the task of making up for the diplomats' failure to establish an honest meeting of minds with their allies. It was hard to imagine any successful business operating in this way.

I had by now become a regular visitor to the American embassy, which I could see from my office across Thong Nhat Boulevard. A certain routine had established itself. Bunker would invite me to his imposing private office, seat me amongst the ambassadorial memorabilia, signed photos of heads of state and presidential meetings in silver frames, and in his informal patrician way brief me about the world situation in general terms. He exuded a kind of avuncular authority. Often we would digress to sailing on the South China Sea, which both of us loved. Once, in a storm, with a novice crew overcome by sea-sickness, the octogenarian Ambassador had stayed alone at the helm on deck the whole night long. I could well imagine his sharp face set against the punishing spray. I even offered to buy his yacht whenever he moved on, but unfortunately it was not his to sell, being the property of the US Navy. After coffee, he would ask his secretary, the redoubtable Eva Kim, to take me to Tom Polgar's office for more specific talks.

Polgar was no patrician, and totally different in his approach. Although his office was as large and deeply carpeted, and fitted out to the same opulent standards, it felt workmanlike and closer to reality. Polgar liked always to understate the awesome power of his agency by hanging caricatures of himself, bogus mementos and comical photos on the wall, of five Vietnamese youngsters balancing on a Honda scooter in peak-hour traffic. After acting the sympathetic host, he began chatting about developments, not about the embarrassing Buu incident, which seemed as if it had never occurred. The North Vietnamese offensive had failed, as we knew. Chou En Lai preferred a divided Vietnam to one dominated by Hanoi, which could become a nuisance to China. Unhurriedly, he rambled on: even Brezhnev wanted *détente*, because his economy was going nowhere. As a result, North Vietnamese delegate Le Duc Tho had to make real concessions in Paris, so that prisoners could be exchanged and America could be extracted from the war with its honour intact. All that remained were local skirmishes and Nobel Peace Prizes for Tho and Kissinger! That was the big picture, as sketched in five easy minutes by Polgar.

However, just for my private information he hinted at something more interesting on my micro-level. He seemed more alive now. Without my seeing how he had alerted her, a trim businesslike senior analyst came in right on cue. She extended a metal pointer, tapped the wall-map impatiently for attention, and began a well-rehearsed survey of terrorist activity during the last weeks, a bomb explosion here and an electrical power line broken there – the usual. Tom looked keenly interested, as if he was hearing it all for the first time. The point was that all these enemy sapper attacks were aimed at civilian targets: rice depots, electrical works, roads; there had been not a single attack of military interest. The reason, according to 'incontrovertible' electronic evidence – Tom favoured the phrase – was that the attacks were meant to put economic pressure on the South Vietnamese to accept the peace agreement. Details from intercepted written communications confirmed this picture. The attacks were to culminate in attempts on oil-tankers and on the great Shell installation itself. For this purpose, the élite Dac Cong sappers had now been deployed in the Rung Sat, ready for action. He had, of course, alerted Admiral Chon, whose few means to protect us made him irrelevant. So we would have to fend for ourselves. Beyond giving adequate warning, it was not his concern any longer. 'Welcome to economic warfare', smiled Tom.

The presence of better-trained enemy sappers in the Rung Sat was another major challenge for the installation management, but it did not appear a priority to our friend and official protector, the ARVN colonel in charge of military security in the swamps. In his often-stated view, the area had to be cleared out by infantry every few years, but he had no troops to do it. The Americans had left him an ultra-sensitive anti-personnel radar system, but of course the few ARVN soldiers could not stay alert all the time in front of the monitors. And even had they detected enemy movements, the colonel could not have taken action on his own, because the Navy had overall command in the area. Rung Sat not only fell between commands, but the South Vietnamese had no adequate resources for the task.

Thus we had no option but to walk the familiar path to the shed near the river, guarded by hissing geese and an emaciated alsatian on a chain, which was the command post of our friends, the long-suffering installation guards, the same guards who had participated in the Nha Be celebrations. We discussed the threat with the captain, who agreed to intensify night patrolling around the tanks in return for increased amenities. But his suggestion that troops be admitted to the installation, although militarily correct, had to be turned down because of the unmanageable opportunities for increased theft to which it would have led. The free-fire zones between the outer and inner security fences were meticulously cleaned up, however, and radio communications with our private army improved.

As a sign of concern, I ordered an expatriate executive presence in the installation at night in the period of high risk until the signature of peace, to keep an eye on things. This last measure also had the favourable, if wholly unexpected, side-effect of temporarily stopping all pilferage by military barges at night. In addition, it provided a stream of operational improvement suggestions, which could only have occurred to insomniac expatriate brains in the course of a boring night watch.

9

A Tanker
Under Attack

Inevitably, as foretold by Polgar, one bright morning a crew of North Vietnamese sappers lay in ambush behind a clump of palm trees, bellies in the mud, on the edge of the shipping channel, waiting for our tanker, the *Clintella*. They let the advance escort patrol – a deep floating camouflage painted relic of the French war with old tyres hanging over the side – pass unhindered. A South Vietnamese sailor, in jeans and baseball cap, scrutinised the very spot where the squad lay through the sights of his .50 machine-gun, but from 30-metres distance saw nothing unusual. After the patrol-boat's passage, the sappers could safely rise to their knees to aim the RPG 7 rocket launchers. The steel hulk of the oil tanker already loomed at the river bend, slewing sideways, heading for the ambush site with its own 17-knot maximum speed augmented by 3 knots of the incoming tide. The water bulged in front of the snub bow and crashed in crowned waves through the reeds upstream. The mighty rhythm of the marine engines at full emergency power must have thudded through the wet clay under the sappers' knees. As the bow swung past, the iron side momentarily blotted out the sun. The ardent young sappers, mentally reconciled to their deaths in the forthcoming explosion, supported the rocket launchers by an elbow on the left knee and peered through the sights. No need to fear any reaction from the unarmed colossus. They could also safely disregard the man in white uniform with gold stripes on the high bridge who looked directly down at them through field glasses, and seemed unaware of his destiny to die with them. At 200 metres, the target was unmissable, like an elephant at close range.

But tankers, with all their heavy safety features, are in fact much harder to sink than battleships. Had the sappers been knowledgeable, they would not have been attacking a loaded tanker, as direct hits in the oxygenless compartments merely fizzle out. An empty one on its return, with a belly full of explosive gases, would have been a better target.

In the shortness of time, however, the sappers' political instructions decided their aim. They sent the finned rockets into the gleaming officers' quarters behind the bridge, fully expecting to be engulfed in the resulting liquid fireball. Faultlessly directed, the rockets' two-kilo warheads slammed with hammer blows through the steel wall. But the explosions sounded strangely puny, and the ship's engines did not miss a beat. In spite of the perfect hits, the unarmed moloch remained steadily on course for Saigon. No reaction could be seen or heard, none at all. Of course gratitude at still being alive on a beautiful day, with birdsong in the reeds, should have filled the sappers' hearts. Instead, bullets from the escort vessel, which had raced back, began to slice through the undergrowth to spoil their day. There was no time to feel elated. They ran inland in bewilderment and humiliation. Behind them, the patrol-boat gunners, unable to see even a glimmer of a target, eventually stopped their blind firing, and in the following silence a similar sense of futility and failure began to envelop them.

Two minutes later, when the captain radioed with a request to evacuate a wounded officer, it was my turn to feel failure. What had begun for all of us as a promising day faded into failure and slapstick comedy. Clever little David had attacked Goliath with a sling. According to the bible, he should have had no trouble killing him, but Goliath just wiped the blood off his brow and David had to run for his life. Such slingshots, however, would occupy the company for days on end with insurance claims, staff compensation and worried questions from Shell Centre in London. Moreover, an escalation of pin-pricks could tie even Goliath down. I dreaded the bureaucratic battles about appropriate reactions, but the first priority was to hurry to the scene.

The transition from the rotting outskirts of Saigon to the fresh countryside never failed to surprise. After two bridges over tributaries into the main river, the city lost its airs and graces and became a line of mean buildings and sweat-shops. Sophisticated city women gave way to old hags with toothless smiles, wearing black pyjamas. The old Mercedes clattered with difficulty over the perforated metal sheets of a third hunch-backed bridge which had long ceased counting the times it had been half-destroyed and repaired again. On top loitered the usual arrogant soldiers. Below, in the mud, fishing boats exposed their scaly bottoms, lying sideways between rolls of barbed wire. But then – miracle – on the other side, the eternal countryside suddenly took over. Bridges there had similar criss-cross approaches and sandbagged positions, but these were obviously guarded by fresh local boys. In the hamlet markets, the old women in black seemed to carry real authority, and we were back in the eternal Mekong delta again.

From afar, our large petroleum storage tanks dominated the horizon. On entering the installation, I found the *Clintella*, correctly moored in the churning yellow water along the jetty, discharging 30,000 tons of fuel like a contented cow. But the captain was livid. Having bundled off his only casualty, the wounded first mate, with accompanying wife, to the Saigon hospital, he felt free to vent his frustration by bellowing about the inadequate protection of his ship against military attacks and bewailing the absence of helicopter protection as in the 'American days'. In fact, he and his officers had been delighted to be chosen for the lucrative Singapore-Nha Be run, and to draw the double salaries on offer because of the increasing war risks after the 'Vietnamisation' of the conflict. They had keenly volunteered for the opportunity, considering it a risk-free pleasure trip at double pay. Apparently they were now even taking their wives along, against all rules and common sense. I did not need to point this out. The captain changed tack. He had seen with his own eyes through binoculars 'those Vietnamese terrorists', so very nearby, so unbelievably arrogant and at ease when aiming their tubes at him. He swore that he could identify them in a police line-up, which both of us knew would never take place.

I suggested that if he could see the attackers so clearly from up high he must have been in an excellent firing position, and that therefore he should perhaps consider taking on board half a dozen Vietnamese machine-gunners at Vung Tau for proactive protection. The best example of such self-protection lay moored nearby. I pointed at three rusty river tankers with Cambodian crews. Between sandbags around the helmsman's position and the machine-guns, the crews' children were playing hide and seek. These boats carried our oil 200 miles upriver to Phnom Penh, without any external protection at all, right through enemy territory. When shot at, they just shot back, and kept going with negligible losses so far. They had no extra pay, and their families joined them because they had no other place to live. They might be mud lizards compared to our gleaming *Clintella*s, but their poor crew, unlike ours, had at least looked war risk straight in the eye and had drawn the hard conclusion about how to protect themselves.

The *Clintella*'s white officers might well consider these boatmen throwbacks of an existence too miserable to imitate, but were we not all equals in the war-zone, and were we not in the competitive business of survival? And if, from an economic point of view, our Caucasian lives were too valuable in salaries and insurance, not to

mention education and medical expenses, were we not pricing ourselves right out of the war? We all knew that one effective hit with a
score of deaths could bring the European seamen's union out on strike
and halt all supplies to Vietnam. This was my business and my livelihood as well. If we wanted to continue trading, the pragmatic solution
would indeed be to bolt machine-guns fore and aft on deck and
operate with a Vietnamese semi-military crew under volunteer company officers.

This was unthinkable within company policy, of course, and mercifully further arguments were cut short by a young Vietnamese-speaking
CIA American. They seemed to pop up uninvited at key moments. Had
he heard of the incident by listening in to the ship's radio? How had
he passed through the installation's security? In any case, he was
there, congratulating the captain for being in command of the first
merchant vessel to be hit by an RPG7. Amidst our argument, we had
completely forgotten to look at the impact itself, and now we trooped
sheepishly behind this uninvited weapons expert. The rockets had
entered the starboard side, punching a single hole through two inches
of steel, after which, split into multiple hot fragments, they had punctured successive bulkheads through the whole width of the ship to
shower an officer in his bunk, all the way on the port side, with ragged
shrapnel and liquid metal. We were lucky that the North Vietnamese
sappers, after so much planning and preparation, had bungled their
mission by choosing the wrong target and the wrong weapon.

I went to see the ship's officer, who, his uniform caked with blood,
had been brought to the best French hospital in Saigon, the Grall. A
sickening smell of disinfectant hung in the stagnant hot air. Patients
lived in lines of yellow blocks with corrugated red iron roofs under
dusty trees. A few nurses moved indolently amongst the families doing
the cooking and caring for their relatives at their own expense.

He was lying face-down in a dark room, attended only by his
desperate young wife. A bunch of flowers, sent by the company, lay
scattered on the floor. All morning she had complained to French
doctors and Vietnamese nurses who did not understand a word of
English that her husband was being left to die in his bed. Nothing had
been done, and on finally seeing a Shell executive she broke down
sobbing. I button-holed a junior doctor, just out of medical school in
France, who explained patiently that our man was in no danger, that
the harmless shrapnel embedded in his flesh had to come out by
natural action, and that, besides, the Grall needed its beds for more
serious patients. When I drew myself up and argued our company
employees' inalienable rights to instant and complete medical treatment, wherever in the world, he laughed. Oh, was that so, the doctor
drawled teasingly, an extinct Gaulloise hanging from his lower lip. In

that case, he himself would be honoured to oblige, on the sole condition that I would act as his medical assistant, because the nurses were at lunch. 'Allons-y!'

I proved a willing but inept orderly. As we wheeled the first officer on a stretcher into an empty operating theatre, cockroaches scuttled off into corners, but the doctor switched on the operating lights and the ceiling fan as if he was in a spotless private clinic in Paris. Humming a pop tune, he donned a stained white coat and gloves and held a needle aloft. The half-sedated officer, eyes bulging and very frightened, was slurring enough four-letter words for the surgeon to stop his good-natured humming of 'Mamie Blue' and inject the needle without further ado. The pretty wife slid into a faint, while the doctor, humming 'Oh Mamie', set to work on her husband. He worked quickly, taking the larger pieces of metal out with pincers while I dabbed the wounds with mercurochrome, leaving the deeper ones untouched. Quarter of an hour later, everyone's honour saved and the operation finished, we wrapped the patient in blankets, installed him in the back seat of the Mercedes, his head on his wife's lap, and waved them both goodbye. Tao delivered them to the *Clintella*, just in time for the good ship to borrow the ebb tide for her return dash through the Rung Sat. Back in Singapore, the officer would duly receive a hero's welcome and a decoration.

In their base camp in the Rung Sat, the North Vietnamese held their usual after-action self-critique, a *kiem thao*. When we heard the details later from a captive, I was awed and fascinated. These sessions formed part of the iron system of self-criticism in front of one's comrades, the idea of which was to learn from experience by analysis, and improve one's own and others' contribution to the cause, without ever questioning the cause itself. The latter restriction was necessary to keep higher ranks beyond criticism. At working level, however, blame was eagerly accepted, and this helped to build a deep internal discipline and commitment into troops, one that went beyond the discipline instilled through intimidation and military drill exercises I myself had undergone in the West. From three days' quiet discussions emerged the conclusion that if a hit to the brains of the beast did not work, perhaps a stronger blow to the belly might do the trick. After all, that's where it kept its petrol.

More weeks of intensive preparation followed during the wait for a moonless night. The plan was for five frogmen to go back to the river. Their leader would be in his twenties, but the others were younger still, mere fifteen-year-olds. A sampan would be waiting for them, with a fisherman in the prow and in the stern, hunched over their paddles. An engine was ruled out for its noise, and was in any event superfluous because the in-rushing tide would take them effortlessly enough to

Nha Be. The sampan rowers would bring them as close as they dared, but would stay well outside the patrolled areas within the installation's protective lighting. There the divers would await the beginning of slack tide. They would slip overboard and swim under cover of clumps of water hyacinths, breathing through tubes, to the tanker, magnetic mines of Russian make, resembling small car wheels, fixed to their belts. They were confident that the land-based South Vietnamese sentries could not see them, nor shoot at every single bundle floating past the tanker at slack tide. Moreover, they had ascertained that we still, unaccountably, failed to station marksmen on top of the tankers, from where they would have had a more commanding position to shoot down into the river. The divers had to fix the mines to the hull well below the waterline within a quarter of an hour, set the delay fuses at 30 minutes, and swim back to the sampan with the reversing current. They were to carry survival rations of cooked rice in plastic bags for any unforeseen emergency.

10

The Price of War

An Estimate of Outside Economic Support to the Belligerents

December 1972 was a fateful month. With insane fury, South Vietnamese President Thieu first rejected the peace draft, then submitted to it on condition that certain petty changes were made. By then, however, the North Vietnamese Politburo was refusing any further changes, and President Nixon had to make the cold decision to unleash the ultimate fury of the B52 bombers against Hanoi military targets, bringing howls of protest from all over the world, but forcing the North Vietnamese back to the table.

Meanwhile, on our micro-level, Cong Ty Shell's Corporate Plan, like that of any Shell company in the world, was duly emerging from the collaboration between Saigon executives, who had first absorbed London's interpretations of world trends, before developing their own ideas and specific targets for Vietnam. These were to be summarised in a prestigious-looking booklet and presented to London shareholders as rational objectives for the next five years. The procedure might seem academic, or even a waste of time at the climax of a civil war, but this was our equivalent of *kiem thao*: a way of promoting positive thinking throughout the company while keeping an eye on South Vietnam's survival chances.

I was participating in the internal discussions, though without much faith in extrapolating from the past, as most of us were doing. In talks with outsiders too, I kept looking rather for a flash of insight to place things in perspective, in the same way as a salmon's leap can reveal what is upstream. Everyone has such moments, when, after a long search, the truth of the matter literally leaps up. The stakes we were playing for in Saigon were high. Many people from different walks of life, of independent mind and with ample local experience, were drawn in to shape my thoughts, but one Australian stood out above the rest. Down-to-earth and inquisitive, Ted Serong could explain the politics and the fortunes of war better than most. The sturdy ex-commanding general of the Australian brigade, a cool unconventional professional, saw the war neither apocalyptically as a prelude to World War III, nor cynically as an international testing ground for officers (he was retired), but for what it was: the local struggle between two Vietnamese sides with incompatible ways of life. Hardly any war was total armageddon in his eyes. On the contrary, war was a normal state of affairs in many countries, and his life had been full of such Far Eastern struggles, with the incompatibilities ranging from religion and tribe to political dogma.

In Vietnam he had, in unusually close co-operation with the South Vietnamese Army, cleared the Vietcong out of whole provinces, committing his units to constant training in improved platoon tactics and night operations. Eschewing the spectacular, he had used small innovations like tracker dogs and specialists for tunnel networks, and stressed constant routine surveillance. But above all, he had used artillery sparingly, to keep the population on his side.

He was the only successful general on our side applying everyday moral and economic concepts to warfare. His first consideration in keeping a war sustainable and morally winnable was the application of 'commensurate force'. You can destroy a palm hut with an artillery shell worth twice the hut's value, but if you do that all the time – or worse if you do it with B52s – you will certainly be losing the war. Common people will not only hate you, but it will wear out your own side rather than the enemy. Better let the hut stand. The illustrious Ho Chi Minh had grasped the concept of war economics early on, pushing it to its logical conclusion by attaching different values to human lives themselves. 'If we kill only one expensive Frenchman, for every four expendable boys killed of our own, the overall balance is still positive,' he had observed. At the end of his tour, Ted Serong was in such demand that the Rand Corporation and President Thieu retained him as their military counsellor. This exceptional officer, now a stocky grey-haired man, with solid arms sticking out from a short-sleeved civilian shirt, explained to me the basic errors on our side, which had so sadly increased the length and nastiness of the war.

It stood to reason, he argued, that money was a prime mover in the outcome of war. Why should war be different from business or any other human endeavour in this respect? Business and scientific judgement has to be backed by capital, and even art flourishes better with a wealthy patron. Clearly, with human resources on both sides being roughly equivalent, as in Vietnam, outside patrons dispensing military aid decided the whole issue.

He pointed out that initially Vietnam had been an easy victim for France. In 1873, Francis Garnier was able to take the citadel of Hanoi and half of North Vietnam with only 200 Frenchmen because the Viets had, as yet, no generalship and no weapons to speak of, and the population had been totally disaffected. But 80 years later, after Vietnam had been modernised and politicised up to French levels, the colonials were seriously deluding themselves in continuing to believe in their superiority. Unlike Ho Chi Minh, they had taken their eyes off the economic equation, believing that they were still stronger and better equipped for the fight. Although their expensive expeditionary corps of 150,000 foreign soldiers and their rickety Airforce could indeed inflict massive damage wherever they went, they were inappropriate and clearly unaffordable in the long run. The annual costs, rising from $1.2 billion in 1952 to $2 billion in 1954, had to be subsidised by the US, who did it to bolster France as an ally in the European Cold War. Fighting in this expensive way, The French could not afford a long-term strategy, while Ho could bide his time. Moreover, the French were ill-equipped for the real war of small-unit actions, less mobile across terrain, and even outnumbered by the Vietminh army.

Behind the scenes, Serong continued, unnoticed by almost every observer, Russia and China were already matching the French and American expenditures in direct aid to the Vietminh. The Communists knew that no local revolution prospers without serious outside backing. The Vietminh regular army could only grow to 200,000 men with donated Russian arms, while 15,000 Chinese instructors shaped it up in training camps in Southern China and on the artillery ranges of Ching Hoi and Paise. Up to 150,000 Chinese coolies assured the supply line into North Vietnam, no fewer than six Chinese generals advised the Vietminh on the battlefield, and the Chinese took responsibility for feeding the civilian population of North Vietnam into the bargain. Translated into dollars, that Communist aid was well superior to the American and French expenditure in those early days. No wonder that the Vietminh, with the sustained weight of outside economic support in their favour, prevailed against the French.

The Geneva peace, concluded in 1954, between a Communist Northern and a quasi-democratic Southern half, lasted in effect only till 1960. During it, South Vietnam became a republic, and the US replaced the French as its protector. Democracies, however, have a distressing habit of losing interest in the balance of military forces in peacetime, and do not realise that thereby they invite attack. Thus practically nobody in the Western democratic camp in that 'peaceful' interval between 1954 and 1960 saw the continuing military investment in the Communist North as a serious threat. Like in Europe in 1939, democracies could not budget for the probability of war. Only eccentrics like Ted Serong bothered to denounce the small American military aid to the South, compared with the huge Russian and the Chinese aid to the North during that deceptive peace. Financial analysis, inexact to be sure, should have made obvious at the time why the victorious North Vietnamese war machine continued to grow in peace even faster than in war. Through Russian and Chinese aid, to the tune of $500 million during each year of peace, it could double in size to 400,000 men and start to infiltrate the South in preparation for a new war.

By contrast, the situation south of the seventeenth parallel after the French had washed their hands of the affair was utterly relaxed. The new republic's chief military advisor, US general 'Hanging' Sam Williams, did not ring any alarm bells. He complacently wrote off the Southern Army as a 'heterogeneous assembly of perhaps 100,000 men', and did nothing to improve it. And while in 1960 President Kennedy verbally pledged to pay any price to support the United States' allies anywhere, he only spent his money in Western Europe and in Korea. To South Vietnam, where President Ngo Dinh Diem clamoured for help with the armament and training of at least 200,000 lightly-armed men, to stave off guerrilla attacks, Kennedy sent one advisor. On his return, four-star general J. Lawton Collins merely gave Kennedy the welcome advice that the Southern army could safely be cut down even further, to 77,000 men.

Anyone totting up the differences in material support at the time should have decried the resulting disparity of military power as a recipe for disaster. It was a disparity that would eventually suck America itself into the war. However, amongst foreign advisors a remarkable complacency prevailed. General Collins totally underestimated the Asian ability to raise very large, cheap and effective armies. In the seventeenth century, the Nguyen warlords of South Vietnam, from less than half the current population, had raised no fewer than 260,000 armed men, supported by war elephants and fleets of rowed armed vessels. That was four times the number Collins allowed for South Vietnam in the twentieth century against a superior enemy. The US advisors despised the local forces to such extent that they did not even recommend training the few existing ARVN soldiers, on the strange basis that the Saigon government was too weak to warrant a trained army. And worse, they shaped the remnants of the ARVN in the American image: heavy and road-bound to repel a conventional attack from the Chinese Communists, rather than what President

Diem really needed, an army able to fight a lightly-armed guerrilla threat.

Quite apart from such errors of judgement, however, and strictly on the basis of comparative investments alone, the South had already lost the war before it re-started. In 1955, US Ambassador Donald R. Heath in Saigon wrote that President Diem needed at least $500 million of military aid a year for the bare maintenance of his own forces, which was only a third of the military aid with which the French expeditionary corps had lost its war against the same enemy. Yet actual US aid amounted to a mere $140 million in that year, and to no more than $160 in following years, derisory assistance in proportion to Communist aid to the North. But disciplined diplomat Heath, like good soldier Collins, deferred primarily to Washington's own needs and perceptions. Saigon was full of weak American advisors like them, who watched helplessly the loss of the undeclared war. They allowed a local South Vietnamese guerilla operation to turn into a disastrous international involvement in a war of attrition, and attrition against expendable Asian armies was the equivalent of defeat. Somehow they seemed able to back a war with money only if American, Israeli or West European lives were on the line. Thus the neglect of the South Vietnamese army in the so-called years of peace during the Eisenhower and Kennedy mandates laid the basis for the future waste of 50,000 American and hundreds of thousands of Vietnamese lives.

Suddenly, listening to Ted Serong's analysis of Vietnam's recent history, the salmon started to leap: we were about to enter another of those false-peace periods. After the signature of the peace treaty and the withdrawal of its troops, America was bound to lose interest again. What if, in this year of military stalemate, 1972, and during the armistice to follow, South Vietnam were treated by her allies as she was in 1954 all over again, starved and abandoned for the third time, under the pretext of a signed peace? With foreign troops safely withdrawn from a disastrous involvement, all further interest of the American congress in South Vietnam's survival might well cease, and the country would be abandoned again. But at least we now knew what signs to look for. We had an early-warning system. We could predict the course of the war, and of the peace-keeping, not by sticking coloured pins on maps, but by tracking the military aid figures. We were a very important item in these financial figures, which I had to discuss each week with the inhabitants of MACV, the American command, in their air-conditioned windowless offices. To be explicit, we estimated annual current aid to North Vietnam at over $1 billion, and growing. Aid to the South was declining, but still above the $1 billion danger mark which Ted and our own staff estimated as the minimum required to hold the line. As yet, we felt reassured that there still was a valid balance of power and that at least we would get an early warning of any deterioration by watching the numbers.

So there I stood on a podium one morning, in dark suit and white shirt in front of the luminous screen with coloured graphs, beaming back at the staff in the darkened auditorium the conclusions they had reached. And I dared to express confidence in a forthcoming military stalemate, going hand in hand with prosperity, without dwelling on the darker side. I took a ceasefire for granted before it was even signed. While this confidence trick was perhaps excusable *vis-à-vis* overseas shareholders, it did raise the hopes of vulnerable local staff whose lives were on the line and who believed in me totally. Every Vietnamese face in the audience seemed to look up at me in the touching belief that I saw their future from a higher vantage point, and that the company knew best.

That night I packed my bags for the presentation in London and for a Christmas holiday with the children in Holland. During their last stay in Saigon, the old Phan Dinh Phung house had temporarily forgotten its ugliness. The servants dearly loved family life. They liked the little girl who swam in the pool like a water nymph, especially when it rained bubbles and they gladly suffered the pranks of the teenage boys. When they left, a pathetic tearful line-up had seen them off. The water nymph waved goodbye to the little green snake in the tree and her washed-blue eyes smiled for the last time on the staff, and on the crestfallen house. Since then, the silence in the empty house had weighed heavily. By now, I was so well organised, that I almost resented the perfect service, the impeccably ironed shirts laid out over a chair in the bedroom with the pressed trousers and the polished shoes underneath, like a ventriloquist's dummy, ready for the next morning's performance. The performance the following day would be a welcome break with routine. An early morning flight to London would see me pampered in an Air France first-class cabin, allowing me to go through the details of the presentation one more time and to daydream about the family reunion with my children over Christmas.

No sooner had I fallen asleep when I was woken by a terse telephone call from Nha Be. The news was sickening: a tanker moored at the installation was believed to have one or more underwater mines stuck to its hull. With half of the cargo still aboard, it could become a fireball in a split second. Vien, the installation manager, and the tanker captain had ordered all personnel to abandon ship and man the fire-fighting stations. Listening to Vien, I could well imagine them fleeing down the gang-plank in panic, convincing themselves that they had ordered the retreat of all those who followed, but as the end result did indeed reduce numbers of lives at risk I commended him warmly. Then I ran to the car and took to the empty streets of the curfew. There was the risk of trigger-happy soldiers, but luckily the guards on the bridges knew the white Mercedes, which crawled up to their check-points slowly with dimmed headlights.

Nha Be was visible from afar, lit up like a football stadium, with powerful lights concentrated on the tanker. For the last half hour, all movement had been frozen and the hundred-thousand-ton storage park and its personnel awaited their fate with stoical calm. Only the senior staff and tanker officers, crouching behind a brick wall, were arguing noisily and inconclusively amongst themselves.

The tide had turned, and the seaward current made further diver attacks impossible. Army frogmen, who had first sounded the alarm, had succeeded in detaching one mine from the hull and disarming it, but had not dared to look for possible others. Their sampan had kept a respectful distance for the last fifteen minutes. Meanwhile, the aban-doned tanker, floodlit from all sides, hung in its white mooring lines, helpless, like a fat caterpillar in a web. As I watched that silent ship, an irrational anger rose in me. What stupid cowards we were. A mine with a time-fuse of more than half an hour stretched the credulity. More likely, I thought, there was no mine at all, and even if there was one we should now be busy emptying the ship. But I think it was mostly the fear of ridicule that made me get up suddenly and walk away from the chattering officers towards the deserted jetty. It felt good to be on my feet again, and even better when I heard the steps of a ship's officer behind me. Only when arriving at the towering hull did we realise that we could do nothing except justify our action by appearing to check the shore side of the ship. So we started looking severely below the waterline, trying to pay no attention to the yells from the sampan crew.

Seconds later, a thunderclap issued from the steel wall, so powerful that it threw us down onto the concrete floor. Dazed, we sought each other's eyes. It was no oil explosion, but what was the hissing sound, like air escaping from a giant balloon? More seconds passed, while the inrush of water through the shattered hull forced petroleum fumes out of the open air vents on deck. The whole ship began to list incredibly quickly over us. The officer sprinted up the gangway, shouting for me to help him close the enormous valves on deck by hand so the ship, now a punctured bag, would stay afloat on trapped air. Other crew members rushed forward to finish the job and minutes later we could all peer incredulously over the railing at a hole in the hull, larger than a doorway, through which the river was slopping in and out. Rapid pumping to empty the undamaged compartments lifted the hole completely above the waterline, and in that condition, without any repairs, the sturdy old tanker was to steam back to Singapore.

It must have overtaken a fishing sampan on the river, with two heart-broken men at the paddles, perhaps giving a desultory wave. The gaping hole in its side was the only proof the sappers would ever have that their comrades had hit the target, because there were no survivors amongst the divers.

By this time a half-circle of thoughtful men had formed at the river's edge, amongst them, in faded fatigues, the admiral commanding the Rung Sat region. The sampan crew, who had thrown grenades at the divers and army swimmers were dragging bodies out of the river and laying them out for inspection, like game after a hunt. The gleaming white bodies of five enemy frogmen were outwardly unhurt, but their lungs had been crushed by the percussion grenades. They were dressed in black shorts, with diver's watches and plastic bags, filled with cooked rice still in their belts. They seemed to slumber, almost god-like, awaiting an unceremonial and quick burial. The workers and soldiers, whom these teenagers had held in such terror, filed past expression-less, for a look and a silent prayer, almost respectfully.

Just before I went home, that Christmas of 1972, catching my flight after the adventures of the previous night, the B52s had started to bomb targets around Hanoi, to force the North to sign the peace agree-ment. Only a determined cold warrior could have issued the order, while at the same time a tearful Thieu was paradoxically telling the Southern population on TV that Nixon was delivering them into the hands of the Communists. I caught an exceptional glimpse of the air operation from the cabin of my Air France Boeing 747 on the way home. The watery Mekong delta had disappeared, and we were over-flying Cambodia in brilliant sunshine when the shocking reminder of war appeared. On a parallel course, a flight of obsolescent eight-engined B52s, a generation older than our 747 but stuffed with rejuvenating electronics, was descending to their base in Thailand. They looked their age. Protruding radar and machine-gun domes and jungle cam-ouflage paint heightened their ugliness. Some engines trailed smoke. Having reduced the bridges, railroads, fuel dumps and power plants of North Vietnam to dust with electronic precision, they had lost a distressing number of their own to the new SAM missiles. All that violence for the signature on a piece of paper which the two warring parties themselves did not want. But that is what outside military intervention will always be about: imposing a ceasefire against the local leaders' will.

On touch-down at Heathrow after my connecting flight from Paris, the world was perfectly normal again, the weather foul; but the bombing was front page news, with angry reactions from Western allies. The Centre, however, marched to an entirely different set of pre-occupations. This time it was all about who owned the oil under the desert. A gradual nationalisation of Middle Eastern oil sources was in progress. Not surprisingly, the Arab governments firmly believed that increased ownership of the oil sources would automatically maximise their revenues. While they were inflexible in their demands, however, they seemed content to leave the messy detail of production, transport, refining and marketing to the former owners, the international oil companies, who were also asked to draw up the necessary legal language on compensation payable in oil.

A Shell team had been formed to 'negotiate' the transfer of ownership, and a whole new language had sprung up to distinguish the various categories of compensation oil, the different values attached to each and the agreement of production schedules, of which I was as woefully unaware as any Vietnamese peasant. Luckily, a team member brought me up to date with the essential jargon of 'equity' oil, 'shortfalls', 'buy back', 'phasing' and 'bridging' oil, all describing the same product from the same fields, but justifying different price tags. Pricing had to be more devious than ever, with phasing oil at 'tax paid plus 25', bridging oil at 'quarter way plus 7' and 'overlift' (the lifting of more oil than allotted) at posted price, to reflect the infinite shades of ownership and production rights. Prices were hard to calculate in real time, and were therefore routinely adjusted after the product had already been sold and delivered, if, in retrospect, they had not correctly reflected the arrangements at the time.

Compensation for the loss of ownership of oil in the Middle East proved just as elastic as price. Under pressure from the Yamanis, Attiquis, Khalifas and Oteibas of OPEC, the Western oil companies had made a concession to raise Arab participation in the billion-dollar installations from 20 percent to 51 percent over five years under a nebulous compensation arrangement hidden beneath lawyers' formulas. Conveniently pushed out of sight was the fact that the producers and marketers of the oil would have to be the current owners, the same despised companies for the foreseeable future. None of the participants had an inkling that within a year most of these artificial arrangements would be swept away by the 100 percent nationalisations which were to follow the 1973 Arab-Israeli 'Yom Kippur' war.

In these distracting circumstances, our Vietnam Plan and Budget were quickly approved by a yawning Vee, as Far East Director presiding over a large meeting of finance, marketing and other functional executives. As long as our Vietnam company provided dividends and required no financial assistance from Shell Centre, it was allowed to exist in its own fashion, regardless of the rising public outrage against the unpopular war. The executives concentrated on the speculative issues, which I juggled in front of them – the possibility of fast growth after peace, openings for exploration, refining etc – without going into current operational detail. Vee and I kept it that way. Besides, the plan chimed with all the latest notions of Central Planning, and I had learnt to speak the new jargon convincingly. And naturally one issue was never raised: the leakage of Shell's oil into the Vietnamese black market and ultimately the depots of the Vietcong and the North Vietnamese.

In the corridor, leading to the office of Gerry Wagner, the Chairman, I passed an old painting of Hong Kong harbour, with sailing junks and satisfying mountains of red and yellow oil drums, a light-hearted reminder of our humble beginnings in the East. Wagner was a charismatic Dutchman in his fifties with a square face and a shock of grey hair, but his London office was furnished in a very neutral style with bland woods and beige carpets, avoiding vivid colours and distracting individual taste. He and his British, Dutch and American predecessors had risen through the ranks, and seemed cut from the same nondescript material: approachable, tolerating no nonsense and discouraging anything leading to the personality cult so beloved by financial journalists. In fact we liked them in that disembodied way. The checks and balances of the system, which alternated British and Dutch chief executives, made our global top executive a superior type of *apparatchik*, unable on his own to commit the company on concrete issues without his colleagues' agreement written into the minutes. But his influence behind the scenes was enormous. To me, by way of introduction, he was the only one to mention in all seriousness the public pressures represented by outside board members to pull out of Vietnam, even after the peace signature, because our mere presence in the war-zone seemed a worse public relations liability than our presence in South Africa under apartheid. Perhaps it was impossible to build fire-walls between our activities in South Vietnam and the outside world after all. The Vietnamese civilian market represented only a few percent of sales worldwide, but to the world it meant active involvement in a most unpopular war. Were the profits really worth it?

His words marked a possible change in corporate attitude. Up to now, as long as we kept London out of our affairs we were left alone to generate sales and bring in the profits. Could it be that public relations pressures were now getting to Wagner?

My strong reaction merely amused him. I was opposed to terminating our historical presence in Vietnam just because it was unpopular with the media and current public opinion, my main ethical argument being that without people like us there would be no peacetime reconstruction at all. The North understood war economics, living off handouts from the Russians and Chinese, but not peace. I handed over the silly 'industrial policy' statement contained in a major speech delivered by the Northern head of government, Pham Van Dong, on postwar industrial development to make my point. Pure French undergraduate

Marxist stuff, ascribing great significance to heavy industry, arbitrarily allocating plants to manufacture export products with no markets, long discarded anywhere else in the world. But neither did the South, under Thieu, know how to take advantage of the peace. Both sides started from a backward agricultural base with great unrealised potential, but lacked the knowledge and the capital to make a successful transition on their own, for instance to explore for oil and to produce coal and power plants.

The Chairman rolled his eyes to heaven. He commended my efforts amicably enough, but warned in the same breath that I should not count on his co-directors to support any investment. They seemed much to prefer the predictability and respectability of the European home companies. Don't be discouraged, he said, and the interview was over.

PART II

Year of the Buffalo

11

Peace Celebrations

On 27 January 1973, when the peace agreement was signed in Paris, all activity stopped throughout Vietnam, as if by magic. Tet, the Vietnamese lunar new year, had arrived with flower buds and sweet scent in the air.

People were a little breathless, and reeling from the sudden fall of the ugly old certainties, rather like cripples told to walk without a stick. The agreement's clauses were meticulously spelled out by each transistor radio in each apartment, each hut or wooden boat, and each of us strained through his tears to understand the deliberate ambiguities, wishing fervently to believe in peace and happiness for the year of the Buffalo. To the North Vietnamese sappers in the Rung Sat, the text was presented by their political officer as a reward for their sacrifices. They too must have felt lumps in their throats, dreaming of family reunions and of an end to their sub-human existence in the swamps.

Officially, all offensive action had ceased, and prisoners of war would be exchanged within 60 days. However, as the agreement did not even mention the Peoples' Army of North Vietnam, whose presence in the South had never been admitted, they did not officially exist. Their stand-down was an optical illusion; but its soldiers cheered nevertheless at the mere thought of going home.

The ceasefire agreements provided for joint supervisory commissions, staffed by the former combatants, reporting to a neutral International Commission of Control and Supervision (ICCS). In the first instance, each former combatant was provisionally left in control of the ground he currently held and this was Thieu's main objection. He wanted immediate control of all of South Vietnam, including the bits he had never been able to conquer. Usually these were pockets of jungle and thinly inhabited areas, controlled by the so-called Provisional Revolutionary Government (PRG), which formed 'leopard spots' on the main body of his South Vietnam. The rice-growing areas and cities, with 90 percent of the population, already belonged to Thieu.

As to the future government, the two former enemies, joined by a third 'neutral' Vietnamese contingent (an intriguing concept, as true neutrals were hard to come by), promised to form a Council of National Reconciliation and Concord. This was supposed to restore democratic liberties and to supervise free elections to decide the colour of the future government, a tall order for a body that could only decide by unanimity. While unlimited opportunities for trickery between Vietnamese thus remained, the bottom line for the Americans was that they had successfully extracted themselves from the war, leaving behind an internationally acclaimed framework for supervising the reconstruction of a just society in South Vietnam.

It might just have worked if President Nixon had retained his credibility as an enforcer, which was soon to be destroyed by Watergate, and if Thieu had grasped his last chance. Thieu was unable to seize the advantages the new ground-rules for peace gave him. After his tearful denunciations, he issued the defiant and daft state policy of the Four No's in clear contravention of the agreement: 'No negotiation with the enemy; no communist activity in South Vietnam; no coalition government; and no surrender of territory to the enemy'. That gave him a soaring short-lived popularity rating in Saigon, but no flexibility at all to take advantage of the peace. Neither, of course, could the old men of Hanoi be credited with much positive thinking. They too wanted total military victory.

As Giu and I were listening to the specious clauses, schoolgirls were playing their favourite stealth game in the courtyard below. One wisp of a girl stood immobile, with her face to the wall, only her *ao dai* moving in the soft breeze, like the tail of a stalking cat. Behind her back, the other girls were trying to move closer without being detected. Whenever the girl at the wall sensed movement, she would turn in a flash and anyone caught in motion would be dead. The survivors would freeze, until she had her face to the wall again, then slide closer. When, at last, one could lay a hand on her shoulder, the girl at the wall was dead and another would take her place.

Giu and the Vietnamese executives took it for granted that stealth was also the name of the peace game. They firmly believed that committees of mentally arthritic politicians and generals would remain immobile, intent on sabotaging the peace, and that the people had to make the running behind their backs. The peasants could only make peace work by helping themselves. And their justification lay in article No. 11, which gave them freedom of movement for the first time, and in article No. 4 of the military protocol, which allowed local commanders to agree to local accommodations. The pent-up demand for goods in the Communist areas was such that a wide interpretation of these articles could get the ball rolling, open the roads, clear the mines and get the people involved. If allowed, they would rush and buy food, oil and technology, and plant rice again. And once there was momentum for economic integration, it would be hard for higher-ups to clamp down again. We acted immediately, starting before our own government prevented us. Our dealers' lorries and sampans began trading with the leopard spots at once. Trade soared.

Around this time, Madame Thieu was advised by her fortune-teller to celebrate publicly the shotgun wedding of her daughter, and the presidential couple, still basking in their newly-won popularity, made a rare public appearance together. The frigid image sticks in my mind as the worst kind of presidential performance. Thieu, as Head of State and the embodiment of Virtue, was taking tribute from us, a long line of dignitaries, waiting to present our compliments and gifts. Dressed in traditional silk robes to emphasise his nationalistic background and his obeisance to the imperial tradition, he kept pressing and dismissing hands with an absent-minded smile, resembling ever more his isolated and unfortunate predecessor Ngo Dinh Diem. In another vast ceremony, I saw him distributing legal title to agrarian land 'to the tillers', a very popular programme among the peasants. In full uniform on a podium with Ambassador Bunker, who had provided the money, Thieu had the new landowners lined up in squares to applaud him.

On his orders, meanwhile, the official North Vietnamese negotiating delegation, under General Tra, languished inside a military compound without access to anyone. Also on his strict orders, ARVN General Ngo Dzu automatically rejected all attempts at integration of the leopard spots. The window of peace, small as it might be, was slammed shut by the Vietnamese leaders themselves.

But the public mood remained deliriously happy at the approach of Tet and peace. The year of the Buffalo was about to begin, and you could feel the intoxication of the whole continent – a quarter of all humanity – totally involved in the festival of renewal. Household altars carried abundant offerings, to appease the house spirits and to welcome back the ancestors on their annual descent from Heaven. In these first days of peace and Tet, homesick soldiers deserted both armies in their tens of thousands. Even I, wandering around the house in shorts, could feel the excitement gripping Sao and his helpers as they polished the floors until they shone like mirrors and turned the garden into a showplace for the following day's new year reception.

For my part, I hoped I had masked my personal detachment by duti-
fully assuming the role of benevolent businessman. Red envelopes with
stiff new banknotes lay ready for presentation to the servants' families,
and a bamboo pole complete with hoop and streamers had been erected
outside as a centre for the next day's outdoor celebrations.

Unexpectedly, a Vietnamese friend came to survey my spotless
house. She also surveyed me on the eve of Tet with a critical eye. The
house looked a bit like its master, she explained with a sly smile,
perhaps steady in the line of duty but not exactly reaching out to make
others welcome. Tet was renewal, exuberance and warmth for everyone, she proclaimed. Failure to clean the soul of negative thoughts, or
to embrace a positive spirit would bring business failure too. People
would blame me if my garden looked correct but unhappy, the house
clean but not lavishly decorated and if I went around with a long face.
On this happy occasion I should tip my servants much more than they
deserved and start living to the full. The house and garden badly
lacked rows of new orange trees, may blossom flags and an abundance
of decorations, which I could pick up in the market for a song.

So off we went to the teeming market of downtown Saigon, where
millions of people, from all walks of life, jostled together in the fragrant
air. In the shaded sidewalks I saw fantastic wares on offer: wild bear
cubs on chains, talking birds, crayfish claws and goldfish, and in the
thieves' market, stereo equipment and petrol in glass bottles, sold by
eight-year-olds. With dozens of flowering plants in the open boot, I
returned victoriously home flushed with excitement. Sao and the
other servants caught the spirit and sent us back for new treasures,
ceramics, ribbons and glitter to bury the severity of the house. On each
return, they clapped their hands in encouragement until the ground
floor was a festive market itself, overflowing like the horn of plenty.
The year of the buffalo had a propitious start.

On the morning of the first day of Tet, after a dive in the pool, I
happily put on my brand-new clothes to begin the ceremonious round
through the house handing out envelopes with gold characters for
peace and prosperity. There were gasps at the number of stiff banknotes
inside. I kissed the children as my own, and filled their hands with
sweets. Then I drove through the streets, crowded with people in conspicuously new clothes, to Nhung's apartment to wish her well and
have a late telex decoded. She was hesitant at first to open the door,
because the first person met in the New Year determines your luck. My
smiles, however, removed her doubts, and she offered the obligatory
sweet rice cakes. After a few more visits, joyful and happy, I went home.

In the garden, coloured ribbons fluttered from the bamboo pole and
tables stood in the shade, groaning with food. Music started and the
workers from the office and from Nha Be, with their families, started

to arrive *en masse*, eager for entertainment. The food disappeared in a wink, the garden was trampled by a thousand feet and the new potted plants in the interior were overrun. At a roll of drums, a dozen men formed a military square on the grass, under Giu's direction. Longest-serving employees, with tight faces and medals on the lapels of their new suits, stood in front. In a somewhat stilted ceremony, every bit of it as traditional as a presidential reception, I had to go through their ranks, pinning 18 carat gold Shell badges next to the other medals and handing service certificates to men who kept staring straight through me in the disconcerting fashion of soldiers standing to attention. After this, however, ranks broke and I became lost in the crowd, free to drift.

The sound of firecrackers and wailing music approached, and through the garden doors a multi-coloured pop-eyed paper dragon entered on a dozen feet and started to undulate above us. Chinese acrobats began climbing the pole and jumping off in backward somersaults. Others held stylised sword-fights. Finally, a crescendo of sound announced an attempt by a famous karate expert to cut through a stack of bricks with his bare hands. Glistening with sweat, he lifted his right hand like a sword, psyched-up by the drums and the shouts of his comrades. On the first try, he failed, bloodying his hand. Nobody minded. On the second and third attempts, he broke through gloriously, ensuring Cong Ty Shell's prosperity for another year.

12

Leopard Spots

Everyone talked about the 'leopard spots' on the map of South Vietnam. In the rich Mekong delta, where relations between enemies had always been influenced more by the rice cycle than by grand military initiatives I thought I had an opportunity to see for myself.

When I asked the manager of our delta operations, to show me how the former combatants managed to live side-by-side, he was taken aback at first. Being an intelligent and cautious man, he lived in a police compound in Cantho on the great Hau Giang river, one of the four mouths of the Mekong, where he often spent sleepless nights angling for minute fish from a rickety jetty under a roaring generator exhaust. Reluctant to expose me to reality, he arranged to take me on a family guided tour instead, with his uncle, the commander of the Cantho airbase.

At the desolate living quarters of the base, Colonel Le, a peaceful-looking man even in Airforce overalls with a revolver in his belt, was waiting for us. His wife had already brought the baskets with cakes, wine and napkins to the helicopter. Its empty machine-guns were hanging dejectedly down on each side, but flying conditions looked great. A few reconnaissance planes were landing, but apart from that, we had the whole of the immense ex-American base to ourselves. Without much of a pre-flight check, Colonel Le started the engine and began lifting the shaking platform into the air. Soon we had the court-yards of the villages under our boots.

We flew leisurely over the choppy brown river to the rice lands on the other side, where most roofs among the palm trees bore the red and yellow government colours for protection against air attack.

94

As we rose higher, the sun jumped out of a bed of yellow haze. In spite of the peace, from force of long habit, Uncle Le still gained altitude over the 'leopard spots' to avoid possible small-arms fire. So we did not get a close-up view of them, but to me they looked like all other hamlets.

After an hour, he brought us down in the territory of the Cao Dai religious sect, a spot chosen by our manager for its absolute security and prosperity. The Cao Dai demonstrated the feasibility of keeping out warriors from both sides by employing their own private militia. They practically opted out of the war, and the result was instant wealth. A local dealer walked us along the well-kept irrigation ditches, showing us the fabled land of the four rice crops a year. In these conditions, peasants could keenly experiment with new rice varieties, and become rich enough to afford the necessary fertilisers.

Our accompanying ladies, stumbling on high heels over the sun-baked clay, had no interest in farming, however, and enticed us back to a courtyard amongst citrus trees, to tables loaded with drinks and hammocks invitingly stretched between branches. They seemed to be in charge. Behind our local '33' beers, we sat in easy chairs next to a glass fish tank. Salted crab and lobster from the tank were served, with snake meat, highly recommended for its aphrodisiac qualities. This was not what I had requested. For my entertainment, two little boys laid on an impromptu cock-fight, which finished with the losing bird saving his life between my feet while the winner was held high and kissed by its triumphant owner. To top it off, Uncle Le suggested a siesta in the hammocks, but luckily the women insisted on consulting the *bonzes* of the black virgin pagoda near the Cambodian border and he had to get his party airborne once more.

We now flew due west, towards pink clouds mirrored in the tributaries of the Mekong, to the blue hills on the horizon, which had to be Cambodia. The unmarked real border was moving ever deeper into that unhappy country, with the encroachment of Vietnamese rice planters, but that was hardly remarkable any more. More relevant, according to Uncle Le, was Cambodia's renowned excellence as a preferred battlefield for the Vietnamese. Fighting on your own terrain, he explained, meant that you had to destroy your own kin and property in order to get at your enemy. Every battle in populous South Vietnam, therefore, was a defeat in human and property terms. So far, the South had suffered half a million civilian casualties, against only 25,000, at most, in the North, which was why thinly-populated Cambodia was such an irresistible battleground to the South Vietnamese. As the Americans, however, strictly forbade them from crossing the border in force, the South Vietnamese had reluctantly to leave it to the enemy, who used it as a sanctuary.

A large black mountain had meanwhile begun to dominate the view. Uncle Le landed near its base and rummaged around in the bush for a couple of hidden oil drums and a hose to fill the tank. We flagged down a soldier with a jeep, and left the chopper in the care of a local youth. The soldier, a careless driver, seemed proud to leave an imprint of his tyres through as many bundles of live chickens as he could manage, oblivious to all protests. Apparently the mountain and its pagoda had changed hands as a gunnery platform so often, and at such cost, that the combatants had finally hit upon the compromise of declaring it a religious zone, demilitarised by both sides. Since then, civilians had pursued their own interests without much interference. The soldier belonged to an ARVN artillery unit in the valley, which apparently had artillery fire for sale. The North Vietnamese Army, who were at that moment a little short of heavy weapons, had paid it cash to fire on its own fractious allies, the Communist Khmer Rouge. To the soldier, both were enemies, and their internal quarrels did not concern him. He did not care who gave him the target co-ordinates, as long as they paid in dollars.

On top of the mountain, a large gate opened onto a prosperous pagoda, with carved dragons and yellow walls with pictures of peacocks. Initially the cool breeze refreshed, but soon the heavy rhythm of gongs from the inside began to numb our senses, and the incense to sting the eyes. Women emerged from the old wooden building in tears, still hypnotised by the monotonous sound of male bass voices in common prayer. We went inside. Countless candles lit a grand red and golden structure, beside which Buddhist *bonze*s, half-clad in orange robes, officiated. Money had to change hands for each small favour, and for each joss-stick. Flowers filled even the recesses of the hall with heavy scent, and our ears reverberated with the drone of prayer. An old *bonze* sold our ladies the right to shake and empty a cupful of sticks. From the position of the sticks, as they fell hap-hazardly and hit the ground, he could tell the thrower's future. He made it so dismal that they demanded another try, but still the old man continued spitting out dire predictions, collecting their money, until, enraged, the ladies gave up on him and stormed out, claiming it was a good thing that they did not believe in fortune-telling anyway. We followed. The view over the immense plain restored our mood, and gave Uncle Le the brilliant idea of taking the chopper for a picnic on the Ha Tien beach.

Once again, the character of the landscape changed: the mud roads became winding, and were lined by wooden houses on stilts. Obviously we were taking a shortcut through Cambodia. Clouds began to obscure the sun, and the light dimmed. At last we flew over a recog-nisable landmark, a cement factory, and from there to a palm-lined beach. Uncle Le had boasted that he would clear it of trespassers with the down-draft of his rotor, but that was not necessary, and we landed unopposed on a totally deserted beach. After switching off the engine, the only remaining sound was the occasional whisper of wavelets on the fine grey sand. We had a lazy lunch, to which an old French wine made a melancholy companion. French wines travel badly in the tropics, but were considered essential for elegant picnics.

Afterwards, as I was floating belly-up in the listless sea around a promontory, I heard voices and, wading ashore, came upon a large and elaborate grave, built from eroded sandstone, overgrown and cracked by jungle roots. To my surprise, some village women were placing fresh flowers on the grave-stones and brushing the path, in a half-hearted sort of way, smiling coyly. According to them, a Chinese pirate lay buried here, where he had waded ashore with armed companions, three centuries earlier, to conquer the province from the Cambodians. His name was Mac Cuu, and he was a renegade from the Ming empire who paid tribute to the Vietnamese court. He had brutally subdued the Cambodian population, yet, many generations later, unpaid Cambodian and Vietnamese women still came here to worship their conqueror, about whom they knew nothing but his name, and with no justification other than a reverence for his supposed powers. I could not comprehend: Indo-China was either morally superior to us, or just plain hopelessly confused. Neither war nor aid would change a people who worship the killer of their own ancestors. I wondered when a shrine for the American B52 airmen who had bombed Hanoi would spring up somewhere in the depths of North Vietnam.

After lunch, in case I insisted, our manager had indeed negotiated safe passage to a company service station, which had been out of reach in enemy hands for many years. This was it. The two of us travelled over a badly deformed road in the direction of some thatched huts. Somehow you could sense the crossing of a line by a change in the atmosphere, even in the absence of material differences. We came to a stop at a pre-war, hand-operated petrol pump, where a small reception committee had been waiting, perhaps all day. Polite but not excessive greetings were exchanged. In the shadow of papaya trees stood the house of the station operator, a matron who appeared with her two daughters on the veranda. They invited us in. In the cool interior, a table with sweet, garishly-coloured rice-cakes was set. After our eyes had adjusted to the dark, we became aware of a number of men standing against the wall, and they were introduced to us simply as comrades. The daughters went around with the brandy, and we cautiously toasted the revival of the long-lapsed dealership.

Outside, the rice fields still lay fallow after the December harvest, while in the government-controlled areas they had already been seeded, begging the question why Communist rice was planted so much later here. A solemn young man, who seemed to speak for the others, answered me that the land could simply not support more than one crop a year, and that it needed to lie idle until June, while adjacent identical land under government control was producing two harvests. This patent untruth made all of us a little uncomfortable. He claimed moreover that the colonial regime had never produced more than one harvest a year, and that in those bad days the profits went to the rich landlords, while the labourers had to spend their piastres on drink and gambling, as in rural Europe a century ago. However, the revolution had chased the parasites away, and had distributed the land to the tenants, who were now free to enjoy the revenues. Of course, all unemployed men had 'volunteered' for the Vietcong regional defence forces, so that male idleness too was a thing of the past. In fact, only very old men and women, it seemed, were still occupied with the harvest.

The young man had spoken with such finality that, at first, no-one cared to take issue. Suddenly, however, there was a commotion, and a heavy man, with the round face of a village buffoon, surged forward. He seemed to carry a different kind of authority. In any case, they allowed him to give his own contradictory explanation as to why they had to be content with one harvest a year, instead of the two harvests of the average free farmer. At first he digressed. It seemed that his father, a big land-owner in colonial times, had been executed by the revolutionaries. In those days, before the establishment of the Vietcong (he called them by their popular name, rather than Provisional Revolutionary Government), the wealthy owners had indeed produced two harvests, before they had been eliminated by Trotskyists, religious sects, by Ngo Dinh Diem's police, or by the Vietcong. He insisted on lifting his trousers to show the scars on his ankles caused by iron shackles. But all these persecutions, right or wrong, could not obscure the basic truth, that all the land we stood on had been water-logged jungle before colonialism, before his father had come here to invest his money in a drainage channel, which alone made farming possible. Without his capitalist father and French investment, there would have been no farmland and no harvests at all, he insisted. Since then, the farming situation had only deteriorated.

I wondered if he was some sacred fool, who risked his life to answer my stupid question, but the young cadre, without a hint of embarrassment, introduced him belatedly as the elected chief of the farmers' union. By their election, the peasants had probably saved his life, I thought. Apparently he also owned two lorries, and bought the petrol for the pump on the black market; he was our true retailer here. And suddenly the pieces of the puzzle fell into place. I recognised the outlawed entrepreneur whom no despotic regime can do without. Like the comrades, the man was drinking heavily, and beginning to enjoy the recognition. The peasants had to make do with only one crop a year, he now bellowed happily, because the Party forbade the use of American water-pumps, fertiliser and seeds, which could have given them two, or even three, crops. The Party kept economic improvements out in order to stay in control.

During past centuries, he further asserted, population growth had stagnated only through starvation, until the French, acting with people like his father, had increased the rice acreage ten-fold in 60 years, allowing the population to triple. The introduction of capital and the technology to dig channels, with the help of 'lackeys' like his father, converted brackish land into useful land. They also introduced roads, railways and remedies against malaria. The colonial system had indeed produced large and efficient farms on land which was now stagnating once again, unable to maintain even the lousy one-and-a-half tons of paddy per hectare obtained earlier. The second agrarian revolution was obviously passing the leopard spots by.

The brandy was undoubtedly having its effect on all of us. The farmers' chief had lapsed into French several times and, thinking to slip a question past the censorship, I asked him, in that language, for how long the land would be left in the hands of the small peasants. To my utter surprise, the young cadre himself answered, in excellent French, that the PRG would not allow the emergence of a new class of small owner-peasant. The much-vaunted land reform had only been a means to destroy the old order, to allow some social engineering, not to increase production. Initially, the Party took land from the rich and gave it to the poor, although it was obvious from the start that they could not work it economically. The poor therefore immediately 'gave back' their unworkable parcels and 'volunteered' for the Vietcong armed forces. A 'rectification campaign' arbitrarily transferred the land thereafter to 'friendly' big owners, who were allowed to work it for a while. But as the Party's grip tightened, those friendly owners in turn were persuaded to 'donate' it to co-operatives which, alone, could obtain supplies and permission to sell the product. Thus, large regimented production units sprung up, and more boys could join the army and be relieved by women. But yields declined through neglect. The managers and the remaining men attended managerial and political meetings, while the women worked the land, as they had done through the ages. In accordance with its doctrine, the Party then ordered the combination of those production units into even bigger super-co-operatives, or *Xa*, where everything was state-regulated, from work to sex, where no-one was allowed to earn money, and 'merit points' instead were awarded by those at the top. But now some farmers were allowed their own plots again.

I could not help but marvel at the inexhaustible patience of the long-suffering people, pushed around by political overlords, turned from independent peasants into soldiers, or to unpaid peasants in communes. But according to the smiling cadre, the circle would never stop: as soon as the Chinese tired of sending Vietnam the rice which the inefficient *Xa*s could not produce, they would have to go back to a system of private exploitation again. It was a merry-go-round. Apparently, the Communists had no fixed land policy. Already, even *Xa* labourers were allowed to grow vegetables for the black market on the small plots around their dwellings.

He was now too drunk to look surprised at his own audacity. The comrades and even the entrepreneur were scratching their heads in doubt, and I thought that perhaps we had gone too far in one session. But then he started to smile, and suddenly all of us burst out laughing. The hostess laughed, lady-like, behind her hand, and the daughters passed the Martell bottle. Many toasts followed, in Russian fashion, to the competition of two systems in peace and to everlasting peace. The cadre however, with an eye on one of the daughters, confided to me that no-one could expect to win the peoples' hearts by economic performance alone.

There was a better way to conquer the hearts and minds. Whenever the Communists took a contested area, they let their soldiers sleep with all available – and not always willing – women, married and unmarried. These women would then remain loyal to the fathers of their children. That was, he claimed, how Binh Dinh province was held. Though the ARVN had nominal control by day, the Vietcong could move anywhere, from bed to bed, at night. Looking close up into their bloodshot eyes, I realised that we were all having a rare good time. By now there was tremendous fraternisation in the ranks, like at Christmas 1916, when German and British soldiers kicked a ball around between the trenches in Flanders before going back to the slaughter. We had to get back to our cocktail party in the provincial capital, however, and the sun was already going down. So we stumbled out of the room past a guard of honour, with eyes and ears reddened by alcohol. We quickly shook hands and drove away.

The reception for the provincial notables was already in progress at our manager's house in the police compound. His vivacious wife, a Catholic Vietnamese, was looking after our interests. Obviously, however, the sturdy and combative head of the national police in the delta, Colonel Huyen Thanh Son, had been informed of the afternoon excursion, and as soon as we entered made his objections crystal-clear. The people we had consorted with had been fighting his own police-force for many years, and would continue to do so. The peace agreement itself meant nothing to him, because he took his orders from the

President himself, whose policy of the Four No's was simple and explicit: no accommodation whatever. Therefore, we had trespassed. I could be forgiven, as a foreigner, but our branch manager should have known better.

The hostess was at our side in a flash of silk. She gave the policeman a handsome wide smile and took me protectively to the new American consul general, Wolfgang Lehmann, who had just flown in from Germany as part of the advance party of the new American Ambassador. He still had all the self-assurance of a right-hand man, unimpeded by local knowledge. As a hardened cold warrior from Europe, he did not see the point of making the Kissinger-Le Duc-Tho peace agreement work, convinced as he was of the uselessness of all contracts with Communists.

Peering through gold-rimmed lenses, he confirmed that the peace agreement, allowing contacts between former combatants, ran counter to local government, and therefore embassy, policy. State Department officer Lacey Wright and CIA operative Norman Achilles were standing nearby. The State Department seemed to have an insubordination problem on its hands, I suggested only half in jest. How could ranking American officials condone the ditching of an agreement made by their own Secretary of State? In Lehmann's view, however, Thieu's rejection of the treaty proved him to be one hell of a far-sighted politician. But if Thieu could sabotage the settlement with local American support, how could further war be avoided? I protested. It seemed, declared Lehmann, that I had no appreciation of the subtle power game that Thieu was playing. He was, in contravention of the treaty, holding 10,000 Vietcong prisoners up his sleeve, as a bargaining asset, and he would release those only if the North agreed to his additional demands. In Lehmann's opinion, they were bound to do this, because in addition the Americans held the ace of a secret $4 billion aid offer, which the North surely could not afford to reject, as reasonable men.

13

South China Sea

The First Oil
Exploration Contract

The Vietnamese part of the South China Sea was the least explored oil basin in the world. Its tantalising prospects had been protected from the drill by war, border disputes and the absence of special legislation. Once peace had been signed, however, oil company prospectors flew in by the dozen.

Minister Pham Kim Ngoc needed exploration activity to boost the economy. To speed things up, and even though I was an interested party, he asked me to act as a sounding-board for the innovative ideas of the new executive director of the National Petroleum Board, Tran Van Khoi, who was fresh out of a US engineering college. Ngoc's main concern was to get private company investment up and running as quickly as possible, in strict accordance with the new petroleum legislation.

When I climbed the worn steps to the Board's office, however, my heart sank as I glanced through the shabby windows. At communal benches, row upon row of thin clerks, surviving on rice handouts, worked on hand-written papers. Typewriters functioned as status symbols for the supervisors. Messengers carried leather-bound volumes extremely slowly between the floors, and the whole organisation seemed absorbed in processing mineral exploitation requests from the previous century. It had no relevant output that I could see.

I found Khoi in a nondescript office on the first floor. We sat down on a plastic sofa to discuss matters. He had a broad engaging smile and dark-rimmed glasses, which he had to push continuously back up over his flat nose. As a new director in his first month in office, he had wisely not distracted his worthy staff from whatever they were doing.

Shortly before, the UN and international legal experts had helped draft a general petroleum law which laid down the framework for oil exploration and production, and for eventual profit sharing. Having passed both houses of parliament in quick-time, it had been signed by President Thieu in December 1970, but had lain dormant during the military offensive which followed. In this time, the bidding procedures and documents, put together with the help of executives from the Iranian National Oil Company, had been circulated to interested companies. An English expert from a reputable petroleum economics firm in London had worked with Khoi on cashflow models and production and cost projections. Now, Khoi's immediate and delicate problem was to divide the South Vietnamese offshore area into blocks on which oil company exploration tenders could be safely invited, excluding such areas as might be disputed by North Vietnam, China, Indonesia, Malaysia, Thailand, Cambodia and the Philippines. His problem, in talks with some of these nations, was no less than the delineation of their sovereignty over the whole offshore area. This depended not only on the mainland coastline and borders, which were obviously under dispute with North Vietnam, but also on which nation claimed sovereignty over the many uninhabited offshore coral reefs and islands, such as the Spratleys and the Paracelles. He realised that the whole issue might not be settled in his lifetime, but his overriding need was to get the ball rolling for South Vietnam.

While a number of speculators were prepared to bid for a financial stake in the action, only the international oil companies were able to carry out the work itself. Protection from war risk being their primary concern, naturally they wanted to keep their offshore platforms well away from any disputed zones. Even so, Caltex, a company with a major marketing investment in Vietnam, declined to tender at all. For them, the American withdrawal had taken the safety pin out of the situation. This left mainly Mobil and ourselves and a few other international companies in the running. I was in favour of bidding because whatever the arrangement between North and South, the zone would eventually be explored under any regime, and first-come-first-served. The bid would naturally be supported by Shell's exploration department, which had never yet turned down a work opportunity. But I realised that our international board would have to agonise over the risks to life and property.

To diminish these risks, we took unorthodox action. Giu suggested asking both the North and the South Vietnamese governments if they were prepared to support either a combined exploration operation or separate agreed operations in the Northern and Southern offshore areas, so that neither side would have an incentive to attack the other's oil-rigs. Although this was in the co-operative spirit of the peace agreement, we were not even sure how such a proposal would fare *vis-à-vis* the Southern government's policy of the Four No's. And so far, the North had never shown an awareness of what offshore exploration might accomplish for it. When we checked with Minister Ngoc, however, he surprised us by his support for a multinational company such as ourselves approaching the Northern and Southern governments on equal terms, like East and West Germany. The minister and the whole government were anxious to conclude a major business deal under full public scrutiny, to show the world that South Vietnam could develop its economy in keeping with highest international legal standards. We now needed a positive reaction from the North Vietnamese government.

Giu flew to Paris, ostensibly for medical care. In the tangled web of Vietnamese-French relations, the chances were that he would call on one of Paris's 700 Vietnamese doctors, while back in Vietnam a similar number of French doctors took care of the Vietnamese population. Relations between French and Vietnamese of Northern or Southern descent, of communist or democratic persuasion, were still intimate, with constant exchanges between Vietnamese families in France and Vietnam. When knowledge of his arrival spread in left bank *émigré* circles, Vietnamese graduates from good French universities flocked around him, begging for employment in Saigon. The prevailing feeling amongst Vietnamese was that the peace would hold. Soon, through a medical doctor, a contact was established with the office of the North Vietnamese peace delegation in Paris, where Giu proved a perfect match for his old authoritarian acquaintances, the high-ranking communist diplomats. The result was an invitation from the Hanoi government to discuss exploration in the North, which would have guaranteed the security of all company operations in Vietnam.

The suggestion went to London through my personal channel, but it ran aground straight away. Members of the international board were chosen for their prudent views. Prudence was now the watchword. The directors were as worried to extend operations in South Vietnam as to be be seen dealing with Hanoi.

But then the wondrous wheel of fortune made a full turn. Out of the blue, the Vice-President for Exploration and Production of Shell Oil, the American Shell affiliate, descended on us in Saigon for a first ever visit. The American affiliate maintained a special arms' length relationship with the rest of the Shell Group to protect their outside shareholders' interests, and we, the rank-and-file, were not informed of each others' business moves. Without informing us, the American operating company had closely studied the draft concession agreements and the South Vietnamese government tender invitations. They had independently evaluated the opportunity and decided to bid for the acreage on their own. The Vice-President arrived with a $12 million bid in his pocket, and an offer to start drilling in two prospective blocks within six months. He and I looked at the dates. The document had been agreed at a Shell Oil board meeting in Houston, under the same chairman, Gerry Wagner who, a few days before had been instrumental in turning down our own proposition at an international board meeting in the Hague. The American bid, moreover, contained none of the guarantees we had so carefully sought, and all the points on which the board had objected to our proposal still applied in full. I could only wonder at the way our horn-locked bureaucracies had the power to force our chairman to reverse his decisions so quickly.

The bids were publicly opened, certified and signed on each page to minimise opportunities for corruption, by all Board members including Khoi. We were delighted that Shell Oil had outbid the competition on three blocs, although somewhat embarrassed at the $10 million we had 'left on the table'. The next bid for the same blocks being only $2 million. With such a large difference in our favour, the official award by the National Resources Commission, the ultimate arbiter, should have been a mere formality and the Vice-President flew home after a job well done, asking me to keep an eye on the shop.

Days later, however, the award still pending, I received a warning from Khoi's office, that certain ominous changes were in the air. Apparently, some Commission members had been in favour, in a closed session, of awarding the main one of 'our' blocks to a fabulously wealthy Texan independent instead. 'Special Incentives' which sway the minds of decision-makers are usually a matter of common knowledge only after the event, but in this case I was forewarned. I knew the Hunt brothers' operating methods from Libya years before, when they had obtained a large oil concession through favours to the aged King ldris, including the restoration of a green oasis near his ancestral desert home. Being only interested in financial gain, they had farmed out the actual operation of their concession to BP. In Saigon this time, their representative had not only influenced the members of the Commission, but also the English oil adviser from a reputable oil economics consultancy.

In the few hours available, I cornered the adviser, a dignified weasel, with the message that I would obtain his immediate arrest on charges of corruption if he did not comply with his own published rules. Saigon jail was no laughing matter. Then I called Ngoc, who reassured me that he stood by his guarantees of strict adhesion to the bid criteria, and that he would preside over the allocation himself. The Hunt bid was disqualified. The Commission duly awarded the blocks to the highest bidder, Shell, and that night Ngoc proudly held the $12 million cheque up to the TV cameras for all in North and South to read.

By then, the Hunt brothers' representative had left town, perhaps a few thousand dollars lighter with nothing to show for it. In retrospect, however, he and others whose bids failed walked away with the prize. The following year, Shell discovered some non-commercial oil, but before it could be evaluated the fall of Saigon obliged it to beat a hasty retreat. A Mobil oil discovery was given for exploitation to a Vietnamese-Soviet joint-venture which is still producing today. After spending millions, the geological puzzle of how much oil existed under the virgin sea remained unsolved for another 20 years. The real losers were a generation of Vietnamese tipped into poverty. For a long time to come, the numbers of subsistence clerks at the Board's offices would increase and continue to shuffle limp papers in a mouldy building without fresh air.

14

Organised Theft
and a Dinner

After the successful bid, Cong Ty Shell's future seemed bright enough
to staff. For other Vietnamese however, spring had truly clouded over.
Hanoi recalled its top delegate from the henceforth useless Joint Peace
Commission in Saigon. General Tran Van Tra accused President Thieu
of sabotaging the mission, before going back to his headquarters
across the Cambodian border to command the Communist forces in
South Vietnam again.

The leaderships on both sides heaved sighs of relief that they did
not have to bet their survival on democratic novelties like free elections
which, in our staff's opinion, the Southern government would have
won. Thieu was therefore the bigger loser, but he did not seem to
mind. From their side, the Americans did nothing to make him realise
that peace was a workable last chance, probably because his visceral
anti-Communism was secretly admired by the hawks of the embassy.

In this climate, the international commission to supervise the
ceasefire could fare no better. From the date of his appointment, the
Canadian president, Michel Gauvin, who had become a friend of
mine and a celebrated figure in Saigon, failed to get co-operation to
implement even the most basic of the peace agreement's terms. He
often publicly warned of the dire consequences of failure. When
nothing changed, however, he began to drown his frustration in drink,
and the press corps were all over him, like flies, for his latest biting
sarcasms. When Communist forces shot down one of his clearly-
marked white helicopters on a peace-keeping mission, he had to
spend weeks in formalities, cleverly devised by both Vietnamese sides,
just to retrieve the dead bodies of his Polish officers. Finally, rather

than serve the travesty of supervision, he made good on his threat to pull Canada out of the commission. And that, together with his own departure, marked the formal end of the peace treaty.

At the time, we were comparing the amounts of aid received by each Vietnamese client state from its patrons, to see if the balance of power was still in place. Unfortunately, the similarities between the latest ceasefire and the 1954 version – which, by unilaterally disarming the South, had incited the North to restart the war – were multiplying. Whereas the CIA estimated that South Vietnam needed $3 billion a year in civilian and military aid, the actual military figure was falling towards the $1 billion mark, while Communist aid was increasing, and ran at double that figure. Moreover, in spite of protests from the head of military aid in Vietnam, General Murray, the American aid figures included large amounts of infrastructural cost, such as the general's own mission costs and Washington overheads, unconnected with the actual war. The Russian and Chinese figures were estimated on the basis of real supplies. All these decreases, and the decreasing orders for oil, were the subject of frequent discussion between me, General Murray and Bill Sharpe, the head of civilian Aid.

If peace depended on the maintenance of a balance of support, the prospect for peace looked gloomy. The North Vietnamese were building 5000 kilometres of oil pipeline through Laos, Cambodia and South Vietnam to supply their troops in the South. Other Communist war supplies now travelled south in Russian trucks over all-weather bitumen roads, unmolested by bombardments. From our own Shell figures, we knew that the South could hardly afford the fuel for its airforce, on which its infantry, shaped in the American image, depended for their fire support. In parallel, American civil aid to Saigon seemed to decline faster than our ability to track the figures. Subsidised civil imports appeared to have fallen by 50 percent in three years. Precipitate, almost unplanned, American withdrawal, forced on a weakened US president, left hundreds of thousands of Vietnamese jobless in the streets.

The worse the figures became, the more our staff felt drawn to redress the situation. Instead of submitting to the inevitable, one of our best executives volunteered, at the urging of Minister Ngoc, to run large refugee relief programmes, designed by the government and the American services. I became uncomfortably aware that this management assistance was becoming more than an ordinary business commitment.

At the Nha Be installation, the armed thefts recommenced as soon as we had withdrawn the expatriate night watches on the signature of peace. The economic motive to steal was simply too compelling. After two alerts on military barge arrivals by young Trung, and after two failed police attempts at intervention, it became obvious that the military gangsters were receiving advance information on the traps from a mole within the company. Some sleuthing revealed that our beloved but ineffective operations manager had been unable to kick the peacetime company habit of always keeping staff informed of operations. He was a grey-bearded Englishman, emotionally involved with his Vietnamese subordinates to the point of shedding tears whenever they had a problem. Constitutionally unable to switch to wartime secrecy, he had passed word of the ambushes to the installation manager, whom we suspected of complicity at the very least. Not only was co-operation with the police now compromised, through repeated failures, but Trung's own unconventional policing role, to which staff must have realised I had agreed, had become untenable. The irate installation manager, whose guilt was still unproven, vowed revenge, and even the devious mandarin Giu set out to destroy Trung for his juvenile lack of respect towards the Vietnamese hierarchy, and he soon found a righteous cause.

Allegedly, Trung had collected money payable to the company from a contractor and had kept it, overnight, against the rules. When questioned, Trung, no fool in these matters, could prove that he had duly deposited it next morning with the company. But Giu, no fool either, countered with the accusation that the receipt was signed by a cashier, a girlfriend of Trung, who had probably pre-dated the company receipt to save her lover's neck. Presumably we could have clarified all this in the time-honoured way with a lengthy, acrimonious and salacious witch-hunt, of just the type Giu was aiming to lead. However, that would have diverted our energies from hunting down the main fraudsters. So the cashier was moved to a less sensitive job in the telex room, while Trung received a written warning. My reactions were becoming more oriental and inscrutable by the day, and I did not like it.

Discussing the logistics behind the military thefts, which occurred also in Esso and Caltex installations, my American colleagues and I agreed that there had to be a 'laundering' network of entrepots and civilian helpers in or near Saigon, to break down the barge loads the same night into innocent small parcels like drums and jerrycans, for onward sale to the black market. Some prominent Vietnamese were bound to know about it. Rumour had it that the president of the War Widows' Association had allowed the use of her lands for this purpose. How else could she afford her life style? I thought about this. Up to the present moment, we were mere social acquaintances. However, as in Vietnam little could be achieved through ordinary channels, observing ordinary social conventions, I risked a shot in the dark. I rang Kim Chi and informed her that a barge with 50 tons of stolen product had left Nha Be the previous night. Could she please help us trace it?

As if this was the most conventional conversation in the world, she advised cooly to report any thefts immediately to the police. Why had I not done so? she asked with a trace of amused irony. I pointed out that police involvement had unfortunately failed us already, and that we knew the barges to be military. With her high connections and influence in military circles she could be of crucial importance, if she wanted to help, at which point she cut in to ask how much her help was worth to us. I was now crossing an invisible line. Ten percent of the value of the recovered product, I offered grandly. She let out an appreciative chuckle, and said she was prepared to discuss things over dinner at her house that night.

When I arrived at the house, the entrance was unlit. No-one was there to show the way, except an old woman, squatting by the door on her haunches like a peasant, who ignored my presence. She was quietly drawing on a cigarette, revealing an unwrinkled forehead and coal-black eyes in the glow of each inhalation. I waited. After a while, a servant out of nowhere silently pushed my shoulders around and led me around the house to the garden, to a table laid out for two on the lawn, picked out by a spotlight. It was my turn to chuckle at her artful way of dealing with barbarians, as I looked around. The tree trunks caught reflections of the blinding tablecloth, but everything else was in deep shadow. The principal actress took her time to join me, but when she made her entrance, it was in a blinding white *ao dhai*, with a single strand of red coral for a necklace. A boy immediately placed iced bowls with shrimp cocktail and chopsticks before us, and another brought a lit candelabra and extinguished the harsh spotlight.

In the candlelight we tried to appraise each other. Now I began to see that house and garden were peopled by silently moving shadows. Obviously she was well protected by her personnel, and feeling entirely at ease. Her manner, though businesslike, was somewhat off-hand, as if to indicate that what I had raised was an unimportant matter between us, which could only hurt us if we delved too deeply. The barges, she admitted, were indeed operated by military acquaintances, in cahoots with low-ranking company people. I should not trust my own staff. In the past, they had used the farm as one of their entrepots, but she had put an end to that long ago. Having cut her relations, she could not help us any longer, except perhaps by warning that doing anything too drastic – she offered it casually – would lead to bloodshed. That was all she could tell. I believed every word, and pushed her no more.

Presently, it began to dawn on me that as a mere businessman I was to her practically a second-class citizen. I began to understand that her Confucian upbringing, reinforced as it was by French intellectual schooling, had conditioned her to regard the politico-military élite as the only guiding lights of society, and businessmen as lowly people to be dealt with, at arm's length, through Chinese middlemen. She told me of her education in the countryside of North Vietnam. Her father, Nguyen Huu Tri, a governor of North Vietnam before the French defeat, had left her happy memories from his earlier days as a mandarin in the provinces. As an absolute ruler, he was still judging petty criminals, including Communists, in public sessions, and when she herself had finished studying for the day she had to bring soup from her mother's kitchen to these same men in the stockade next to the family house.

Her mother, who had looked me over in silence, and whom I had unfortunately ignored at the entrance of the house, had known General Giap and Prime Minister Pham Van Dong of North Vietnam from that period. The latter came from an excellent mandarin family too. Later her mother had been much sought-after as a celebrated beauty by the French generals and foreign diplomats of the day. When things went badly in the North, however, her father had safely married his daughter off to an influential Southerner. However, a plot against President Diem had landed her husband in jail, and as she did not believe in chaste suffering Kim Chi had divorced him at once and married, by her own choice this time, General Do Cao Tri, for whom life with his troops was much more important than domestic bliss. Only his violent death had finally opened her eyes to the necessities of ordinary life. She now spoke from the heart. Her direct and amusing ways had eclipsed from my mind the original reason for my presence.

The staff kept serving meat and herbs, which she wrapped with nimble fingers in vine leaves and smilingly pushed into my mouth across the table. The wine glass in my hand remained filled by the serving shadows hovering around. While she hardly wetted her lips, I drank it like water, and began to feel in control of the universe. Instead of intimidating me, the theatrical setting seemed to inspire me to tell my best stories like a bit actor, with more attention to lines, gags and timing than to truth. I had suspended the search for rational truth, and was obeying other laws. People who feel attracted to each other do not feel the need to act on a rational level. Even fish hide their motives behind a welter of colour and performances. When our purpose is so transparent, the way of the telling matters more than all the substance.

This night, however, I outdid myself. I listened to my own voice as if from on high, from the rafters in the night sky, enjoying fragments taken from real experience, dressed up for her, like clowns, to be rewarded with a laugh. No single response from Kim Chi escaped my eye, hyper-conscious as I was of her smallest gestures, the way she put the glass to her lips and the exact voltage she radiated. I ate, drank and spoke like a lord, strutting like a peacock on her stage. Eventually a sad-eyed servant, pouring into my cup green tea with a bitter taste that cut the flow of words, signalled the end of the act. I followed her into the dark house through corridors with shadows flattened against the walls, into a back room with a rack of gleaming guns, to a field bed.

15

Another Attack
on Nha Be

Resignation of
a High Flyer

Some military people believe that wars are won by dropping large doses of explosives on primary objectives. In line with this belief, the American command had not seen fit to pay much attention to decidedly secondary areas like the Rung Sat swamps, and the ARVN had adopted a similar attitude. This left Cong Ty Shell on its own to face the hundred North Vietnamese sappers who had different ideas about the Rung Sat swamps. But even for them, as we were to learn soon, 12 months of deprivation, without definite orders, had almost been too much. Gut diseases and boredom had taken such a toll of the troops' morale that without immediate combat action their political officer feared he would lose control over their minds.

From the safety of Hanoi, the Northern leaders could speak loftily of the need for peace, but their bloody-minded soldiers in the Run Sat compared their own plight with that of their lucky comrades at home. In the South, they felt time seemed to be working for the ARVN. Where once the mechanised US army had waltzed over the underground positions of guerrillas without much of a fight and without breaking their will, the ARVN was at once a more sloppy and a more tricky enemy. True, in the image of their masters, they still relied too much on air support, but they kept the terrain occupied to protect their own people. Their clever *Chieu Hoi* ('open arms') programme worked on the minds and attracted increasing numbers of Communist deserters, and their deadly *Phuong Hoang* ('phoenix') programme killed more experienced fighters than the airlifted American army Operation Attleboro had ever done.

As we came to know later, the Northern captain decided on the armed reconnaissance mission to improve the morale of his troops as much as to inflict damage on Nha Be. He had no orders for a major attack in peacetime. On a suitable night, with a three-quarter moon affording enough light for observation, he led two platoons across the river. The rising tide lifted them to a creek two kilometres upstream from the installation, where they disembarked and covered their sampans in the reeds.

The second-in-command, a lieutenant, took one platoon. In black silks, without insignia or personal belongings, with AK47s at the ready, they blended into the night. After an hour of slow wading through small streams and sticky clay, they got within 600 metres of the outer fence. The lieutenant climbed a tree to observe the Nha Be tanks, drenched in orange neon floodlights, and the guard towers, with guns poking through the firing-slits. The plan was to creep forward, survey the installation defences at leisure, cut through the wire and dynamite a tank or two before running back to the rendezvous point. They expected the enemy to fire, but not to pursue, for fear of ambush. The major risk came from the ARVN's infernal habit of laying down pre-arranged mortar fire over the likely approach and retreat routes when something disturbed their sleep.

The mosquitoes were biting in earnest, but nobody slapped at them as they advanced in silence. At the end of the elephant grass, they froze. Before them stretched a levelled, well-lit killing zone without any cover. Concertina wire protected the fence and the whole installation was bathed in a lethal orange sunrise, almost unbearable on the eyes. They tried to hide their awe in whispers about puppet soldiers, not daring to mine the zone for fear of casualties amongst themselves and the population. But at 100 metres from the fence, the security lighting was like daylight, and they felt small and vulnerable.

Just when they had settled down to note the intervals between ARVN patrols, unexpected steps were heard on the earthen firewall inside the installation, along with the crackling of a hand-held radio. Flattening his thin body, the lieutenant looked up, and what he saw made him grin widely. Silhouetted against the brilliant metal of the tanks walked a carefree Vietnamese from a different planet, a healthy well-dressed civilian, obviously a class enemy, a foppish intellectual from his horn-rimmed glasses down to his buckled shoes. It was Trung. The young lieutenant controlled his instincts and allowed the happy individual to continue on his merry way, whistling a pop tune.

The captain's patrol had made slower progress through a fishing hamlet of wooden shacks recently settled by refugees, and therefore not marked on his map. The men could not see their feet, and splashed through the water. From inside the hovels came voices and the ubiquitous smell of Vietnam's national shrimp sauce, *ngoc mam*. Unfortunately, after the main body of the platoon had already passed, a dog began to bark, a chicken panicked, and someone opened a high window and placed a lit petroleum lamp in it, like a beacon. The captain and one man had to rush back at once to eliminate the tell-tale lamp and its hapless owner, a woman with a son in ARVN. The ugly business finished mercifully quickly, they moved mechanically through the airless grass until they too arrived at the blazing fence. The captain hit two bamboo sticks together to signal his position. They too saw and smiled at the fashionable decadent-looking young graduate. Then they went to work.

A first man crept forward to cut an opening in the fence, with cloth between the scissors to deaden the snap of the wires, bending them back for others to pass easily. The captain now had the satisfaction of feeling the whole installation in the palm of his hand.

But an ARVN sergeant had decided to stretch his legs. His buddies were too full of sleep to raise their heads over the parapets. Although the active part of their job as first line of defence was to spot the enemy and fire first, they had, through boredom, resigned themselves to their secondary passive role of being detected and fired at, mere human tripwires to alert the company base to fire the mortars and bring up the reserves. By this time, they tacitly assumed, they would probably have ceased to exist. The sergeant's fatal problem was that he could not sleep; he felt too much alive. He started out on a walk along the fence alone, and the captain saw him too late to recall his men. His vulnerable squad lay stretched out in the killing zone, holding its collective breath and hoping that the sergeant would pass as the others had done. But the ARVN sergeant could not fail to see the hole in the fence, and as he stopped in disbelief he noticed the pale face of a slightly built youth in black, staring at him from a distance of only 20 metres. The unreal sight made no sense to his brain, but instinct made him crouch, point the MI6 and squeeze the trigger. The black-clad youth's gun too was spitting fire. Bullets whined and ricocheted off the steel walls in a pungent haze of cordite, but such was their marksmanship that when they took their fingers off the triggers after a three-second burst both, still unharmed, stood facing each other open-mouthed in the unearthly light.

The captain had to cut the ARVN sergeant down with an aimed burst. He aborted the incursion, and both columns of sappers broke and ran back along the paths, over which the rudely awoken ARVN gunners, who had made the same evaluation of the terrain as the sappers, laid down their accurate prearranged fire. One round wounded the lieutenant and dispersed his squad. In a dazed state, he was captured at daybreak, trying to buy soup at a roadside stall.

Trung, who had assisted in the army sweeps during the sleepless night, saw a returning patrol dragging a boy of his own age, his hands tied behind his back. At once he felt sympathy and an over-riding curiosity. He probably saved the lieutenant's life, by arrogantly claiming the right of first interrogation, against all military instructions. The soldiers ceded to his authority. Back in the office, he undid the ties and held out a cup of black coffee and some nevaquine tablets to the malarial human bundle in front of him. At first, the lieutenant was sullen. His pallid face with the burning eyes, and his suffering cal-loused body, seemed beyond material inducements. A moment later, however, he took the coffee and swallowed the malaria pills, and when Trung kindly introduced himself as a civilian, with parents in Hanoi, the lieutenant suddenly relaxed. He too had been a student at Hanoi University.

As they spoke, and the lieutenant gripped his coffee, he told Trung that his men had had Trung in their sights and spared his life. Taking a sip, he said that he was now pleased that they had done so. Unfazed, Trung said, 'So we are now even'. He already knew as much about the sappers' organisation and numbers as the lieutenant himself, who was now quite happy to talk man-to-man about life in the Rung Sat swamps as a North Vietnamese sapper. But Trung was not interested in the lieutenant's outpourings on military life. Squatting down on the floor, bringing his near-sighted eyes right up to the lieutenant's face, he finally asked the question that really bothered him: what moved them? What motive could they possibly have, after the peace treaty, to attack an installation that would be needed in any future Vietnam? At once, the prisoner withdrew into unshakeable conviction. If the people of the South could not liberate themselves, he almost recited, they would have to be assisted, even against their will. One aim was to destroy the enslaving capitalist economy. The higher aim, however, was to socialise production. The new society would not need hardware half as much as it needed remodelled man. Surely Trung had heard of the Communist *Dau Tranh* programmes, aimed at the rectification of man himself? Trung had indeed heard of those mind-bending pro-grammes, and a despair deeper than he thought he could ever feel gripped his throat. Something snapped in his mind.

'Brother,' he said slowly, 'I hate your cause, but your brainwashing is so perfect that only a bullet can stop you'.

'That's right,' answered the lieutenant brightly, and when the soldiers came to take him, he was still smiling and shouting, 'You are my brother too – how can you be so wrong?'

That afternoon, Trung burst into my office. I had received reports of the attack, and was in the process of informing London that the ARVN had suffered one fatality, against two North Vietnamese sappers killed and one officer captured, and that we had no material damage. Business as usual. I had suppressed my instinctive desire to go and

116

have a look for myself. Eye-witnesses get involved, and it was some-times better to keep a distance. Trung, however, came in like a true witness of God: unshaven, his pupils wide and feverish, his slight frame shaking. He began deviously, by apologising for having dared to involve me in his misdirected attempts to stop the Nha Be pilferage. At first, I failed to see the connection. Such attempts, he now claimed, could only hurt our friends and allies, because pilferage was positive in a wider sense. Who were we to begrudge an ARVN soldier a gallon of stolen oil if it served to keep his family alive? Last night, one such soldier had died for freedom in Vietnam and for us at Nha Be. It was a God-sent signal to see clearly, to drop our moralistic attitudes and to concentrate on survival alone. All the rest was a waste of time!

If he had immolated himself on the Chinese carpet in front of my eyes, I could not have been more shaken. I told him that he was over-wrought and out of his mind with fatigue. I berated him for posturing. But with his hand on his heart he assured me that this was not so, and he announced that a new calling forced him to offer his immediate resignation. So far, he had only wasted the company's time. With all respect, we did not have to replace him, because anyone else in his place would automatically do the same useless things. With the country in civil war, as surely as bad money drives out good, brainwashed youngsters, crawling right now on their bellies in the mud, would make short work of our efficient company and all of its clever graduates, he claimed. That left only two options for a true Vietnamese: to become either a soldier or a monk. I suspected that his slight chances in the conflict with Giu also had something to do with his decision, but as much as I pleaded that he pull himself together, the resignation remained irrevocable. He was no longer a subordinate, but already an altogether different individual, embarked on a different course. I would never see him again. Although we had not been close, I had counted him as one of the brightest lights in the company, and I felt the loss personally. Moreover, the wider implications of the attack and of Trung's resignation were inescapable.

Coming right down to it, our principal activity was fuelling the war, inevitably both sides, one through legal contracts with the Southern armed forces, the other one through the black market in products diverted from their stated destination once they had left our facilities. There was also the stealing of fuels directly from our instal-lation right from under our noses which Trung and I could only shrug at. All of us recognised that oil, like rice, was essential for life, and therefore likely to be fought over to the death. From the company point of view, our duty was limited to denying as much of it to the enemy as possible, provided it did not undermine our commerce in the process.

Seen from the moral stratosphere in which Trung had now positioned himself, however, we were absolutely central to the survival of the nation, and the pilferage might even be beneficial to our side even if it fed the enemy. This was no total war. Short spasms of conventional military activity in the dry season alternated with much longer periods in which rice, oil and medical supplies were far more important than bullets and were traded between the opponents in various ways. Plentiful supplies led to the 'popularity' of one side rather than the other, to 'control' over the population. More was gained by deals, threats and pressures than by naked bullets.

I had little doubt that beyond my limited horizon, outside Vietnam, similar two-sided trade-offs were made. Shiploads of oil products from refineries in the Southeast Asian area were freely sold. Consider the dire supply alternatives to the communists: supplies from Russia were geographically out of the question; China was severely limited by its own shortages, and had an antiquated transport system. One could argue that trading with the enemy on our terms was good for the empoyment and growth of the Asian democracies, and that it was bleeding the enemy of substance and hastening their collapse in the end. There was no limit to the ways in which we could rationalise and explain away our unwillingness to pull out.

Trung's departure caused me to look again at our business proce-dures, appropriate to a normal peacetime world, which Vietnam was definitely not. Survival was indeed the main issue here, with a lot more than Nha Be's existence on the line. Pleasant but soft graduates, like the current manager of Nha Be, had to be replaced by iron discipli-narians like Phuoc. In ordinary times, such replacements would have been seen as retrograde. Especially to the young Vietnamese students who had met Giu on the rive gauche in Paris, the current manager of Nha Be was a shining example of one of their own, a university graduate, who had made good, and proof of our progressive policies.

When discussing my change of heart with marketing manager Eric Precious, he summed it up nicely. According to him, I found myself on a perfectly normal downward learning curve, jettisoning sophisticated but useless ballast learnt in previous normal appointments. Every passing day, I sounded more like my predecessor, who trusted nobody. He would surely have applauded my choice of Phuoc, the butcher of the *bonzes*, as the new manager of Nha Be, and would have berated me rightly for not doing it right then and there.

16

The Flower of
American Generalship

General Frederic Weyand held a farewell barbecue at the MACV compound – the 'Pentagon East' as it was called – to celebrate the end
of American advisory responsibility for Vietnam, and to present his
successor. It was a symbolic occasion: the last four-star American
warlord and commander of American troops, leaving the field with
his high-ranking friends and their Vietnamese courtesans, now transferring what little remained to a modest two-star logistics general,
John Murray, an administrator, in charge of a team of civilians of
doubtful quality, who pored over the details of our fuel contracts.
Farewell to an era.

The compromise peace was not what Weyand had wished, but then
outright victory had never been a real option. In the nuclear age,
Weyand was never allowed to go all the way. Some claimed that
his mission had merely been to nurse the professional army and its
doctrines, more or less intact, through a messy war, and to help diplomats extricate his country from a sorry affair.

I had been invited to the party by one-star US Airforce General
Holland, who, because I had been a Dutch airforce pilot in Nato and
a fellow graduate of the US airforce fighter pilot school at Williams
Airforce Base, Arizona, accepted me as a paid-up member of that
brotherhood. A US military background was always useful in Vietnam.
On this occasion, I had chosen to bring another brother along,
Vietnamese Airforce colonel Van, whose miserable salary could not
even pay for his children's education, and who needed a break from
long solitary hours of flying obsolete reconnaissance planes over the
North Vietnamese supply line through Cambodia and Laos. He was a

boyish-looking fourty-year-old with whom I often compared flying experiences. After exchanging his flying overalls for khaki trousers and a sports shirt, he tagged along, looking like an awkward teenager.

Both of us followed the white-helmeted MP over a red carpet through an echoing hangar between brand-new command trailers, which had once housed flag officers, but stood empty now. At the last trailer, our host appeared in boots, jeans and a lumberjack shirt, though his bearing and his close-cropped military hair immediately gave his true profession away. While he jovially beckoned us in, I noticed that he looked twice at my guest. The air-conditioned interior had the stark look and cold feel of a cockpit. To make us feel at home, he tossed us a couple of beers from a fridge, but under the jovial smiles on his confident command face, however, he seemed at odds with himself.

The day before, at Guam, he had welcomed back some of his pilots, prisoners of war, released by the North Vietnamese after years in the infamous 'Hanoi Hilton'. All over the world, the drawn faces and proud bearing of these physically, but not mentally, broken men on TV had raised feelings of commiseration and anger. It hit us in the pit of our stomach to see our brother airmen in that state. So we drank without joy the general's sarcastic toast to the end of the $30 billion air war. Never before, he intoned with Churchillian accent, had so many pilots dropped such a weight of bombs – 6.3 million tons to be precise, or three times the total tonnage of world war two – on a country with a gross national product of scarcely $1.5 billion, to accomplish so little!

The party in the nearby compound was a great old-fashioned gathering. Weyand and friends were standing around the large barbecue fires, under a towering red-and-white water reservoir, lit up as a beacon visible from afar, practically an invitation to destroy the flower of American generalship with a few rounds. But the top generals, huge self-assured men in jeans and boots, behaving like cowboys after a hard day's ride, did not worry. Only junior ranks wore uniform. My friend Van and the other Vietnamese officers, half their size, felt patronised or ignored. It seemed they were at a stranger's party. So they tried hard to be invisible amongst the foreign top brass, who were out to enjoy themselves, drinking and gnawing at T-bones.

The commanders of the naval task-forces, including the nuclear carriers, were present. CINCPAC himself, Admiral John McCain had come over, and also the rotund and famous General John Vogt of the 7th airforce, based on Guam, architect of both Linebacker, the final US air offensive, and the secret bombing campaign in Cambodia. A *Newsweek* reporter was asking him how he could be sure of hitting any Khmer Rouges at all with his high-level bombing. The general reined in his temper. Flames were dancing on his face, and the steak on his plate oozed blood. Simple, he roared: during the rainy season only a few places stuck up out above the water in God-forsaken Cambodia, and those he hit with full force because the Khmers Rouges had just gotta be there! (with the rest of the population).

In between the smoking fires, accompanying Vietnamese women discreetly operated to keep the party going. They spoke hardly a word to their own countrymen; Colonel Van did not seem to notice them as he concentrated on his food. But their slender figures caused a ripple wherever they went amongst the tall Americans. Skilled at avoiding conversation, they were like log-jumpers in a stream, from one patron to another. No sooner had one heavy-set American turned to compliment them on their grace than they had flitted to another.

17

Cambodian Operetta
and Black Tragedy

In the West, with the passing of dictators like Stalin and Hitler, the art of the big lie had fallen into sad disrepute, but here in Vietnam it was alive and well. Asian public life makes fascinating use of the big lie, the Orwellian lie, which calls war peace and propaganda information. 'The North Vietnamese Army was never in Cambodia', though aerial photographs showed their troops and tanks. Negotiators used that lie to conclude the peace treaty for Vietnam, by sweeping intractable subjects under the carpet. The resulting 'peace' turned out to be war at a lower level. By comparison, simple truths, of accountants, jealous husbands and historians, are sparrows amongst peacocks.

No wonder the people distrusted official and media information and were ready to believe the worst. Once, the Saigon boulevard press accused Thieu of pocketing rent from me for my supposedly government-owned residence. The south Vietnamese press was amazingly free and outspoken, though not always accurate with its facts. The house was company-owned and no rent was ever paid to anybody, but the story just happened to fit into a largely fictitious article on Government corruption that the public wanted to believe. When Ngoc asked me to issue a denial (President Thieu's denial in the circumstances counting for less than our own), our staff objected that we should not weaken a good media campaign against corruption by unmasking one single part of it as untrue. When I contributed our denial nevertheless, my Vietnamese friends thought it a ploy to obtain a gasoline price increase. Another time, when Hanoi radio quoted me as saying that South Vietnam could not produce oil within a year, the South Vietnamese government denied the self-evident fact because it did not fit their childish propaganda. In fact, the government preferred to believe to the end that the riches resulting from local oil production would pay for the war and make it sustainable.

One question that could never be answered truthfully was what was going on in Cambodia, where fighting was officially non-existent since the peace treaty. It seemed that Khmer Rouge troops in large numbers had suddenly appeared around the capital, Phnom Penh, and that this had caused such panic that its fall was expected in a matter of days. For years we had underestimated the threat, because Cambodian government petroleum supplies, from our Nha Be installation, continued to sail right through the war-zone unharmed. My English colleague, the promising young President of Shell's Cambodian affiliate, had always sent us optimistic reports about the situation.

It came as a shock, therefore, to have his Cambodian deputy calling me suddenly with the news that his boss had bolted to the safety of Singapore, with his wife and without leaving instructions. This executive, now nominally in charge, belonged to the handful of Cambodians with a Western university degree who had chosen to work in their own country instead of making money in Europe, a mistake for which he would pay with his life when the Khmer Rouge took over. But although the Communist shelling was audible over the telephone line, he appeared only preoccupied by his possible failure to complete the company's five-year Business Plan and have it in Shell Centre in London on time. His and his family's survival and the evacuation of staff seemed nothing beside the completion of the Plan. I hastily convinced myself, therefore, of my duty to get to know the real situation, and accepted his invitation to go and see what I could do for them.

Giu, however, immediately ridiculed my good intentions to save the Cambodians from themselves. Cambodia as a country should never be taken seriously! Think of it in terms of comic opera, he suggested. The head of state, Prince Sihanouk, was a dancing, singing puppet, cast in the leading role by the wife of the ex-French governor, who thought him *plus mignon* than his cousin, who was awarded the prime minister-ship as a consolation prize. Playing the god-king for his people, literally in song and dance, Sihanouk always slavishly followed the line of the dominant regional powers, Japan in the forties, China and North Vietnam in the fifties and sixties. Only when the Americans began to show their teeth did he acquiesce in the not-so-secret bombing of the North Vietnamese sanctuaries in thinly populated areas of his land, and finally close his ports to Communist weapon transit to Vietnam. He even ordered his worthless army into action.

But then a number of farcical Cambodian misunderstandings led to a sinister turn of events. The hard-line chief of staff, General Lon Nol, and the Deputy Prime Minister Prince Sirik Matak, over-eager to get rid of the Vietnamese intruders and their Khmer Rouge protegés, deposed Sihanouk while he was on a tour to France for a health cure and to Moscow for 'friendly' discussions. The chief of staff had counted on American support in training and military hardware supplies, which had been denied his army in the past. The US embassy, however, declared itself totally surprised by events, and refused to endorse the coup. In frustration, the Cambodian army started its own crusade against Communism by murdering thousands of Vietnamese peasants in revenge for centuries of encroachment. Their bodies, floating down the Mekong, horrified his potential South Vietnamese allies. Meanwhile Sihanouk, stranded in Beijing and in search of another role, allowed himself to become the mascot of the Khmer Rouge liberation front. In the now familiar pattern of US neutrality and Communist covert build-up, the Khmer Rouge armed forces, trained by North Vietnam, increased from 15,000 in 1970 to 40,000 by 1972, and with help from two North Vietnamese divisions were able to expel the poor Cambodian Army from all the territory east of the Mekong. The belated US response was more secret bombing, which cost many times more in money and in Cambodian civilians lives than timely aid to the Cambodian Army would have done.

The only realistic help came from the South Vietnamese Army, which made a limited incursion under its best commander (according to Kissinger's memoirs), General Do Cao Tri, which was decided and announced in advance by the Americans to be no more than 30 miles deep and of less than 8 weeks duration, allowing the North Vietnamese to withdraw safely and come back later. Unpaid and unaided, the Cambodian Army could not hold out indefinitely against superior forces, and this had now led, in a reversal of expectations, to the fear that Phnom Penh would fall to the Khmer Rouge sooner rather than later. The capital, built for 500,000 and enfeebled by the influx of two million refugees from the countryside with insufficient access to fish and rice, undeniably presented a ripe target.

Why the Khmer Rouge should want to collect the prize at this particular moment, however, making their troop concentrations unmissable targets for Vogt's bombers, was another one of those Asian enigmas to Western experts. Even the Khmer Rouge had to be aware of the US Congress decision to cut all funding for US Airforce bombing in all Indo-China, including Cambodia, as from 15 August 1973. This would make any direct US military action illegal in Vietnam, Laos and Cambodia after that date. With any common sense, the Khmer Rouge should have waited the few months until that date to march in, practically unopposed, instead of which they attacked now and exposed their massed troops to American carpet bombing. At the same time, they indulged in turning against their North Vietnamese backers.

I paid a visit to the third floor of the US embassy to ask Tom Polgar's advice and help. With the customary self-confidence of important small men, and in his booming soothing voice, Polgar reassured me. Although commercial flights had been suspended, CIA personnel still flew routinely in and out of Cambodia. He seemed not in the least put out by my request for transport, and sympathised with my need for contact with the abandoned affiliate. I did not ask for, and he did not offer, any guarantees or help from his organisation. Each of us had his own network and responsibilities, but his friendly advice was that given such irrational opponents, even the weak Cambodian Army might hold out this season, and that Phnom Penh was safe for me to visit after all.

In the absence of commercial services, the CIA knows how to run a good airline, and I was only too happy to fly with them. We had to fasten ourselves to the military webbing inside the unmarked DC3, backs to the wall, next to unknown agents and personnel with missions sinister or banal. On Air America there were no plastic lunches and soothing voices. In-flight service was a shared thermos of hot coffee. While the technology was as old as the pilots, the handling of the plane was noticeably professional and alert. Approaching Phnom Penh, the box patterns of B52 bombing, two miles by half a mile of devastated red earth with neatly spaced craters, came in sight, but those imprints apart, few signs of war could be seen around the encircled city. The pilot made a corkscrew dive to the Pochen Tong runway, landed and taxied very fast past the smouldering wreck of a passenger plane. All was perfectly quiet.

Inside the yellow stucco airport hall, with its blown-out windows, the senior Cambodian Shell executive, a softly-smiling young man with a smooth brown bespectacled face and a golden Shell clasp holding an expensive tie to a billowing shirt, was waiting. I easily recognised him as a member of the Western university educated élite that Shell likes to recruit in developing countries. From his point of view, I was the stodgy representative of mother Shell, reassuringly normal, even if arriving by unconventional means. We played an elaborate game of normality. He apologised for the deplorable state of the pock-marked building, inquired studiously after my health and comfort during the trip and took me to his air conditioned limousine. First, he insisted, we should inspect the battle-scarred oil depot. Three days before, it had survived being machine-gunned from the back of a lorry driven by a few youths around the perimeter fence in one of the desultory attacks the Khmer Rouge mounted during siesta time. The government soldiers guarding the place hardly stirred themselves, so the depot's survival was due only to the Khmer Rouge's apparent lack of purpose. Many of their soldiers, fifteen years old and younger, and maybe on drugs, could hardly be blamed for not thinking straight.

We approached the immense shanty town of rural refugees fleeing the Khmers which had sprung up around the city. At a junction of roads, two government howitzers were firing at the other side of the river. Grinning barefoot boys carried shells to guns, and wives tended the cooking pots for the soldiers. Empty cartridges were sold on the spot for two dollars apiece. A handsome boy lieutenant was smiling into a field telephone, with his back to where the impacts could be observed with the naked eye. Millions of refugees depended on such amiable boys for their protection.

We drove through the residential quarter, where the Russian and American embassies stood guarded but virtually deserted. Their personnel had left. Ruins here and there were reminders of sporadic 107mm rocket attacks. Otherwise, the wide avenues retained the looks of the attractive, sleepy, French provincial town Phnom Penh had always been. It was a struggle to accept that this was dangerous territory.

The easy-going executives, the chatty secretaries, the clerks and the doormen of the Shell office all delighted in showing how seriously they were at work in their cocoon. The service was still excellent; I could choose from various local fresh fruit drinks and coffee and cakes. From my presence, they concluded that they had nothing to fear, just as I concluded from their behaviour that my own fears were overdone. Thus, instead of addressing realities such as the imminent fall of Cambodia and the emergency evacuation of personnel while there was still time, I allowed myself to be buried in an avalanche of business statistics pretending to portray the next five prosperous years. All nonsense, but the clever presentation and the happy smiles on the intelligent Cambodian faces, and Polgar's prediction that the unlikely status quo might last, made me back off from upsetting the contented staff. Instead, I helped put in the commas and crossed the t's of their lovely Plan.

Later in the afternoon, to work off my frustration, or perhaps to show off my faith in the normality of the situation, I asked if they thought the Khmers would mind if I did some water-skiing on the river. The senior staff, like all old-regime Cambodians, appreciated manifestations of eccentricity, and assured me, with a thousand smiles and without the slightest curiosity as to the real situation, that the whole of the Mekong was secure. In truth, the Mekong's security was somewhat circumscribed, as the people living on its borders would tell me. Every ex-French colony or protectorate has a smart 'club nautique' as a hub of its social life. In Pnom Penh, however, the club grounds, upstream of the bridge, had been taken over by refugee shacks with their out-houses open to the water. The club was deserted, except for some old servants. At that point, the front-line was so close that club employees and a crowd of onlookers could point to individual bushes on the far side occupied by the Khmer Rouge. The driver of the old speed-boat said he would hug the safe side, and would not go beyond 500 metres, because at that exact point we would come under gun fire with clockwork certainty. Rising out of the brown water, speeding towards the bend, I felt comforted by his local knowledge, and by the thought that if I fell, the current would sweep me back to friendly territory. At a sharp turn near the bridge, I did indeed fall flat on my belly. This so delighted the friendly guards at the bridge that they began throwing anti-personnel mines in their excitement, at what they thought was a safe distance, but which the cracks in my rib-cage told me I was lucky to survive. The crowd warmly applauded the caper, and I began to feel convinced that nothing was ever serious in Cambodia.

At dinner, that conviction was badly shaken once more. As one of the precious few visitors from the outside world, I had been invited by what remained of the foreign, mainly French, community to an old mansion, where I took place between alcoholic planters and lean Catholic missionaries who had fled from the interior. Drinking the last and best of the wines as if there were no tomorrow, they were exchanging recent experiences and predictions of approaching disaster around the swimming pool. French missionaries always knew the up-country situation better than any spy services, because they were living with villagers all their lives without self-seeking motives, speaking their languages.

Even these hardy men of good faith, however, were dumbfounded by the malevolent changes which had taken place among the naive, illiterate rural youth. Asked who the Khmer Rouge leaders were and what they stood for, the Catholic fathers could only rub their unshaven chins in bewilderment. Not even they seemed to know their leader. Names changed every year. Was Pol Pot really Saloth Sar, who had replaced Tou Samoth? The latter had been murdered, but by whom? They knew no more than what the peasant children could tell them: that Angkar was the sinister master organisation that had taken possession of their souls. They still referred to as 'children' those fifteen-year-old killers who sullenly eliminated intellectuals (people with glasses) and accepted to die for the organisation. Angkar preached a vision of a world without money, a totalitarian kingdom on earth for those allowed to live, although many would have to die first. Whoever the Holy Church failed to convert to Christ was reaped by the other side at the point of a gun, and forced to fight for the Devil.

If the words of these priests were anywhere near the truth, a great catastrophe was imminent. One stern missionary, raising a bony hand at me, quoted the Bible, Revelations, on the fall of Babylon. 'Men who became rich from doing business in that city will stand a long way off, because they are afraid to share in her suffering. They will say: how terrible, how awful for the great city! She used to dress herself in linen, purple and scarlet and cover herself with gold ornaments, precious stones and pearls. And in one hour she has lost all this wealth.' The words stick in my mind.

In spite of these terrible predictions, however, Phnom Penh miraculously would not fall that summer of 1973, or during the whole of the next year. Instead, it would continue teetering on the brink till the very end in 1975.

18

The Laotian Dream

Just as Shell in Cambodia depended on us in Saigon for supplies, so all the Shell operations in South Vietnam, Indonesia, Thailand, Hong Kong, the Philippines and Japan depended to some extent on the big Shell export refinery in Singapore. It was to Singapore that the London directors called Shell managers in these countries for a regional meeting on 1 October 1973. It was a final chance to close ranks before the battle over the world oil trading system burst upon us. Of course, we could not know that the first shot of the battle would be another Middle East war, just one week later.

In the cinema-like auditorium of the Singapore Company, most of us were already seated, with an acute sense of foreboding about the climactic events to unroll. The director in the chair on the podium, Bob Hart, an earnest American with a penchant for endless repetition, was flanked by executives and oil philosophers from London, who waved at late-comers. We, Chief Executives, filled the oval rows in front.

As the ceiling lights dimmed, one man and his charts remained in a mild spotlight, a microphone attached to his lapel. Like a jack-in-a-box, he sprang to life, pointing at us, shouting a controversial open-ing phrase. Pierre Wack, the bald, saffron-coloured Frenchman, one of the founding fathers of business scenario writing, could seduce even the most critical audiences with his mesmerising eloquence, conjuring up exotic visions, which might conceivably become reality. Sharp and agile as a court jester, he limbered up our minds at the start of important meetings. His French accent and newly- fashionable jargon – with words like 'societal' and 'environmental' hand-written all over his view-graphs – were part of the show. With him, it was easy to lose a sense of time, and sometimes the line of argument as well. On this occasion, he was impressing on us the inevitability of fundamental change. Pierre concluded his presentation with a dramatic flourish: the absolutely unthinkable was bound to happen, like in Singapore, 30 years before, when all the guns were pointing out to sea while the Japanese swept all before them from the land behind. The audience applauded, which they did for no-one else at company meetings. When the lights went up, Pierre just stood there, wan and exhausted, now the colour of a yellow wallpaper rose, his task done and with no part in subsequent proceedings.

The serious business started after coffee, with more greetings from colleagues and dashes up and down the ranks of seats. The big question was what our Shell Group should do, given OPEC-induced scarcity and upward pressure on prices, and in particular, how to explain ourselves to angry demoralised customers and consumer governments. World demand could not be satisfied if OPEC further restricted production, and with Shell supplying well over 10 percent of it, we would have to face a lot of irate customers. The supply director now took the floor, flanked by executives who set the prices to every group company in the world, or more often rationalised them after they had been set by OPEC, whose captive customers we were. Even after the glaring failures of the OPEC talks in Teheran and Tripoli, Shell continued to reach for another agreement with OPEC thus to avoid a wild bidding up of oil prices, and to hang on at all cost to the small, regulated, and predictable increases of the past. Without a single challenge from any of the affiliate company managers, the supply director proposed that the OECD consuming governments could simply not 'allow' drastic price rises, because even if they did, the demand for oil would prove 'inelastic' to such rises, as no free market mechanism existed to bring supply and demand back to balance. But there was a nagging feeling of unreality. We, the affiliates, had never tried to buy oil on a free market, we merely 'indented' from the Centre at prices adjusted for quality and transport differentials retroactively. But could that artificially controlled system hold in the forthcoming crisis? Now at last the scene was set. The lights stayed up so that everyone could look everyone else in the eye. The free ride was over, and we felt apprehensive.

One of the supply experts outlined the dark scenario of failure to reach agreement with OPEC. This would result in a world wide scramble for oil directly between OECD consuming governments and mighty OPEC itself, in which the oil companies, with heavy investment on both sides, would be squashed in the middle. In order to survive at all, we would have to take sides, and it was clear that our main weight lay with the consumer governments. We were therefore admonished to be prepared to help them 'distribute' the foreseen shortfalls fairly, and at the same time to resist any market-driven price rises. This scenario should have provoked one of us to rise to his feet and ask if, in view of our failure to negotiate price or anything else with OPEC or with the consumer governments, we should not consider giving the free market a try. The resulting price rise might have brought supply and demand into balance without the need for government intervention, be it at the expense of the weaker economies and customers. Such a suggestion, however, would have been mercilessly struck down in 1973. Nobody in the auditorium remembered, or could imagine, free markets. It seemed downright unpatriotic in times of cold war to claim freedom for prices and markets.

Pierre's warning had not sunk in. The director swept a grim glance over his unenthusiastic audience. In the despondent spirit of the time, when Vietnam loomed as a strategic defeat in the global struggle, the free market was an orphan. Only one man, an alcoholic with keen eyes in a florid face, rose ponderously to his feet to predict that within a year scarcity was likely, as always before, to turn into abundance once again, with all distribution schemes be forgotten. He was right, but at this moment he was considered a mere curiosity. The rest of us simply tried to drown our doubts at a luxurious dinner in the $10 million home of our Singapore host, in the secluded park in the city centre.

Afterwards, we went to the lively bar of the Goodwood Hotel, with its Chinese serving girls dressed in Scottish kilts. Now bored by problems, we reverted to gossip and our own home-made solutions. The best recipe against oil crises, claimed the Dutch general manager of the Indonesian company, was a round of golf with President Suharto. Energy scarcity benefitted Indonesia, as a producer, and gave it an option to mine and sell Sumatran coal to Japan. But although he was an experienced executive with a good record, he was considered by his peers to be a middle-aged intellectual lightweight. So we indulged him and moved on. The Japanese executive muttered about commodity-poor Japan working itself into a state bordering on panic. As Japan lacked its own international oil industry, the Prime Minister himself was already traveling through the Arab countries negotiating for assured supplies, and was said to be ready to offer a high price to take over our Vietnamese exploration venture. The offer was eventually turned down. The Chief Executive of the Cambodian company, now looking a little sheepish, took me aside. He had returned to his post as soon as the perceived danger was over, and hoped that no-one would know of his short holiday. He seemed preoccupied, not so much with the fate of Phnom Penh as with the possible damage to his career, in which Phnom Penh was a just a stepping-stone.

Meanwhile, our athletic Hong Kong man was loudly challenging members of an Australian swimming team to a relay race in the hotel swimming pool. To the amusement of the lean sunburnt girls, he bet them a few bottles of champagne that his middle-aged friends would beat them. While the teams were chosen, he found a moment to commend me for cutting Hong Kong in on the proceeds from the Vietnamese contracts. We had transfered some contractual accounting work to low tax Hong Kong after the expiry of a tax holiday of the Singapore service company we had used before. Such cross-border courtesies were routine between us. Then we dived into the pool, and by cheating outrageously swam to a disputed and rowdy victory.

I flew back through Bangkok with Henny de Ruyter, the eager Chief Executive of the Thailand and Laos affiliates. He was an enthusiastic talker with a great singing voice, which he used to advantage in pleasure-loving Thailand. An engaging bandy-legged physical appearance, a slight stammer and an infectious grin made him irresistible to men and women. Prosperous, easy-going Thailand seemed an ideal staging post for his career, with its large investments in oil exploration and diversification into tin mining. The country was judged to have a great future, and so the more money he invested the more highly he was regarded. His main problem, he sighed, was steering clear of daft pro-posals favoured by Shell's wealthy Chinese business partners, such as the atomic blasting of a canal for tankers through the Malayan isthmus. By contrast, Vietnam's investment opportunities, he regretted to say, were nullified by war risks. Even so, I remarked, it produced and repa-triated more profits than Thailand would do for a very long time, and if it ever emerged as a free economy it might well overtake it.

In the same half-frivolous vein, Henny offered me his light plane, in which to go and savour the ultimate in outlandish investment climates, Laos, which depended on him for supplies and had no pre-tensions of ever making it to the economic big league.

For me, this was an irresistible offer. Gentle Laos and its royal capital Vientiane floated before my eyes like an opium-induced dream on the fringes of the world. It was a vision of a 'kingdom of a million elephants and a single parasol', according to a quaint French description. I had heard of the nebulous mountains and of a beautiful prince (chosen by the same discerning governor's wife who had the young Sihanouk appointed in Cambodia), overseeing a happy land of easy-going peasants in the upper Mekong delta. But I knew very little of the tribes in the Laotian mountains, over whom the prince also pretended to reign. According to travel descriptions, they must rank amongst the most admirable misfits of our time. The fiercely independent mountain people, the Meo and the Hmong, have no written language and no courts of law, and owe allegiance to no government. Despite borders on maps, they have migrated freely, a few million of them, since time immemorial over the whole Indo-Chinese mountain spine between Yunan, Burma, Vietnam and Laos, holding fast to their customs and their ancient lifestyle of hunting, slash-and-burn agriculture, promiscuity and opium production.

For their tenacity in clinging to outdated vices and virtues, they are a thorn in the side of all modern governments in Laos, China and Vietnam. Warm-hearted hospitality for the underdog is said to be their greatest virtue, but it surely has also been part of their undoing. In 1941, they sheltered the Vietminh from the French government, and in March 1945 the defeated French from the Japanese army, but neither of these grateful guests would leave them alone after the war, which was all the *montagnards* ever asked for. The French ignored their freedom by creating the fiction of rule by the royal Laotian house over the mountain tribes. However, in the following disorders, while one prince supported the Lao Issara from a safe distance in Bangkok, and another prince supported the communist Vietminh, while the King himself relaxed under a triple parasol in Luang Prabang, the mountain people had to defend themselves against both. Many years later, when Savannarath was re-confirmed in a peace conference by all parties as the constitutional monarch in Vientiane, his own brother Souphanouvong, urged on by his North Vietnamese wife, continued to lead the Vietminh sympathisers, the Pathet Lao, against him, and the *montagnards* had again to defend themselves. Thus it became all too clear that whereas the lowlanders did not mind submitting to king, or communist, or to whoever else appeared to have the upper hand, the Meo and Hmung would fight for their way of life.

As it happened, their interests coincided for a while with the French army's need to keep the North Vietnamese out of Laos. However, the French generally took a jaundiced view of their allies, not realising that protracted conflict in mountainous jungle could only be handled by local forces with knowledge of mountain warfare and survival. Their own heavy expeditionary corps was gobbling up the whole of the military budget, leaving nothing with which the Meo could be allowed to re-place their flintlock guns. The expeditionary corps, which could well have defended the accessible lowlands, went to its defeat in the remote highlands, at Dien Bien Phu, in 1954. Largely because without a screen of local scouts, the Dien Bien Phu command was eyeless, and the Vietminh could stretch their vulnerable supply lines without fear of interdiction. The massive defeat might have been avoided if the French had seriously supported the *montagnards*, instead of merely selling them old arms for opium. Right up to the fall of Dien Bien Phu, and even after, the French quartermaster general only helped the Meo by secretly trading old French guns for Meo opium, which was transported by military planes and sold in Saigon through the Binh Xuyen gangs and the Corsican mafia. Everyone took a cut in the revenues. General Salan defended this activity in his memoirs by claiming that if he had not bought the Meo's only source of revenue, the Vietminh would certainly have done so.

French commanders could hardly credit the evidence that the Meo, with their inadequate weapons, had already forced the withdrawal of two Chinese Army and three Vietminh divisions from the highlands around Samneua, because it had been achieved not by battle but by ambush, harassment of supply lines, surprise, mobility and starvation. Yet the Meo took higher casualties than the French corps itself in these campaigns. In spite of the evidence of *montagnard* effectiveness, however, the myth that the expeditionary corps did most of the fighting persists to this day. At that time, the French high command, like the American later, were totally in the dark about the superiority of local troops on their own inaccessible terrain.

Western army officers do not see straight in this matter. On the one hand, they acknowledge the superior hardiness and cunning of local militia in the defence of their own villages; on the other, they blame them for 'dissolving' in a hopeless battle when they should have sacrificed themselves to cover the retreat of a foreign armed column. At the heart of the problem, perhaps, lies our concept of discipline, which is unsuited to guerrilla conflicts. Since Frederick the Great, we have drilled our soldiers as weapon-carrying robots for set-piece battles on Western plains. For good measure, we clamp a helmet over his eyes, hang a flack jacket over his shoulders, add 50kg of regular issue and tell him to stagger off into foreign jungles to find 'Charlie'. He gets himself killed on the first home-made land-mine the local people forget to tell him about.

The local soldier presents a disconcerting contrast. He fights for nothing in economic terms, but, in his own opinion, for the highest stakes of all: for freedom, family and tribe. As a native hunter, he has all the instincts of a guerrilla who can smell the enemy. Barking orders at him is counter-productive, because he already knows why and how he must fight in each instance, and also when not to fight. His appearance is usually disconcerting too: a Meo warrior would wear his hair in a pigtail and, apart from arms, carry nothing in battle. He walked barefoot. Not surprisingly, after the defeat of the French regular army in 1954, the incomprehensible and uncouth allies were dropped altogether, and the Americans, after initial support, also washed their hands of the Meo. President Kennedy signed a hollow international treaty in 1962, which recognised them as subjects of the neutral Laotian government of Souvannah Phouma. The main characteristic of the treaty was its lack of teeth. The North Vietnamese used the 'peace' to carry their war into the Meo highlands.

Poor, easy-going, gullible Meo. In 1970, the CIA began to use them once more to help expel 70,000 North Vietnamese troops from the Plain of Jars. Again, with proper help the *montagnards* accomplished the job and fought well. Now recognising them as intrepid fighters, the CIA was anxious to continue support. It was therefore with the utmost reluctance that the CIA had to obey orders from Washington to stop all military supplies a few years later. The orders had been implemented, in fact, just before my visit. Once more the mountain tribes had been betrayed by their Western friends.

Our Cessna was descending over the miles-wide expanse of the Mekong to land on the other side, where Vientiane slumbered, literally: the policeman in his booth, the labourer in siesta and the prince on his silk cushions. In a Land Rover, we crossed the green provincial town with the dusty avenues so beloved by French city architects. Traffic in the centre was waved on by wardens in white, with effeminate hand movements. The Russian-built hotel had no active reception clerk, but it was empty and we could choose our own rooms. Even the Shell depot, walls splashed with red mud by last season's rain, seemed to be dangling at the far end of a long chain of command, without much in the way of graphs and records to show for itself. It was surely the only Shell company in the world without a Plan, nestling comfortably in a country with endless festivities and no future as we understood it.

The American Ambassador in this backwater, Charles Whitehouse, a friend from the year before when he was deputy to Ambassador Bunker, and an ex-US airforce pilot like myself, had invited me to a pool-side lunch. His reception room with polished wooden floors evoked the pre-civil war estates of the deep South, straight out of Hollywood. But what was lacking was a gracious hostess. The good lady had chosen not to accompany her husband to this back-end of the world. Whitehouse, as he came in through the garden doors, was irrepressibly elegant, as always, his lined face wrapped in welcoming smiles.

We sat with our cold drinks in comfortable rattan chairs in the shade of a hardwood tree, interrupted occasionally by a raucous bird-cry. Our conversation was drifting around to the subject of Asian women. Regrettably, we noted, Souvanouvong, the Laotian prince, was manipulated by his North Vietnamese wife, who was a Communist agent. But could Asian husbands ever resist female dominance? Even the present-day Chinese empire was ruled by Jiang Qing, the ex-actress wife of the senile Mao. And what about the dominance of Imelda Marcos, Dewi Sukarno and Madame Nhu, through their men, over the affairs of state? Did we, from the West, ever accept the realities? I expressed surprise that the Saigon embassy had never established direct contacts with President Thieu's very influential wife (who had not been above seeking me out in my office, accompanied by a general staff officer, to force my hand on a minor business matter or two).

Whitehouse patiently explained that it no longer mattered. He and his colleagues represented a great nation more and more intent on withdrawal from Indo-China at whatever human cost. Personal friendships could be an encumbrance at this stage. His own nomination had been delayed by six months in congress because of the suspicion that he might be a 'hawk' and too sympathetic to the local allies. 'And what possible difference would that make?' he asked ironically. The time was past when a hawkish US Ambassador could send targets for bombing by the Seventh air force, or arm the *montagnards*. Nevertheless, he had to swear to the gentlemen of the Senate in Washington that he would never recommend the use of military force in Laos. It sounded like another repetitive tale.

After lunch, it had become oppressively hot even in the shade. Great yellow cumulo-nimbus clouds towered in the sky. A few heavy raindrops evaporated as quickly as they fell. If I wanted to see it all in a nutshell, suggested Whitehouse bitterly, the shameless withdrawal of a super-power and the fig-leaf of humanitarian aid to former allies, I should see for myself how they dropped food on the last defenceless Meo tribes still holding out against the North Vietnamese Army.

He drove me personally to an old Air America transport plane at the airport and introduced me to the grey-haired crew. They gave me an exaggerated welcome as I descended from the limousine. To their regret, they could not offer me a seat in the cockpit, as befitted an ambassador's friend, but they could use a 'kicker', someone to open the doors and kick out the rice bags when they switched on the red warning light. The flight plan was simplicity itself: follow the Mekong below clouds to Paksane, then strike out north along the valleys towards Samneua and drop supplies on three settlements of Meo women and children whose men were still resisting the North Vietnamese somewhere.

The engines coughed and started after some backfiring; the leaked gasoline on the ground caught fire, but the propellers blew it out. Once airborne, I had a limited forward view between the shoulders of the pilots, from where I was in the belly of the plane, amongst the rice bags on the wooden pallets mounted on rails. Drizzle from the woolly clouds mingled with ground-fog rising from the jungle, covering the perilous mountain ranges on either side. It was no flying weather, and not a suitable terrain for low flying. The plane, however, reacted smartly like an old warhorse to the rudder kicks. The pilots seemed madly determined to find the settlements, and I began to curse them for trying to kill us all in their crazy support of a few *montagnards*. Suddenly they cried out simultaneously that I should prepare the first drop. Seeing nothing through the rain-splattered windscreen, I lurched in a sideways slip to the door, fell against the pallets, bled, loosened the ropes, hooked my harness to the fuselage and opened the door into the slipstream. The red warning light came on, and still without sign of a target, or a even a break in the jungle, I kicked out a pallet and had the instant satisfaction of seeing the freed bags arc downwards very gracefully. At that moment I also noticed the small scar of red earth of a clearing in the bush and the canvass cross at which the pilots must have aimed. The only view I got of the result of my efforts was of those bags bursting in long stripes of white rice against red ground, bang in the middle of hundreds of children, running with upturned faces. Some of them must have been hit. As far as they knew, poppies grew on earth and rice fell excitingly out of the sky.

There was nothing else to see, none of the famous Meo-long houses, which had been abandoned for tents in their long retreat during 20 years of fighting. It was all over in seconds, and two more drops remained. By now the exhilaration of flying between clouds and hill-tops had taken hold, enhanced by the emotion of dropping food for children. I marvelled at the skill of the pilots, flying at a hundred feet. I was sliding tons of rice over the rails, kicking out the sacks, yelling at every bullseye hit amongst the children. The half hour's elation soon gave way to other emotions. With my back against the shuddering fuselage, I was crying uninhibitedly at the uselessness of our mercy mission on the edge of the known world.

The limousine and the elegant figure in the white linen suit were waiting for us back at the hangar. The famous ironic smile still hovered over Whitehouses' lips. He was sorry to have sent us up in such weather. The pilots, true brothers now, waved apologies aside. And all I wished to know was how much longer he thought the persecuted *montagnards* could last. A bored professional look: 'Oh, another thousand years, with luck and without other do-gooders trying to save them,' was the nonchalant answer. If Cambodia was not serious, Laos surely was only a dream.

19

Vietnam Highland
Defences

I began to recognise a clear danger to my career, arising from my management style in Vietnam, yes; from my being there at all at this critical and uncertain time. A reputation as a manager in our type of business was built on an image of being able to achieve confident growth and promise of further expansion through brilliant acquisitions or investments. Profits alone were not enough. Colleagues all around me were achieving their aims by gaining new markets in promising Thailand, by extending the Singapore refineries, or through dreaming up coal export projects in Indonesia. Essential for all this was to employ armies of high-potential, highly-paid expatriate staff who would vie with each other in drawing up long-term plans and projects, and in introducing the latest business gimmicks to be circulated for wonder and emulation within the Shell Group.

Instead of competing on this level, I was bogged down in discussions with brick-heads on the best security precautions, like adding new lighting, enlarging killing zones and introducing improved types of barbed wire around the up-country depots. I was on the London Personnel Department black-list for rejecting the employment of high-flyers in the fields of retail network advertising and sales promotion in favour of local Vietnamese staff, who knew something about their own markets. I had failed to replace clerks with computers. I had advanced Vietnamese to top positions, depriving deserving young expatriates of a career opportunity to cut their teeth in the field. My name was mentioned in connection with outrageous proposals to put machine-guns on tankers manned by non-Shell personnel, and to come closer to the combat front-line by putting fuel directly into airforce planes at military bases instead of simply selling the fuel to the Vietnamese armed forces for them to fuel their own planes. Furthermore, even when promoting Vietnamese, I did not attach the usual overriding importance to their academic qualifications. And most inconvenient of all, I still believed in a possible future for South Vietnam.

'Going native', as it is called, normally accompanied by loss of a 'proper perspective', is a condition rightly feared by all overseas executives. They are expected to adapt to local conditions, but not to the point of becoming involved beyond the call of duty. They have to keep their home shareholders' interests uppermost in their minds, because that is what determines their future career.

In this light, the starchy American embassy of Elsworth Bunker was a prime example of rectitude, always giving due deference to State-side opinion and not minding a little hypocrisy in the process. It certainly never went native, indefatigably propagating an unshakeably optimistic American viewpoint, backing the South Vietnamese democratic state to the hilt in words, while in practice writing it off completely. Having spent many billions of dollars on the high-minded American effort to save democracy, they now quibbled over a few millions to keep the less-than-ideal, but palpably real, expression of it in Vietnam alive. In conversations with Bunker and his entourage at my house or at his own residence, Saigon's precarious situation and the new measures needed from Washington were taboo subjects. They knew the facts behind the facade, but affected an iron-clad confidence that supply programmes at current levels would carry the day.

This misled even the South Vietnamese leadership into thinking that they could rest in their defensive positions and still have a viable military future. Only a strong offensive against the North Vietnamese staging posts in Cambodia could have saved them. When Bunker was recalled, I had no doubt that cynical minds in the White House had realised that his expressions of confidence were hollow, and tended to mask reality and misdirect the effort. He could never be accused of putting a foot wrong; his actions were always honourable, initiated cautiously and backed by higher authority, but in the end Washington could not have helped but notice that the local situation slipped further out of their hands. He made a lasting contribution in improving the freedom of the press and economic enterprise, and in promoting democratic elections. But he failed to convince President Thieu that US support was waning and that defensive military solutions were no longer possible. Now at last he had been relieved of the thankless task with full honours.

Bunker's successor was his exact opposite, someone who accepted the local situation, warts and all, but believed with his whole being that its protection was worth his life. If not, he could have comfortably retired to a farm in Tuscany. He did not mind berating Washington. 'Going native' from the start, he and his adjudants fought for the Vietnamese. However, although the new Ambassador, Graham Martin, did have plenty of charisma and local touch, even I thought it was a little late in the day for such radical change. It would have meant, for a start, doubling the aid and support for renewed excursions into the Cambodian sanctuaries. In earlier days, in Italy and Thailand, he had been able to make a strong personal contribution to staving off Communism. His compassion and drive could well have made a difference in Vietnam too, but at this late stage it could also prolong the agony. His Promethian and ultimately doomed attempts to convince congress to reverse the decline of American aid to South Vietnam were based on an overestimation of his mandate, every bit as lethal in human suffering as Bunker's underestimation. People would hate him for it later.

To the German embassy had fallen the honour of introducing the new American pro-consul to the locals. Official limousines choked the embassy driveway, and minor dignitaries had to leave their cars half a mile down blocked roads and hurry through crowded sidewalks, clutching their invitations. Inside, diplomats, notables and society women crowded his path to catch a revealing word or witticism from his lips. Courteous with everyone, and thoroughly prepared, when my turn came he even pulled my leg about the high price we had paid for the exploration concession. Then, adding with absolute seriousness that no-one in the world knew as much as he about protection against terrorism, he declared it his pleasure to advise personally on the security of our installations.

That first contact created a friendship which no later doubt about his actions could ever change. All subsequent contacts confirmed the impression of a committed individual, never afraid to play against the odds to win. Even at the very end, in 1975, when evacuated by helicopter from the roof of his embassy, an arrogant but spent force, one could only fault him for having persevered too long. On this night, still at the height of his powers, he renewed our hope, and was loved by us in return. As soon as he left in his car with motor escort and screaming sirens, the party was over and the guests went home uplifted.

Kim Chi had asked me to drive her home from the reception, and as I kept glancing sideways at her pharaonic profile, I wondered what on earth she was thinking. What, I asked, was her impression of Graham Martin? She shrugged. To her he was the same as any other in a long line of ambassadors passing through. Philosophising did not pay the bills. Her house was full of flower bouquets with name cards, crying for attention, and coloured telephones ringing constantly with calls from journalists, family and people to whom she owed money. A cook was standing by for instructions over the intercom. In between, a maid told her fortune from a deck of cards, which she was tapping very pensively with long finger nails, her eyes glued to the peasant girl's face.

Minister Ngoc had invited us to join a group of foreign military observers, reporters and friends in a conducted tour of the Pleiku and Kontum defences in the highlands. I had offered to drive Kim Chi to Dalat airport, where we would join Ngoc's party in their plane to Kontum. Route 20 to the cool and pleasant mountain resort of Dalat had been only recently re-opened, and I was anxious to explore. For many years it had been closed due to insecurity, but now its 300 kilometres could be travelled in safety again, judging from the arrival on the Saigon market of fresh fruit and vegetables carried by lorries all the way from the highlands around Dalat. Moreover, Cong Ty Shell owned a villa up there, overlooking the jungle, close to ex-emperor Bao Dai's luxurious old hunting villa with its vast driveways, immense reception halls and elaborate kitchens. Lack of security had so far prevented its use, and I looked forward to seeing its fabulous setting for the first time.

When I collected her in the early morning, she could easily have been the twin sister of the farm girl who was kneeling to pack her suitcase. Without makeup, dressed in white blouse, peasant black trousers, wooden sandals, her hair tied back with an elastic band, Kim Chi had blended back once more into rural Vietnam. And I was not the only one to be oddly affected by her withdrawal.

In the Hai Ba Trung Boulevard we came upon a car accident. An old friend of ours had hit and slightly damaged a *cyclo-pousse*, one of those three-wheeled bicycle taxis, where passengers sit in a vulnerable basket in front of the cyclist. Our friend was standing surrounded by an excited crowd. Relieved to see our car, he hailed us, stuck his head through the window, 10cm from her face, and without a glimmer of recognition, or awareness of her presence, asked for a ride to the police station. He even came in beside her; she had to shift to allow him in. During the short drive, however, our common friend directed an animated chatter at me, treating her as non-existent. Suspecting a practical joke, I glanced at Kim Chi to see if she was in on it, but found my own gaze bouncing off an expressionless mask. I found it hard to even focus on her, transparent, near invisible as she had become. This convinced me that my friend was not ignoring her on purpose, but that he actually could not see her. Only after we had dropped him off did life flow back into her features. No European can recognise a Vietnamese woman if she does not want to be seen, she explained happily.

'East is East and West is West, and never the twain shall meet', was one of her teases, brought home to me by another incident. En route, we had stopped off at her farm, to inspect some work. I was to wait in the ghastly *kitsch* living-room of the prefab farmhouse, with its plastic-covered seats, framed and signed official photographs and the obligatory gold-leaf Chinese characters for happiness and prosperity on the walls. After a few minutes, there was a commotion outside. Glad of a diversion, I drew the curtains aside. In the courtyard two attractive farm girls were holding a shouting match, shoving and pulling each other. A circle of lecherous men had formed, encouraging the girls to fight it out. Excited by all the attention, one girl escalated the dispute and smacked the other resoundingly across the face. The other responded by ripping the other's blouse and drawing blood with her nails. At the sight of bare breasts, the men went wild with excitement, placing bets on the half-naked women, yelling their support.

But as suddenly, they fell silent when a third barefoot girl jumped into the ring. She took a hold and twisted the hair of the attacker around her fist, expertly pulled and kicked her legs from underneath, and pinned the victim to the ground, crunching a knee into her back. There were no cheers this time, but utter fear. The girls, the men and I stood paralysed, while the third woman kept grinding the open-mouthed face of her victim in the dirt, regardless of howls for mercy. I felt ashamed, like a *voyeur*. Only when the woman rose did I recognise her as Kim Chi. The farm girls were bowing and sobbing for mercy now, the men backing off and shuffling away; the dispute was over. I was still shaken by what I had seen when Kim Chi swept back into the room, brushing past me, cool as cucumber, in a torn shirt, only the veins in her forehead still pulsing. At my first word of reproach, however, she stiffened. In reply, she dipped her face in the fountain, sucked up some water and blew it at me through compressed lips. Then, in a soaring voice, she wailed that she could not afford to pay salaries and pensions, like respectable foreign businesses, that she had to employ deserters and whores because they came cheap. If she had not acted with the violence they expected of her, if she had not physically beaten that girl, it would have meant the end of her farm.

Even I could now see the elemental differences between us. While I had the luxury of presiding over an international business, giving employees security and respecting their dignity, the small Vietnamese employer had to live by his wits and had to have the guts to fight his own employees for a fair share of any half-illegal proceeds. If she had lost her foothold, her business would have been dead by now. The Vietnamese marketplace was violent and devious. Even the largest Vietnamese institutions had to resort to stealth and illegal operations. The Central Bank cashed half a million dollars a day from what it very well knew to be North Vietnamese blackmarket operations, in order to keep the economy going.

We drove on. Route 20 to Dalat bore all the scars of a recently reopened highway. Trees and lush vegetation had been cut on both sides to improve fields of fire, but the few ARVN checkpoints offered no more than symbolic protection. Travel was entirely at one's own risk. The pewter sky was reflected in the cratered, waterlogged road surface. Crowded busses and lorries, to avoid holes in the paved surface, had chosen separate tracks in the soft earth alongside, and had thus created improvised parallel roads. Mined vehicles, stripped of removables, littered the sides, and our pedantic white Mercedes, covered in mud, its exhaust knocked sideways, was sadly and ridiculously out of place. Kim Chi, with her legs drawn up on the front seat, had returned to her indestructible good humour. She was scanning the sides of the road bantering about clever journalists who had a knack of twisting the 'good' information she gave into 'bad' articles. I had no idea what she was talking about, but knew that she naturally liked to laugh at any mischief, in whatever guise, in whatever field. As a child of the great oral tradition, she told current scandal stories larded with appropriate quotes, first spoken by famous men hundreds of years ago. Women of her class were judged by their ability to entertain with salacious historical tales and proverbs. Books were definitely inferior sources for learning Vietnamese history .

For my benefit, she was telling her stories in French, in a racy Parisian slang, saying the punch-lines in Vietnamese first to get the full flavour. Above all she adored double-meanings in Vietnamese, through varying the intonation, by which you can turn 'school' into 'brothel' without sounding any different to Western ears.

As spoken by her, the Vietnamese language was an ideal weapon of the oppressed, used with devastating irony against 1500 years of Chinese and French overlords, as a major part of the nationalist underground. Without lifting her eyes from the jungle edge, she giggled, and asked if I had heard the one about Trang Quynh. It seems he had been a particularly wicked courtier, whose name is warmly remembered even above that of his master, the emperor, for the quality of his practical jokes. (I had listened to similar stories about the early Khalifas from the mouths of Arab storytellers). Apparently, one day the Vietnamese emperor, on his throne in the palace in Hue, was very worried at the approach of the Chinese Ambassador. The problem was, of course, that the emperor knew full well that the Ambassador, as a representative of a super power, would insist on entering the palace through the principal door in the middle, the Ngo Mon gate. And this of all things was out of the question, because he, the Emperor, has just decreed that it could only be used by himself, on his own birthday. All other mortals had to use a second gate next to it. Here Trang Quynh jumps to the rescue. After some innuendo to his emperor friend over the words gate and access to the female body which I could not follow, Trang Quynh rushes outside and positions himself in front of the second gate to welcome the Ambassador. But instead of doing so, he pelts the outraged Ambassador with rotten tomatoes and jokes of doubtful taste. The pompous Chinese becomes very angry indeed. To make him raging mad, Trang Quynh waves his heavy plumed fan in front of the Ambassador's eyes and hits him on the head with it. The enraged Ambassador tries to grab Trang Quynh by his robes, and pursues him into the palace through the second entrance, which was Quynh's purpose all the time. Throwing himself at the Ambassador's feet, the prostrate courtier begs forgiveness. Emperor and Ambassador make up, and an international incident is averted. The story loses in translation, but Kim Chi kept her bright humour.

When the midday heat became too much, we stopped at a cool mountain pass. Around us, the trees fell away sharply, and we could see other ridges descending towards the lowlands. Monkeys were crashing in groups through the branches, crying out at each other. A stream gurgled from the rock face. Judging from old wine bottles lying around, it must once have been a favourite picnic ground, but now we found ourselves alone, with our napkins and chicken salad on plastic plates. Just as she was regaling me with more gossip about an amorous TV announcer, Kim's voice trailed away, and I turned and froze.

Ten metres away, a boy had appeared out of the shrub with a rifle pointed at me, and turning my eyes I could see another approaching with slow deliberate moves. I felt the muscles in my face relax, my eyes widen and my body lighten up. I did not have to think; some centre in the brain had already analysed the details, and was making me rise slowly with empty hands and a happy smile. The boys were half my size, they had joyless baby faces, low foreheads and carelessly formed mouths with widely spaced teeth, their MI6s the only clean things about them. Those and their canvas boots, instead of tyre sandals, identified them as 'friendlies', but not necessarily less deadly than the 'enemy'. When they looked at the food, Kim Chi at once gestured them to take it, talking gently in Vietnamese. Being Meo tribesmen, however, they did not understand, and consulted each other by eye. Their adrenaline level might be diminishing, but their thoughts remained easy to guess. Shall we kill these foreigners and take their possessions, or would that land us in more trouble than they are worth? One shifted his gun and took a chicken leg, grunting appreciatively, and his brother-in-arms followed suit. We added a couple of beer tins, from the goodness of our hearts, and sidled back to the car. But they had already lost interest in us, and allowed our departure with wide grins.

Towards sundown, we arrived at the company's villa in the pure cold highland air of the Dalat forest. It did not seem as wildly romantic as remembered by the older staff. The jungle had receded from it, and the guardian, living in the annex like a squatter, had replaced the famous rose garden by commercial vegetable beds. In his long isolation from Saigon, and without our approval, he had burned part of the jungle, terraced the land and turned it into a market garden for himself. Although our arrival must have worried him a great deal, he and the whole of his family were lining up to welcome us at the massive door, all bobbing and smiling. With elaborate courtesy, we were led inside the clean and well-maintained hall. A thundering log fire lit up the massive beams, the wooden sculptures of Buddhas-in-contemplation, gilded wooden monsters and Chinese vases and bronzes. The furniture consisted of hard chairs and rosewood tables, without any concessions to soft modern luxury. An imposingly austere, but strangely fascinating, reception hall.

The bathrooms were engineered on the scale of Roman baths, in a lighter-hearted style. Gleaming copper tubing from old-fashioned gas heaters led to sunken round baths with descending steps. On the tiled walls, Jugendstil nudes danced with satyrs in flowered meadows. Well designed solid bidets and chain-flush lavatories presided majestically over the accoutrements of ritual ablution. The bathrooms nestled among a range of baronial bedrooms decorated all over with volup- tuous paintings *à la* Rubens. The old French planter who built the place obviously liked his solid luxuries and playful diversions.

Before we sat down for dinner in the hall, and while I was toying with a glass of really cold champagne, our caretaker poured out his fears and complaints to Kim Chi in Vietnamese. I could see his words upset her. She had again dressed in Western style, and was frowning, smiling with her lips only. Some exchanges do not have to be translated to be understood, and excluded as I was from the details of their conversation I sensed the tenseness in her which the caretaker's words produced.

Hours later, after a fresh and light Vietnamese dinner, when we opened the creaking old doors to the cool of the terrace to watch the falling stars, an owl flew through the moon. I could feel her wince at the ill omen, but the bird flew away in silence, and silence, almost too perfect, hung over the terraces. To take in the beauty of the far wooded hills, we were leaning way over the stone balustrade, our heads sil- houetted against the moonlit sky. So mesmerised were we by the majesty of the night that when the supersonic crack of the first bullet hit our ears, it seemed a distant and irrelevant sound in the depth of the universe. The following fusillade, however, had the impact of a train thundering past. We ducked behind the rampart. Explosions now shook the ground. Echoes within the valleys made it impossible to tell where the volleys came from. Then, abruptly, deafening silence reigned again, but a different silence from the one before.

Obviously we took the incident – was it linked to the caretaker? – as a warning not to assume that the property was entirely our own. Daylight investigations, however, led nowhere. The police post next-door had heard nothing at all. Our caretaker suggested that a regional guard had perhaps opened fire, or that the firing might have come from another valley. Night echoes are notoriously tricky, they all said.

Our visit to the Pleiku Kontum enclave of General Phu in the Central Highlands was even more poignant than my previous one to General Truong in Danang, but only increased the same fundamental doubts about a passive defensive posture, which left the initiative entirely to the enemy. Both were successful generals with a lifetime experience of fighting Communists, and although they now held the most exposed front-line sectors in the whole of Vietnam, with an inferiority in material and numbers, they shared the same rock-like conviction that they could hold that line forever.

Small and wiry Phu had served under Kim Chi's husband, and welcomed her as a friend of the family. Not the kind of personality who would dominate TV screens, he was clearly sensitive, and a father-figure to his men. He was a survivor of one insurmountable crisis after another, starting with his parachute drop as a young daredevil into Dien Bien Phu in 1954 when the fort was already as good as lost, only to undergo the indelible subsequent experience of Asian captivity, which he swore never to suffer again. Released after the Geneva peace treaty, he made rapid promotion. His divisions had fought in the highlands with changing fortunes, but had always kept the line. The secret of their success and their motivation was there for all to see: the wives and children of the soldiers lived in the military compounds around Kontum under their sole protection. All their worldly goods, cattle, goats and buffalo grazed under the reach of their guns. Their well-tended market gardens stretched well into the distance. We visited the school for children within the defensive perimeter. They seemed like a forgotten militant tribe with modern weapons, settled in clearings in the jungle forever, waiting and accepting their lot.

Our party of well-dressed foreigners, many of whom were professional soldiers from Western armies, gaped in astonishment at this subsistence fighting, shaking their wise heads in admiration at the always smiling troops. Of course these troops were no longer mobile, they explained to me, and if pushed from all sides by superior forces they would be hard to reinforce: an accident waiting to happen, they said. We had to suppress feelings of pity when Minister Ngoc, as a token of our appreciation, handed Phu a heavy block of newly-printed 1000-piastre notes. Phu accepted the almost useless gift humbly in front of his troops.

Only in private did he point at ominous new developments that would affect the life and death of himself and his troops. The

Arab-Israeli (Yom Kippur) war had started with an Egyptian surprise attack wiping out many of the Israeli's front-line tanks and aircraft. Everyone sensed that the shattered Israelis would be lost without prompt and massive American aid, but luckily, unlike the Vietnamese, they could count on a powerful Jewish lobby and other friends in America to paint the local disaster in stark colours and drum up support for drastic measures to bail them out. Nixon was able to save Israel by replacing dozens of lost F-4 jets and promptly airlifting war material to the value of $2.2 billion over and above aid already budgeted. Phu pointed out wistfully that the US had given more support in two weeks to Israel than to Vietnam in a whole year. Vietnam had no lobby. For him, that summed up American priorities, and the diminishing chances of South Vietnam's survival, but in his task he never wavered.

We flew back to the golden, if somewhat derelict, imperial capital Hue, arriving there as evening began to fall. The last rays of the sun picked out the high walled citadel, the Palace of Everlasting Longevity, the Pagodas of the Elderly Goddess and of the Famous Eunuchs, and the crumbling tombs of emperors along the slow and shallow river. The lowly houses of the living had already evaporated into the dark. The ordinary people of Hue were thoroughly tired of the sufferings imposed by its grandeur. In the 1968 Tet offensive, the North Vietnamese felt obliged to hold on to the imperial citadel for its value as a national symbol, causing devastation and loss of life for 30 days against overwhelming odds and the best of American troops. They executed 5000 of the city's inhabitants as an exit gesture. A modest plaque commemorated the mass grave.

We found, however, that for official visitors and for hard cash Hue could still put on a slick show, like a smart courtesan who may have seen better days. Minister Ngoc had organised a performance of the royal dance group in the imperial palace. An over-aged orchestra struck up, with wailing tunes on flute and cymbals in the torch-lit royal hall, for twelve very young and pretty dancing girls in classic gold tunics. They proudly showed their skills with bird-like sideways movements of head and eyes, curving their long nailed fingers overhead like a lotus, or flashing them before the eyes of us foreigners, reclining in our easy chairs after the tiring day. The classical ballet soon changed into an acrobatic spectacular, with girls flying and somersaulting in all directions like screaming eagles. The most beautiful girl, of course, had to land on top of a pyramid formed by her colleagues, from where she winked broadly at the minister. They really were just schoolgirls. When the top girl found her rightful place in the final line-up usurped by another, she simply pulled the offending sister back by her golden hair ornaments to recover her position.

On our way out of the ramshackle palace, some vendors embarrassed us with offers of engraved imperial furniture, directly from the palace, apparently on behalf of Bao Dai's impoverished mother, who still lived there and who needed the money. I could not help noting that Ngoc casually led his party through the damaged Ngo Mon gate, the emperor's own gate in the middle with the carved phoenixes, although he too must have known the story of the Chinese Ambassador.

Dinner was the traditional entertainment, taken on the 'river of perfumes', the broad expanse of which smelled of rats and stagnant water, with light perfumes of charcoal and *nuoc mam* seasoning. Sampans tied together into rafts lay waiting for us at the sandy shore, their fires already lit. Inside each sampan an old woman under a bamboo cover cooked rice over a fire to serve to her guests. A sampan held three or four, with visitors free to step from one to the next to choose their company. Musicians in the bows struck up their guitars to provide background music of a melancholy kind. Then the sampans were untied and boatmen poled each craft with their guests out into the shallow stream, where they left them to drift in the feeble current. Songs of the musicians were answering each other between the boats. All this seemed a dream. We accepted the glutinous rice from the old woman squatting near her fire, rolling our rice-paper around the minced shrimps with herbs and dipping them alternatively in *nuoc mam* and peanut sauce. The moon made all faces unfathomable. I knew a storm had broken, far away from this scene.

PART III

Year of the Tiger

20

The 1973
Oil Crisis

The October 1973 war in the Middle East and what was now being called the 'energy crisis' had me flying to the London Centre in November to discuss the impact on Vietnam. The word was out that the raft had truly hit the rapids.

On the way to Europe, transit passengers from Air Vietnam found themselves segregated in a distant hangar at Bangkok airport, rather like a quarantine hall for the dangerously afflicted, to prevent the war virus from spreading. Respectable European airlines, it seemed, were shy about doing business with Vietnam, and accepted travellers from Saigon only after delousing and re-ticketing in hygienic surroundings outside the country. Once safely admitted to a reputable airliner, and on the way to a first stop in Zürich, however, I immersed myself in the newspapers. I found that they were flush with the new war and with a new world problem: oil and energy shortages. Vietnam had been downgraded. A diminished foreign press corps in Saigon was still routinely dishing out the daily ration of atrocities to the world, but editorial opinion was set firmly in the mould that Vietnam had no business involving the world in its family differences any longer. Opponents should swallow the peace prescribed by the super powers and return to their empty rice bowls. Failing that, the North, purer than the driven snow because the media could not see what was happening over the bamboo fence, should be allowed to win outright. To all appearances, the Vietnam War had run the public ratings curve, from initial enthusiasm, to heartbreak, to boredom and denigration. It was last year's movies.

The brand new war between Israel and the Arabs, at the very start of the curve, still had all the attractions of a fresh crusade, and on top of that the tangible credentials of oil. The newspapers treated the unexpected price escalations as the consequence of the war, with all the breathlessness of a journalistic scoop. Few seemed to realise that the war was just the last tremor which set off the avalanche which had been building up, unreported, for over a decade, or that oil companies had informed governments all along that something like this could happen. Since 1970, in fact, OECD governments and the oil industry had argued *ad nauseam* about specifically what actions to take in the event of OPEC-induced shortfalls – inconclusively, however. OPEC's belligerence had effectively obscured the oil industry's own need for higher prices, to develop additional sources in Nigeria, Alaska and the North Sea. The Western media now enjoyed polarising the issue by denouncing any and all price rises as a gang rape of the Western consumer by OPEC and the oil companies.

I felt some unease about Giu, whom I had left in charge of the Saigon office. His mind had no space for world crises, and was wrapped up exclusively with his own people whose protector he felt himself to be. Malnutrition was so rampant amongst junior Shell staff that he had undertaken to convert the office attic into a cafeteria where all employees could eat a belly-full at company-subsidised prices. That this brought us into the fast food business did not cause him a one moment's hesitation. He had wasted no time on budget approval, and had pulled out all the stops to finish the work from petty cash in three weeks. Nor had he bothered with building permissions, knowing that the Prime Minister's office next door would never allow one more floor on top of the Cong Ty Shell building, from where it could theoretically be taken under small-arms fire.

The cafeteria, which therefore had to be invisible from the outside, was compressed under the old roof and lit by small skylights. It was so low that only Vietnamese could walk upright in it; foreigners were guaranteed to hit their heads against the beams. Nevertheless, everyone instantly loved it, Vietnamese and foreigners alike. It created togetherness, and Giu, at a special table, greeted all as if he owned the place. I knew, however, that inside him a deep frustration with the war was boiling over. The study to which he had contributed, showed that foreign aid alone kept the war between North and South going, and the humiliation of being retained by foreigners to fight against brothers in a senseless war could work him into a xenophobic rage. When another head hit the ceiling, he would look up almost gleefully. One could almost hear him thinking, 'We are fighting for your cause, consuming less oil, less ammunition, eating a bit less to make do with your diminishing aid and taking 20,000 ARVN casualties in the first year of your filthy "peace"'.

Meanwhile, flying against the spin of the globe, I had slept through the extended night since Bangkok. Was that a pre-landing snack in front of me? I suffered a brief disorientation, but the neat rows of trees in the valleys and the prosperous houses below were unmistakably Swiss, and we were landing in Zürich.

Once past the heavily-armed Swiss soldiers, looking on all foreigners as potential terrorists, we entered the welcoming terminal, full of well-lit displays of quartz watches and chocolates. The *Neue Zürcher Zeitung* was headlining a forthcoming meeting between Arab oil ministers in Vienna. Among the crowd of businessmen, I was not surprised to recognise a financial director of Shell. Off to Vienna he was too, with a 'final' 'top secret' industry offer of a 1 percent price increase, in addition to the 2.5 percent escalation of the Teheran agreement. It was obviously too little too late, as both of us realised, but the American companies were now adamantly against higher increases. Besides, we honestly thought that the international balance of payments could not tolerate the sudden large wealth transfer caused by the high price, and that we manned the last barrier.

The Arab ministers, meanwhile, were totally mesmerised by the war. The Syrian army had been driven off the Golan Heights and the Egyptian Third Army, surrounded and without water, could be killed by the desert heat within days. Buoyed by the billion-dollar Soviet airlift to their armies, the Arabs felt sufficiently emboldened to reject the oil industryís modest offer and decided to help their brothers in arms by wheeling out the 'oil weapon': a price increase of two whole dollars per barrel, with immediate effect. That decision struck panic into the hearts of consumers worldwide. In the following weeks, the Arab ministers, surfing a popularity wave, would increase the world price of oil threefold again and cut production by 10 percent as well. In another era, Europe would have gone to war for less.

My first sight of the London Centre, with its carpeted corridors, hardwood doors and reference-numbered occupants, was extremely reassuring. Being acknowledged at the entrance by blue-uniformed guards who knew everyone already gave a warm feeling. The British obviously knew from long experience how to cope with everything, from power-cuts caused by oil shortages to coal strikes and commuter travel delays. In the lifts, friendly secretaries smiled and executives nodded their lined faces discreetly in recognition. No, in such solid organisations panic can only start right at the top and stay there.

Vee gave a nod of welcome. From the way his thin lips moved I could tell he considered himself in a difficult position. He had ordered the head of our Japanese affiliate to approach the Trade and Industry Ministry in Tokyo to inform them of the inevitable cuts in our supplies to Japan, asking for their understanding and solidarity with the

Western consumers in this matter. But their reply had bitterly disappointed him. The Japanese would pay any price and adopt any unilateral policy that would ensure them full supplies, regardless of what the rest of the world was doing. The mornings' headlines told him that European governments and public opinion might not even allow us to reflect the crazy crude-oil price rises in our own market prices, and he recognised this as a recipe for quick bankruptcy. No-one yet seemed prepared to let higher prices work for improvements in productivity. Everyone bayed for the same volume of oil at the same old prices. In this turmoil, Vee was clearly a distracted man. His customary courtesy was still in place, but his appetite for smalltalk was now depleted. He dealt briefly with my concerns and told me to make an appointment with the Chairman.

People had already whispered to me that my days in Vietnam were numbered when word got around that the Group chairman had asked to see me. I went up and waited for a minute in the outer office, where a female assistant was fielding Gerry Wagner's telephone calls and engagements before she let me in.

I was not at all surprised to find him perfectly at ease behind his regency desk, which carried not a scrap of paper. A Shell chairman needs no ostentation, and his backup organisation is always perfect. To get what he wants he does not have to write, nor even to formulate a wish. Merely projecting a mood is usually sufficient. And even if he does not know his own mind, his executives will figure it out quickly for him, trained thought-readers and body-language interpreters as they all are. When he browses through a dense summary, representing weeks of sweat for a whole department, they watch and exchange knowing looks. When he hands it back, with thanks, and sums it up in his own words, like an actor testing a scenario with selected phrases, the assembled underlings take their cue from the emphasis and the omissions, to deduce what he has accepted, what rejected. And he is not self-conscious about the process at all, because in the 25 years before he became chairman he has been treating his line managers in exactly the same way.

By not mentioning Vietnam at all in our conversation, he was making it perfectly clear that I should be glad to leave the mess behind and move on. More important issues preyed on his mind, like the oil crisis, and without further ado he began to address me as a trial audience for the company's new policy line.

The oil committee of the OECD governments had utterly failed at its October meeting to agree any common action between its member governments for 'apportioning' the oil shortfalls arising from OPEC actions. In spite of our previous warnings, OECD governments were merely sitting on their hands, only too happy to drop the management of the crisis into our laps. The media had already decided on the oil companies as the villains of the piece. He now chose his lines carefully. With mildly disapproving gestures – professional actors needed mirrors to perfect these – he contrasted the impotence of the consumer governments with our own capability and readiness to act like good citizens. I was playing the role of test audience for all I was worth, humming and nodding and sometimes offering different formulations. His line was basically the one we had worked on in Singapore a few weeks before. The international companies had to allocate the scarce supplies equitably to the consumer nations, like the governments themselves would have done if they had been capable of international agreement. I now saw that he was talking about our survival.

We had to dress up our policy as assistance to the feeble International Energy Agency and the EEC, advising them what needed to be done and then doing it for them with their consent. In the full glare of publicity on international oil rationing, we could not take narrow self-interest as a guideline, but had to use some other criterion, such as a percentage cut on last year's consumption, treating each country rigorously alike, as civil servant's dream. It went against the grain to sideline the profit motive, but in times of war shortages and howling public protests we had to put public interest and our own survival first. As he spoke, I saw that Wagner had cast himself in the role of super-statesman, bestowing oil to nations across the globe with theatrical impartiality. Others would take care of the bottom line, he continued, but he would be the supreme arbiter of the rules of the game. At working level, it meant obeying the OPEC oil supply cuts and the embargoes to the letter, whilst making them least harmful in practice, through the replacement, where necessary, of Arab-embargoed oil with non-embargoed oil from elsewhere. But the overall supply cuts were real, and would have to be applied to all nations. Only the five or so largest companies, like ourselves, could shift the necessary oil streams between countries and refineries on a world scale. And you could safely bet that not only the governments of industrial nations, but also the Arab ministers in their heart of hearts, would be grateful to those international companies, indeed count on them to implement the OPEC restrictions judiciously and thus avoid further chaos.

The remainder of our conversation was chit-chat. He lamented Prime Minister Ted Heath's rotten luck at having to face a coal miner's strike with such low oil reserves. OPEC's Sheikh Zaki Yamani had assured Heath that the UK was a 'preferred country' whose supplies need not be cut, but had failed to explain how that could be done in practice. Yamani's ploy was to take OPEC's hard line in public and to bring European heads of state privately the good tidings of their country's 'preferred' position, hoping that we could somehow reconcile OPEC's harsh action with his empty private reassurances. With our diminished supplies, however, we had no choice but to apply the 5 percent cut to UK supplies as elsewhere, thus upsetting the Prime Minister. Faced with the same cuts, the French Government lost all coherence. While President Pompidou lay dying, his ministers played to different galleries. Foreign Minister Michel Jobert tried to make French government oil deals with the Middle East while torpedoing an energy agreement between industrial nations in Washington. His colleagues threatened us with nationalisation and subjected our executives to judicial harassment for not giving France its full oil quota, as promised by Yamani. Only Germany dared to allow a free-market response and the hefty price rises that went with it. Small companies would make a fortune in Germany, by switching supplies from France, while we and others would solidly stick to our policy of an honest 5 percent cut across the board.

An EEC Council of Ministers allowed itself to be lobbied by a pair of Arab oil ministers, on behalf of OPEC, to drop support for Israel in return for plentiful supplies at reduced prices, but during their deliberations OPEC doubled the price again. Enough smalltalk. Before dispatching me, Wagner told me almost incidentally that I would rejoin the Centre again. I knew better than to ask for details, and left.

21

Nha Be Installation
on Fire

A Phoenix

The shrill whistle of the telephone woke me up with a shock. I sat up in the dark, finding myself in an anonymous Tokyo hotel room where I had gone to sleep after the Pacific crossing with JAL, on my westward journey back to Saigon via New York.

The bleeping of the telephone was incessant. After I had groggily groped for the receiver, I heard a crisp Japanese Shell manager on the line. Telexes and calls from all over the place, from London and Saigon, had been trying to reach me. 'Your Nha Be installation is on fire, sir. It has been attacked by the communists. Please, what are your intentions? What are we to do? What shall we tell them?'

A sudden a chill took hold of me. I felt clear and murderous. I rushed to Shell Tokyo's office. The hushed staff treated me like a bereaved parent. Someone quietly handed me the telexes, and for visual impact a Japanese paper and the *International Herald Tribune*, both with front-page photographs of the colossal smoke column rising from my oil-tanks. I looked at them speechless. My Japanese colleagues were far too polite to embarrass me with questions, but they found me a place on the next plane out.

The reality of what I was to find on the ground became clear even before we landed. Still a quarter of an hour out of Saigon, the plane ran into a layer of black smoke. I knew the source even before the pilot announced it. He excitedly followed it down and even made a low-altitude detour over Nha Be to give his shocked passengers a bird's-eye view of our burning installation, before landing at Tan Son Nhut.

At the airport, my colleagues greeted me with gaunt faces, as after a death in the family. From their sombre reports I could well imagine the scene of the day before how they had raced to the scene through the night, like moths to a candle. How Giu's face must have looked in the back of his car, ash-white in the flickering light, with dark pools for eyes. I could easily see, however, that his elemental hatred of the enemy would carry him intact through any defeat. The new marketing manager, Precious's successor, Peter Leach, was a different character, new to Vietnam. Above all, he had felt moral pangs at the wanton destruction he was going to see, loathing the Vietnamese for wasting the fuel the rest of the world was thirsting for and probably cursing me for my absence. Approaching the fire, he had slid in an oil pool, face first, and when he got up no-one had been able to recognise him. Above him, the untouched LPG reservoirs were profiled against the orange inferno. If they exploded, he realised they would all die in a flash. However, they were water-cooled by a sturdy fire team which looked as if they would hold out indefinitely. He made his anonymous way back through an outer ring of frightened soldiers shooting at shadows. His own driver refused him entrance to his car unless he undressed first and piled his clothes in the boot.

I could see that the fire had fused all these different characters and their private motivations together. Wearing helmets and asbestos suits in the searing heat, they had sloshed through the burning mud and bumped into each other. Black oil had stuck to everybody, instantly wiping out any distinctions between them. There was no way they could have guided operations, as everyone was too busy fighting the fire in accordance with the long-established emergency drill. Sprinklers cooled large tanks which the attackers had not set alight. Stinking foam blanketed secondary fires, oil levels in the burning tanks were being lowered by pumping contents into river barges.

While burning steel tanks sagged like failed souffles all over the place, and red-hot pipelines twisted sky high, the fire brigades started pumps and connected hoses to drench the surroundings on their own initiative with moderate success. But by just being there together, however ineffectively, in the face of disaster, I could feel that the Vietnamese, British and American executives had become welded into an instinctive association, having faced a common ordeal. And the complete Vietnamese workforce, who in that howling catastrophe carried out their duties with such frightening intensity that it seemed they were determined to save the installation even at the cost of their lives, were part also of that association. Although nominally in charge again now, I could never be a founding member of that group. Later, when surveying the mangled remains of our installation, I could see encouraging signs everywhere that the fire had opened up hidden reserves of courage and inventiveness.

For myself, I was sorting out in my mind the hospital visits, the endless explanations to London, the claims and counter-claims, the makeshift arrangements, and the TV interviews with nothing to say. We had suffered a major defeat, but it was plain that the action was not over.

Giu, gutted as he was by what had happened, showed a lot of respect for his enemies. From what we were able to piece together through captured prisoners and North Vietnamese messages, the attack on Nha Be was as much an attempt to sustain the morale and fighting spirit of a key military unit as it was to inflict damage on the South Vietnamese and their economy. Diseases and mind-numbing waiting had almost got the better of even these tough North Vietnamese sappers. Consumed by inaction, their torn shirts hung loose over their ribcages, their legs had become covered with ulcers, their faces had yellowed. Young soldiers had shrivelled to the size of the old, who themselves resembled the dead.

After a year of peace, their political officers had realised that political subversion no longer worked in the South. City youngsters, even idle ones, could not be recruited into their subhuman guerrilla existence. The South's abundant economic vitality, which included the black market, threatened to convert even the Vietcong, on whom the North Vietnamese depended. By contrast, the Northern economy lay in ruins. The twenty-first plenum in Hanoi admitted for the first time that worker apathy, mismanagement and corruption had made their way into the party hierarchy. But all that did not really matter, as long as the North Vietnamese Army was held on its feet by its allies, and as long as the Northern population was fed by Russian and Chinese civilian aid to the tune of $1.3 billion per year, which incidentally was twice the US aid to the South.

Obviously Hanoi could not expect the Chinese and Russian aid to continue at these levels, and the only solution remained the quick military conquest of the South. To this effect, military hardware was already moving southwards faster than ever, but it would be months before a new regular offensive could be started. In the interval, the sappers had to give the cause a much-needed lift. A good oil fire is always a morale booster. So a Nha Be firestorm should surely be a great box-office success for the Communists. To the sappers, it was like a lifebelt thrown to drowning men.

We were able to piece together the execution of the operation from a trail of witnesses, materials left behind, inspection of drums, warehouse roof plates, unexploded timing devices etc. The sappers had crossed the river and assembled in the garage of a friendly transport contractor. There they must have practised placing themselves in foetal positions inside luboil drums with breathing holes and lids that could be opened from the inside. Other drums were to carry plastic explosive charges and pencil delay fuses. One late afternoon, the drums were loaded on a truck, passed routinely through the installation controls and off-loaded inside the luboil warehouse, adjacent to the tank farm.

After the installation shut down for the day, they popped cover and did physical exercises in the locked warehouse to recover from the heat, cramp and claustrophobia. When they could be certain that only the small night-shift remained outside, they removed a roof-sheet with pliers and climbed through the hole onto the roof itself and jumped down onto the bund wall around the oil tanks, built to contain the burning oil in case of fire.

Their training left nothing to chance. Each knew his own way through the drainage holes or over the intersecting walls to his assigned objectives, working independently, fixing the charges against the flanks of the numbered tanks, with the fuses set at 15 minutes. The charges would punch holes for the oil to flow out, but as even high octane gasoline might not catch fire spontaneously, they were prepared to light the escaping fuel with flares. The bund wall would contain the fire lake long enough for them to make their escape to the river.

When it was done, they ran to the extreme corner of the installation and huddled together. It must have been a climactic deliverance when the muffled bangs came right on time and at once a sheet of flame shot sky-high. Their ragged forms became visible to our soldiers, as in daylight, but the sappers no longer cared. Victory was theirs. Wild shooting erupted all over the place while they cut through the fence and ran back through the elephant grass, tears of happiness streaming over their malarial faces, awed by the fire they had lit. This time our defence was in total disarray. At last a big explosion sent up a fireball like an atomic mushroom, sending tremors through the wet earth and lighting up far-off Saigon. Apart from one captured later, we never heard from the sappers as a unit again.

We soon found that the destruction of two-thirds of the installation and the threat to all our jobs and careers concentrated the minds wonderfully. In the weeks – and it was weeks – that Nha Be burned, all orders were fulfilled punctually through improvisation by workers and staff, casting off routine and deciding at their own level what to do, then going ahead and doing it even better. This would not have been possible without borrowing and help from our competitors, but any assistance came nevertheless at commercial rates. Before the metal had time to cool, the company engineers, in conjunction with the supply schedulers, had worked out a plan for the switching of tanks and pipelines which made do with a much smaller, but more flexible, installation. I took this as an indictment of myself and past managements, who had often approved expansionary budgets, rather than take the trouble to review the operation as a whole, as we were forced to do now. Past managements had normally gone along with engineers, who always seemed to be obsessed with upgrading components long after the whole complex had obviously become uneconomic.

The new plan indicated that we had been investing in a far too large and cumbersome installation, operated with considerable complacency about its many inefficiences. The most exhilarating experience was the sudden release of staff creativity from the shackles of habit. Wartime destruction is known to awaken extraordinary powers, which made bombed-out Rotterdam the biggest and most efficient harbour in the world and turned Germany into Europe's strongest economy soon after the war. Peacetime innovation unfortunately fades by comparison. But even in peace, a manager or entrepreneur seems only really to blossom after he has faced down some catastrophe, like the bankruptcy of his own business, which is why large and safe companies have so many underdeveloped staff. I myself felt like I had been asleep at the controls of an immensely powerful but under-utilised machine.

Suddenly I found the organisation could produce faster tanker turnaround times and superior integrated supply and storage systems, which halved our stocks and covered peak demand with renting competitors' storage. All of this should and could have been done long ago. Contracts which normally required a year of vetting were signed within a week. The most fantastic proposals floated around, like abandoning Nha Be altogether for a coastal depot, to save tankers the dangerous run upriver, and the building of a safe refinery on an island at sea. The brake on such grandiose ideas was not just Vietnam's less than 'triple A' investment rating, but severe material constraints.

The international oil crisis had also led, through a psychological chain-reaction of panic and hoarding, to a world scarcity of steel. Steel plates for reconstruction of our tanks could not be found at any price. This meant that our solution had to be technical compromise and more intensive use of existing hardware, just as, in their time, the North Vietnamese had replaced their bombed-out coastal depots with intelligent small-scale alternatives. London's laconic reaction to the fire, of 'business as usual', really meant that keeping the company going without one dollar of new capital, whilst repatriating profits to the London-based parent companies, would be considered normal performance. They had kept their cool, the rest was up to us. If we were to decide to throw in the towel, that would be just fine with the Centre, as the oil could be profitably sold elsewhere in the oil-thirsty world.

One young American engineer proposed finessing the steel shortage by rebuilding the lost reservoirs in cheap and easy-to-repair ferro-concrete which, he said, could float without foundations, like molasses, on the swampy ground of Nha Be. As this had not yet been done anywhere in the world, he took us to a Chinese shipyard on the Saigon river, where shrimp boats were being constructed out of that material. Although our engineers remained unconvinced, I was very impressed, while looking around the yard, by a skeleton of a rakish ocean yacht, hanging from the ceiling of a shed like a shark's ribcage, ready for cementation. A similar ferro-concrete yacht had just won the Sydney-Hobart race, and I privately ordered it to be ready for sailing away from Vietnam when the time came.

Before long, in those inventive days, someone remembered the sabotaged steel oil tanks of the abandoned US Navy base at Cam Ranh Bay, now rusting in the sand, apparently unwanted. On close inspection, half of the plates were found theoretically capable of being cut and flattened on site, and of being transported by barge to Nha Be for re-assembly. Western engineers, however, refused to build oil installations from re-cycled steel plate. So we contacted the Chinese from Cholon and their cousins from Taiwan, past masters in the art of metal recovery and conversion, who were very keen and competitive. General Murray, of the US Defence Attache Office, obliged by setting a realistic price for the material, which had already been written off in his books and by accepting payment in piastres.

Those amazing Chinese welders, recruited at nominal cost, finished the Cam Ranh job within a month, working around the clock like ants. At Nha Be, meanwhile, the burnt metal was cut away, new foundations were prepared and reconstruction started at the same speed. Thus in a little over ten weeks we had a new, more compact, faster and totally adequate installation. Meanwhile, our Vietnamese insurance covered the piastre construction costs. And as the burnt oil had already been pre-paid by the US Government, before touching the shores of Vietnam, and its replacement was covered by special insurance, Cong Ty Shell, without a hitch in its operations, survived without any financial damage whatsoever. The venerable installation, built over 70 years and to all appearances destroyed in a conflagration lasting a few weeks, was never out of action. Its workers, withdrawing from all other activities, had just aged a little faster.

22

Singapore Oil Embargo

Cong-Ty Shell was like an ant hill after a good kick. London experts flocked to our assistance, and seemed to enjoy the radical improvisations they so rarely saw in the more conventional companies.

Whatever good tidings might reach the Centre, however, our finance manager, Hans Haerry, kept his Swiss boots firmly on the ground. He knew in his bones that good feelings last only as long as shareholders get their dividends, and thought it high time to remind me of some realities. He had heard that my next appointment would be decided pretty soon. Indeed, ever since the Chairman's talk with me, informed rumour had been flying. This then was the appropriate moment, he hinted, while my next job was still under consideration, to strike, to influence the decision, by making 'them' believe that I was God himself, or somebody with a hold over Him. I must have looked blank. That meant increasing our dividends substantially, he spelled out. But he knew as well as I that last year's dividends had already reached an all-time high. We had transferred only half the amount at the beginning of the year, while the other half had to wait till July, before we could raise the cash. And this year, our cashflow, with all extra installation expenses, certainly would not allow higher levels.

He shook his head with pity at my objections. You are not ambitious then, he teased, you don't want to make a name for yourself? For a moment he enjoyed my discomfort, polishing his thick lenses, before he came out with an offer to help, because, as he said slyly, an unambitious boss could not promote his deserving friends either.

His proposition came down to the following: declare a 50 percent higher dollar dividend immediately, and transfer it all within a month, to really grab the headlines. This seemed impossible, what with reconstruction costs, increased taxes, inflation etc. But he was deadly serious. Had I not learnt from the Nha Be disaster how to turn defeat into victory? Forget the self-interest, if that made it any easier on my conscience, he counselled. The riskier a business, the more money it must make to justify itself in the shareholders' eyes, and heaven knew we, in Vietnam, lived in a war-zone. All our private doubts about our future were arguments in favour of a bolder financial course. We had a duty to milk the present while it lasted, by borrowing from the local banks and using our inventiveness to reward shareholders for exceptional risks taken. We already had too much of our own capital invested in Vietnam. Who would profit from our conservative financial management but the Communists after taking over?

Only once before had I deliberately planned to borrow to the hilt and transfer assets back to shareholders, to frustrate the imminent nationalisation by the unscrupulous Marxist government of Congo Brazzaville which had no intent of compensation. We had changed the normal limited company, which managed operations in five francophone equatorial African countries, into a *groupement d'interêt économique* (the same legal construction as used by the European Airbus consortium). This gave us flexibility in each contributing country to treat its business entirely differently. By over-extension of local credit, I then turned the one nationalisation candidate into a hollow semblance of its former substantial self, repatriating its capital and leaving little worth nationalising. But this was Vietnam, where we might face defeat, but where government was on our side. He had to argue like a teacher to a slow pupil.

A Shell operating company anywhere can borrow enormous sums of money on its name alone, without guarantees from the international parent companies. Next year's repayments would be my successor's worry, if South Vietnam still existed. By then, I would hold an important position in the Centre on the strength of a miraculous performance and would have promoted my colleagues back to civilisation too.

The main feature of the proposition was to increase the profits of the Vietnam company by increasing our charges to our non-Vietnam affiliates, with a bit of creative accounting thrown in for good measure. We could help Cong-Ty Shell to a higher share of the proceeds of the military contracts quite legally by charging a few millions more for our services, which now went, under the terms of secondary contracts, to one of our administrative outside companies. Haerry was amongst the handful of experts with overview and authority over the chain of affiliates through which the working responsibilities were divided and the profits from the military contracts were sluiced back to the Centre. Cong-Ty Shell's fees for handling the product in

Vietnam had been kept low, because it had made no sense in the past to draw good money into the piastre pool and pay hefty income taxes on such amounts. Bringing in more dollars and transferring a high proportion of those back as dividends was perfectly feasible. There was no particular logic in any specific division of proceeds, except that an artificial rearrangement solely to suit our needs of the moment might be unethical.

The mechanics were easy. When the tax holiday of a Singapore affiliate which acted as an intermediary for us came to an end, we would have to make a change in any case. Haerry and I were both directors of that company. We had transferred the work done in Singapore to another affiliate in Hong Kong, which paid only 15 percent tax. We were directors of that company too. It would be reasonable to decrease the Hong Kong fee for services provided to us and increase our own fees for services to other affiliates by a large amount, and that would draw no objections from anybody. The destruction of Nha Be was reason enough for needing more revenues in Vietnam. The Vietnamese Ministry of Finance would be grateful to its honest tax-payer. The price of the product to Uncle Sam would remain unchanged, and the Centre would not worry about details of how the money reached it, as long as the amounts were verifiably and correctly represented in the accounts, and the money reached it in a legal way. It could be argued in any direction.

I let the matter rest. Then, ironically, the whole issue was overtaken by a totally new and unexpected interpretation of the text of the Arab oil embargo. The embargo expressly forbade deliveries of products made from Arab oil, as used in Singapore refineries, to the US and its armed forces. Vietnam had not been mentioned in the text at all. In a fit of excessive zeal, however, to please Saudi Arabia, where they had tremendous investments, or to make more product available for other markets, or even because Vietnam was simply a public-relations night-mare, Esso Singapore had deliberately given the embargo such a wide interpretation that they claimed no longer to be at liberty to supply products paid for by the US government and made from Arab crude to Vietnam. In the same vein, shortly before and during the Middle Eastern war, Esso and the other American companies united in Saudi Aramco had petitioned the President of the United States to stop military supplies to Israel. If that request had been taken seriously, Israel would have been written off.

For Vietnam, however, there was no other crude source on the horizon, and this tortuous interpretation, swiftly endorsed by the Singapore government and automatically applicable to us, suddenly cut the lifeline of oil to Vietnam, and threatened to render the ARVN powerless and South Vietnam defenceless. This came on top of the armed forces already having to reduce operations because the American fuel supply budget had not been increased in line with price rises.

Giu and I rushed for explanations to Esso's Saigon office. With its wall-to-wall carpeting, Western secretaries, bricked-up windows and electric lighting throughout the day, it belonged to a claustrophobic foreign future, whereas our office, with its gilded baroque and open windows, clearly belonged to the easy-going South Vietnamese past. But differences went deeper: the Vietnamese assistant of the president who received us in no way resembled our own abrasive Giu. He was young, college-educated and forward-looking, with faultless English and infinitely more comfortable to talk to, but with none of the nationalist passion of Giu. In the absence of his president, who was in the United States on leave, he regretfully accepted that Esso Singapore had to abide by the implicit ban on deliveries to the Vietnamese army. The fact that after the exhaustion of stocks the ARVN would be immobilised and the North could pick off its units one by one or that the immobilisation of the airforce would make Northern superiority overwhelming did not seem to matter. None of this seemed to touch him personally. By now, however, we knew our competitors well enough to realise that neither they, nor Caltex, would ever question a decision taken by their principals. It meant that only we could get the Singapore government to reverse their decision.

We had limited time left. I phoned my Singapore colleague, but he was away at a meeting in London, so I took a flight to Singapore. After hearing from the product supply manager that Shell had merely followed the lead of the American companies, I drove to government office, where an official explained to me in confidence the entire course of events. He confirmed that the local American oil company presidents, eager to apply the strictest possible interpretation of the embargo, had taken the initiative to cut deliveries to their own navy and the Vietnamese armed forces. To do this legally, they needed the official extension of the embargo to the Vietnamese armed forces. Otherwise they would have been vulnerable to customer claims for non-performance of contract. Therefore, they had pressed the Singapore government for a confirmatory decree. Please make it official, they had begged, so that we can claim *force majeure* with our customers. Oh, and here is your draft decree, already drawn up by our lawyers; you only have to sign and publish it. The Singapore government had merely obliged.

Unfortunately, in the absence of the Shell Singapore president, my own representations carried no authority. The small island state could hardly go against the official advice of the local leaders of the industry on which the whole existence of the state depended. Once the government had signed and published the ban, only a strong counter-force could make them change their minds; for instance, explicit approval for deliveries by an important OPEC member, acting in concert with the US government.

Back in Saigon that night, after the personnel had gone home, I went to the telex room, where the night-shift operator sat in front of her machines. She happened to be the ex-girlfriend of Trung, who had resigned with such panache after the first sapper attack on Nha Be. She had proved totally trustworthy and devoted to the job since her transfer. An idea was forming in my mind while we watched London's messages cascading in. We had to produce an irrefutable counter-argument for the Singaporeans, and after a while I began tentatively dictating an appeal to the Saudi Minister of Petroleum, Sheikh Yamani, with the pompous beginning, 'In the name of our common commitment to democracy in Vietnam...' But this was way overstated; the Saudis were anti-Communists but no admirers of democracy. I therefore deleted the commitment bit and just said, 'In the name of the survival of our staunch South Vietnamese allies'.

No lesser words could do justice to our cause. My methods might be wrong; I had no earthly mandate, the end might not justify the means, and I was a worm, but I let the noble preamble go on line. 'I have to draw Your Excellency's attention to the decision by the Government of Singapore to deny oil supplies to the South Vietnamese armed forces in application of an interpretation of the OPEC oil embargo, which I personally believe to be based on an outrageous misunderstanding of its terms. If Your Excellency agrees with me that the text of the embargo only refers to American forces and not at all to the South Vietnamese forces currently fighting for survival in the free world, and would inform the Singapore Government accordingly, desperate consequences can still be avoided.' The message ended with my name and that of the company. I watched it go, and tried to visualise Yamani's face reading the text.

Years ago, Yamani and I had made reluctant conversation while we were both waiting in an ante-room at the palace in Doha for a private word with Sheikh Ahmed of Qatar. He was called in first as a Saudi minister, a successor to the famous Tariki, but his standing amongst sheikhs was still that of a humble palace servant. Now he was an international celebrity. Whether he remembered or not, he would read my message as a true outburst from the ranks. As for my principals in London and the Hague, who only spoke to him after weighing their words on a gold scale, I could only be sacked once.

Feeding the copies into the shredder, the telex girl and I were joking about our message, and about the odd telexing styles of our colleagues, when suddenly the Riyadh line came alive with an answer: 'In the name of Allah, the Merciful. Grateful if you could address your message to HRH King Faisal. Thanks.' It was unsigned. Perhaps it was only a telex clerk's suggestion, but we changed the 'Excellencies' of the text into 'Royal Highnesses' and let it go again. In for a penny, in for a pound.

We never received a direct reply, but a decisive reaction to the Singapore Government, in the form of official Saudi approval for deliveries of its oil to Vietnam, was duly made, and when several months later the press reported that King Faisal had also made an offer to the American government to pay for all the expenses of the Vietnam War, I was again reminded of the evening in the telex room with Trung's ex-girlfriend. But nothing ever came of the offer. By then, the Nixon presidency had been too weakened by the Watergate scandal to take things further, and to be able to put the financing of the war on a firm footing.

A few loose ends needed to be tied up by the American embassy in Saigon. Graham Martin was, as usual, in Washington lobbying a reluctant congress. His stand-in, the dedicated and indefatigable Josiah Bennett, showed me an intercept of a communication from Communist headquarters in South Vietnam (COSVN) to Hanoi on the Nha Be sapper attack. It described the action modestly as a media event, and not in any way intended to convey that the peace-loving forces no longer respected the Paris peace agreement. But Nha Be was already far behind us.

The immediate task was to delete all mention of American involvement in the oil supply contract with the Vietnamese Government, to help the Singapore government through the embarrassment of reversing its decision. The embassy would clear it with the Vietnamese later. First they put the specific recommendation to the Secretary of State, Henry Kissinger, who happened to be in Tokyo at the time. Kissinger made the telephone call to Riyadh and the South Vietnamese armed forces were disembargoed within a day. The Singapore government were only too happy to rescind their edict. But still, to my amazement, the American companies, sulking from loss of face, or for other reasons, refused to supply their share of the new contract, and thus made Cong-Ty Shell a monopoly supplier by default, at very profitable prices, for a few months, until they could bring themselves to swallow their pride and claim back their legitimate share. Cong-Ty Shell's dividends doubled on this windfall alone, without any resort to creative accounting.

23

The Chinese
Navy in Action

In this ferocious year of the tiger, Great Tiger China found occasion to teach minor tiger Vietnam a lesson in long-term thinking which touched us incidentally.

The Shell supertanker *Copionella* was ploughing the South China sea on a routine crude-oil shuttle between Japan and the Gulf. On the bridge, the first mate kept scanning the sky and water ahead through binoculars. As a professional, he was keen on direct observation of sea conditions in addition to just reading his instruments, but he was somewhat puzzled at an apparent discrepancy between the two. The waves, which should have been blue and docile under the following north-east monsoon, had lost their sparkle and the sky around the low sun had turned sickly yellow: signs of a typhoon. Yet typhoons were rare at this time of the year, and did not show up in any wind changes, or on the barometer or the radar.

The satellite positioning screen gave *Copionella's* position as ten miles east of the Paracelles, a mid-ocean group of arid islands and coral ridges occupied by the Republic of South Vietnam as a legal pawn in the ongoing dispute about oil exploration and fishing rights between nations hundreds of, or even a thousand, miles away. On another screen, a Filipino helmsman was monitoring the autopilot course around the territorial waters and uncharted reefs. The state-of-the-art navigation black box fed deviations off the predetermined course directly to the auto-pilot, which governed the hydraulics of the mighty rudder, and incidentally also moved a token steering wheel on the bridge, smaller than that of a Volkswagen: a reminder of the past. The larger the tonnage, the more atrophied the manual controls.

Human brains and hands were already largely superfluous, and practically extinct on board. The mate was one of three expatriate officers, keeping an eye on the computer, the living quarters and the power plant, and on a few wretched Malaysian deckhands who spoke no English and just cleaned the ship and hauled ropes when in harbour.

The islands showed up on radar exactly where they should, but for some reason remained invisible to the eye. Through his binoculars, he saw only a thin veil of smoke discolouring the evening sky, playing tricks with the colours of the sunset. On deck below, the captain, in T-shirt and shorts, was riding his bicycle forwards and backwards the regulation 100 times. Obesity, lack of exercise and alcoholism are the curses of a modern seaman's life, severely guarded against by company regulations.

Behind the mate, a radio news broadcast was jabbering over the background music about a naval clash between Vietnamese and Chinese somewhere, but he was distracted by an unusually large floating object which had appeared straight ahead. At three miles' distance, it seemed to float soggily in the darkening waves, with lots of small branches sticking out from it, like a giant log. His instinct told him to avoid it. At fifteen knots he had to act quickly. Twenty degrees starboard, he punched into the autopilot keyboard. Behind him, the newscaster spoke of a Chinese victory in the Paracelles. The mate was fully concentrating on the log again, and suddenly the branches were waving human arms. 'Reverse engines!' he cried. 'Santa Maria!' the Catholic helmsman cried, kicking out the autopilot and turning the wheel by hand, full tilt. They spent helpless minutes watching the slowly reacting tanker bearing down almost in a straight line on the shipwrecked sailors, barely missing their overturned lifeboat. They shuddered as the bow, throwing a wave over the wreck, washed several men away. They saw a body come up in the wake of the backward-clawing propellers. But at last, its speed killed, the ship lay inert, wallowing in the swell with the rising shriek of wind over its decks.

The sun went below the horizon, and it would soon be dark. In spite of the wind, the captain agreed to lower a boat. The mate, having plotted the position of other survivor rafts, took torches and a hand-compass and motored off with six Malays. It was his first direct contact with the sea for many years. In those primitive conditions, having to negotiate each wave, the Malays' innate seamanship was far superior to his own, and he found it a new experience to defer to their boat handling, while he navigated and gave the orders.

Communication by gesture and key words sustained their desperate efforts throughout the night. After several sorties, struggling with rope ladders to bring in the wounded in the searchlights, they had recovered some 30 survivors. Not wanting to leave the spot, they radioed Singapore that they were waiting for daylight to see if there were any more. One of the survivors, a lieutenant huddled in a blanket, told them his version of what had happened. At midday, while he lay at anchor, Chinese warships had suddenly arrived, and troops from them had gone ashore, overwhelmed the Vietnamese garrison and torched their huts, killing as many as they could. In the exchange of fire, the lieutenant's boat had been sunk a few miles offshore. He realised that the Chinese would not look for survivors, and had assumed they would die until he saw our tanker.

He was still trying to make some sense of his sacrifice, however, staring hard at the Shell emblem on the big red funnel. Something clicked. Your company is behind it, he concluded with a shy smile of complicity. While admitting that he owed his life to the company, he claimed to know for certain that a prolific oil field had already been secretly discovered in these waters by us, and that had led inevitably to the Chinese attack. In truth, no-one in the world knew if oil would ever be found in these deep waters, but he refused to believe that so many lives had been lost just for a long-term speculation. There had to be a fat prize hidden somewhere. And he was at least partially right, of course. The game is played by international rules which favour the occupant of such worthless rocks with the lion's share of any sub-seabed riches to be discovered in a wide arc around them. It is an invitation to violence in certain parts of the world. And China, already battling the Russians over arid territory on the remote Mongolian border, thought nothing of giving Vietnam, Communist or anti-Communist, a practical warning that any oil found around the islands at some future date, would be the exclusive property of the region's principal power.

Copionella received orders to disembark survivors at Vungtau beach, where a public-relations exercise was planned of the kind at which the Vietnamese excelled. School children were bussed from the neighbourhood, and told to form little groups with flags and flowers for a 'spontaneous' welcome. As the anchor chain rattled out, flares shot up and a survivor's contingent was noisily escorted ashore.

All this formed as much part of the battle for 'hearts and minds' as guns and bullets. Admiral Chonh's Navy had such an inglorious record that it had to celebrate its defeats like victories, turning survivors into heroes and the dead into martyrs. In cold military reality, Chonh knew, there was no chance whatever of retaking the islands, which were out of aircraft range, whilst his Navy was too obsolete to stand up to the Chinese. It had been a grave mistake to tempt the Chinese with the occupation of the islands in the first place.

Of the survivors, those who could walk had assembled near the platform in new uniforms. The band struck up and the Admiral

171

importantly pinned medals on blue shirts. Afterwards, the fit were carted away in trucks, their faces cramped with smiles, the wounded in ambulances. Even the captain of the *Copionella* did not escape a medal.

This was justified propaganda: the survivors themselves required a good face to be put on their defeat. But as a gesture to the nation and to the world, it struck me as a missed opportunity. If the President had ordered the occupation of the islands, he should have foreseen the Chinese reaction and the outcome from the start, and have prepared himself to make capital out of it. One possibility would have been for him to be at Vungtau himself, to present the battle as part of the national fight against the historic enemy. That would have struck a powerful common Vietnamese chord, forcing respect for his government as a defender of the national integrity, thereby driving another wedge between North Vietnam and their Chinese patrons. But General Thieu could probably no longer envision objectives other than 'total victory'.

Had he been really on the ball, he could have made, long before, a grand offer to Peking, or to Hanoi, or to both, of sharing together the sub-oceanic wealth around the islands. That would have positioned him as a wise man of peace, and Hanoi at least would have found it awkward to refuse. It would have shown a mandarins' respect for the high middle ground. A mandarin is taught to think before action about possible outcomes and necessary compromises. But President Thieu lacked the Confucian wisdom to turn defeat into opportunity. The year of the tiger started with bad omens.

24

Ben Cat

A Battle in Which
Each Side Gains

President Thieu also cheated on his own military directives like a Vietnamese woman at *mah jong*. In contravention of his directive never to cede ground to the enemy, he himself arranged, or winked at, the withdrawal of the garrison from Tong Le Chan, a minor outpost North of Saigon, in connivance with the besieging Communist forces. For public consumption, he announced that the heroic 200-man garrison had been over-run, and he even levered that lie into a justification for petty retaliations against the PRG delegates, still sequestered at Tan Son Nhut. We lived with a president who wanted to believe his own propaganda rather than re-think his strategy.

On the other hand, the muddle over military strategy in the North seemed almost as bad. Politburo and COSVN resolutions, which appeared to fall into the hands of the CIA within weeks of being issued, showed the North Vietnamese leaders to be in the throes of a fierce debate between hawks and doves. The Politburo contradicted itself within its own directives, prescribing 'revolutionary violence against the Saigon clique', but 'within the constraints of the Paris peace agreement'. This was a tall order for the field commanders entrusted with practical applications. Firstly there was no favourable climate for revolutionary violence in Saigon-controlled areas, and secondly a regular offensive within the peace agreement was hard to imagine. On the other hand, they could not let an entire field army rot in the jungle through inactivity.

Information from our dealer network amply reflected the strategic confusion on both sides. Desultory attacks on small ARVN outposts, without any pattern, and accommodations with the enemy at a working level were the order of the day. Dealers reported the passage of Vietcong troops through the delta with the obvious connivance of the ARVN.

Suddenly, however, the media erupted with reports of a big conventional battle at Ben Cat in the iron triangle, 40 kilometres north of Saigon. Although the superficial language of the reports, and the stereotypical TV footage, showed that the reporters probably were nowhere near the scene, the official and heroic reports from the ARVN claimed that they were holding their own in bitter fighting.

The battle was accepted as a reality by foreign observers, although no-one could explain what the commanders of the North Vietnamese 7th and 9th divisions in Ben Cat, who had reportedly initiated the fighting, stood to gain from it. Of course, a limited defensive action would have suited them nicely, except that it required the other side to take the initiative, and the general of the ARVN 18th division was notorious for avoiding any initiative at all. His path was not exactly strewn with roses either. How was he to make sense of President Thieu's orders? The Four Nos seemed clear, but from the President down every general evaded them to suit his own purposes.

I needed to know what was going on. If, unexpectedly, big war was to resume, we would be caught short of supplies in our diminished Nha Be storage, and would have to re-schedule our tankers. When in such doubt, Brooks Richards, the British Ambassador was usually my first source of clarification. As manager of a half-British company, and through my attendance of the Foreign Office School of Arabic studies in Shemlam, Lebanon, notorious as an apparent training-ground for spies, I was on first-name terms with half a dozen of his colleagues, and I had often been with diplomats and officials from the Foreign Office, where Arabists have always had disproportionate influence. Richards, through the previous commitment of British troops in Vietnam, was still receiving first-hand military information, which he often shared with me. When receiving British visitors, members of parliament, ministers, or others, he would frequently bring them along to my house. Vice versa, I could always count on him to see my own visitors.

The British embassy was a short walk up the boulevard from my office. Its entrance was guarded by a squad of spick and span, fully-armed ghurkas. Behind the neat facade, however, the interior disappointed a little. The carpets and furniture looked worn, and government issue, though well maintained. Easy informality seemed to reign. Brooks Richards, an ex-naval officer, had a large-scale military map of Vietnam covering one wall of his office. We found Ben Cat, and agreed that its closeness to Saigon made it a potentially dangerous location, but that the battle itself had a peculiar feel about it. Personal observation, he smiled, was still the best, and often the only, way to know and he advised me to go up there under the guidance of his military attaché, a former SAS colonel, a bluff, sentimental and much-decorated hero with excellent ARVN connections. I would simply have to convert myself for the day into a battlefield tourist.

When the good colonel collected me the following morning, in an old uniform, a bit tight around the belt, beaming at the sunrise, he surprised me by shouting, 'Soleil d'Austerlitz!' like Napoleon before Waterloo. I fervently hoped ours was to be a less grand occasion.

With the colonel at the wheel of his old Morris, we grandly set out in high spirits on the road through the rice-fields to Phu Cuong, the provincial capital. It was no more than a village, and we drove straight through it towards Ben Cat, on Route 13. A little further on, some concrete blocks on the road marked the end of our safe and protected world. They formed the ultimate and only defensive barrier against any sudden dash of North Vietnamese tanks towards Saigon. A worrying thought, especially when we found we could zig-zag around the blocks unchallenged by anybody. We could even have bypassed them on either side through the baked clay in the dry season. The countryside meanwhile had changed to soft rolling hills with fewer cultivated areas.

My guide rolled down the windows to breathe the air, and to take in nature and its early-warning signs. His reactions had noticeably sharpened, but as yet there was nothing to be alarmed about. Light clouds drifted sedately in the blue sky. Women in the fields waved, and he waved back enthusiastically. 'Bless you,' he shouted. 'God bless all women!' We passed a couple of shot-up trucks standing unattended on the tarmac. Then a small boy driving two long-horned buffaloes drawing a tree trunk between crude wooden wheels lifted a lazy hand to his tropical helmet in salute. He was the last civilian in sight, and after a few hundred metres we stopped to listen. We knew that women and children could safely work right up to the front-line because they would know the danger better than us. Their absence now was a warning.

The first sign of activity was a platoon of infantry, walking out of the bush in sweat-streaked fatigues, with helmets shoved to the back of their heads. They were grinning happily and making 'V-for-Victory' signs with their fingers. The corporal told us we could go another 300 metres, but no further. We scratched our heads. The troops had obviously been involved in exercises, but still we heard no shooting. On the side of the road we saw a sandbagged 105mm howitzer position, its guns pointing in all directions, including Saigon. Unused and used shells worth a fortune littered the ground, but where was the crew? On leave? By now, the platoon had vanished too, and no living soul could be seen. Somewhat doubtfully, we advanced on foot to the next turn, where the road made a gradual descent into a valley. We saw it climbing up again at the far end in a lazy curve to the blue forested horizon. It was an ideal, indeed Napoleonic, observation point.

The whole landscape had suddenly opened up to our view, and seemed deserted. Under those bushes in the bottom of the valley, however, and between those trees either side of the road, some 30,000 of the most experienced infantry in the world were facing each other. It was unbelievable, even if you knew that these traditional battlegrounds were honeycombed with hundreds of kilometres of tunnels and storerooms. Even in 1966, American divisions had rolled over the terrain without ever catching more than a glimpse of the enemy popping up and down, as if in a shooting gallery.

Finally, my colonel, who had been peering with binoculars through the warm vibrating air, chuckled with satisfaction. 'There they are.' He pointed at a field, about a kilometre distant, where camouflaged ARVN tanks were working slowly around the edge of a dense forest, moving backwards and forwards without firing. The changing pitch of their diesel engines now came to our ears. They were obviously manoeuvring with infantry invisible to us. The enemy remained invisible too, although we now also heard sporadic automatic fire. We sat down at leisure with our field-glasses under a solitary tree, trying to understand the activity. Soon we could pick out friendly patrols as they broke cover, judging themselves out of range.

And then, as if to give us a clue, a single South Vietnamese propeller plane appeared above us. In text-book fashion, straight from the US ground-support manual, a South Vietnamese phosphorous artillery shell arced up, to mark the North Vietnamese target a few kilometres along the plain with a display of pyrotechnics. The fighter-bomber took his cue from this, and made a stilted pirouette in the air before diving without undue haste to deliver, very gracefully, a small bomb on target. What had been impressive on TV last night suddenly seemed suspiciously unreal and ridiculous in the field. This was pure play-acting. None of the radar-controlled anti-aircraft guns, standard equipment for all North Vietnamese units, fired at the plane in answer to the attack, and this was reflected in the pilot's leisurely flight pattern. Several more phosphorous markers were laid down, and each time the pilot used identical headings and dive patterns to deliver his load lazily on target, hurting no-one. Finally, after dipping his wings to friend and enemy alike, he flew home. We shook off the ants and took a gulp from our water cans.

A smile of enlightenment had spread over the colonel's face as he entered into the spirit of the phoney war-game. 'Don't think I blame you, Thieu Tong,' he was addressing an imaginary North Vietnamese general by his proper title, 'I can imagine your dilemma in your lousy underground bunker with all your generals looking over your shoulder.

You tried to show the required revolutionary violence without harming your troops, and you did it by cutting the same old road at the same old place as you have done 100 times before. Your grateful troops know the routine by now and know how to avoid casualties, while you can break off the engagement any time you wish by a small withdrawal. I bet you positively welcome the air attacks for the realistic look they give to the whole operation.'

After another swig, the colonel began to feel even closer to the hard-pressed field commanders having to fight under ambiguous orders. 'And my compliments to you, General,' he now addressed the absent ARVN commander. 'They gave you only one second-rate division to defend Saigon, and you must be grateful that the show is managed by professionals on both sides, who impress their superiors and protect each other's honour by faking battle and killing as few as possible, while you don't even have to leave your house in Saigon to direct the battle. Your troops know the scenario by heart. Gentlemen, please both accept my congratulations for preventing wastage of lives and ammunition while politicians dither. Such a pity the play-acting cannot last, and that sooner or later you will be at each others throats again.'

25

Vung Tau Beach

With my tour of duty nearly over, more than half-way through 1974, I felt as if Saigon as a whole had fallen into a deep depression. Gone was the optimism based on American support and the belief in peace, and back came all the old political groupings, the compromises and the French cliques which had failed before. Night-life was brilliant and empty.

At a 14 July reception at the home of my neighbour, the President of the Banque d'Indo-Chine, the bank vilified by Ho Chi Minh 30 years before but still going strong, middle-aged Vietnamese ministers, clergy, officers and professional men were happy to argue in French once again. With irresistible nostalgia, they celebrated their student days at the Sorbonne in Paris, when everybody was a young revolutionary without a care in the world. Why could I not follow Trung's example and simply step out of this shallow world? But no, I had to be part of it. In my blue silk suit, crocodile shoes and a loud tie from the Air France in-flight shop, I felt right at home in the illuminated garden. Gold-and-diamond adorned French businessmen were milling around, looking like Corsican Mafiosi, which some of them were. Their wives in particular wore much more revealing dresses than admissible in Paris of the day, kissing Vietnamese authorities and *tutoi*-ing them as they never would at home.

Although I meant nothing to her, the hostess threw her arms around my neck, kissed me with a delicate expression and drew me as an exhibit to the centre, where her husband held court with Finance Minister Cuong. I was temporarily fobbed off on a pair of unfashionable Americans with red trousers, white shoes and Elvis Presley hairstyles.

They turned out to be, however, serious and courageous CIA men from the provinces, the only ones amongst us who worked at the sharp end.

Pierre Brochand, the dashing French intelligence chief, noticed me. He had a Swedish-American film star dangling on one arm. As usual, he asked if certain roads in the interior were open or closed to civilian traffic, as I, whose lorries transported oil along all those routes, should of course know. Meanwhile, the actress detached herself from him and, being short of cash (having outstayed her welcome at the British Ambassador's house), auctioned herself off to a circle of admirers for the price of a private free luxury apartment with servants for the duration of her stay. Her breath-taking directness, which was also the greater part of her acting talent, got three offers in no time. And although her eyes clearly still preferred the handsome French intelligence officer, who was averting his eyes, she took the bid of an old Australian wood exporter who had survived four months of captivity by the Vietcong before becoming their hardwood exporting agent. He would surely need all his survival instincts with her.

The honest high-court judge was on show again with his wife, bending listeners' ears with further details of the illegal five percent collected by the Economic Minister on all imports, quoting names of accomplices, sizes of kickbacks and bank account numbers from memory. The wife had that same half-adoring half-forgiving smile for her husband, who would never be allowed to carry his accusations outside these privileged circles. How long-suffering the upright of this country were, and how tiresome. Even the Lord would have preferred an honest sinner.

Nearby in the glittering assembly, the cocky French Ambassador, Jean Merillon, was converting an elderly Vietnamese to his latest political ploy. Speculative games had suddenly become fashionable again. They were all based on the French fiction that apart from communists and anti-communists, a neutral third body of opinion did exist in Vietnam. These neutral 'nationalists' were deemed not only to be acceptable to the Hanoi communists, but fully capable of negotiating with both parties a peaceful settlement to the war. In reality, no such third force existed. The North had merely conjured them up as a smoke-screen for the gullible minds of Olof Palme of Sweden and diplomats in Eastern Europe, and unfortunately Paris too. The French Ambassador in Hanoi, Philippe Richter, never believed a word of it, but Giscard d'Estaing, President of France chose to believe. And so did Merillon.

If Thieu could only be made to resign in favour of General 'Big Minh', he argued, the North Vietnamese would be glad to do business with his successor. Who knows? French oil companies might even be offered the Shell exploration concessions in Vietnam, as they had been promised those in Nigeria if the French-supported Ibo secession war had been successful. Meanwhile, the Ambassador's athletic wife, a head taller than he and showing a full leg through the split of her dress, was looking desperately bored. Her husband, trying to save South Vietnam by spirited intervention, explained that if Thieu would only cede his place to retired Generals Minh or Tran Van Don, both 1960s plotters against president Diem, a coalition government would miraculously save the whole country. Unemployed politicians savoured the Ambassador's intellectual speculations just like the soufflés of the French embassy's cook: if they held the hot air, wonderful; if not, well, just a little mistake. His wife, however, looked around with true desperation.

Graham Martin himself sometimes graced such gatherings, his tragic destiny already weighing on his stooped shoulders. Even he, towards the end, hoped against his better judgement that the Communists would be open to diplomatic deals. At present, however, he mostly listened like a hooded sphinx, and only when he spoke did his grey eyes light up, aiming just above the heads of his audience. The public message was the same as ever, promoting business belief and confidence in the country. From his personal meetings with the Hanoi leadership, he liked to remind us, as well as from CIA intercepts, he could solemnly give his word that there would be no new offensive this year (which in any case had only a few more months to run). So what was the purpose of all those newly-built Communist attack roads in the jungle then, the Australian wondered. Again, Martin issued his flat reassurance that they were for their own survival, not for attack: slanted information from the horse's mouth. A great man clutching at straws like the rest of us.

As my departure drew nearer, Kim Chi and I made one last trip to the beach. We started out on a Saturday morning on the road to Vungtau, congested by the ever-growing numbers of urban middle-class vehicles, driven recklessly each weekend by parents with numerous offspring to the beach. At Xuan Loc, we stopped for a look at the abundant fruit stalls lining the road. I watched Kim Chi haggling with a market woman over a papaya, paying half the asking price and still making her laugh. Hordes of urchins surrounded us, trying to sell black-market petrol out of one litre bottles. I had to admire those little entrepreneurs, much as I tried to cut off their supplies.

After Xuan Loc, the road ambled through shady French rubber plantations, abandoned by the owners, the trees still being tapped haphazardly by the peasants. Its natural cover made it an ideal ambush site. In fact, soldiers of the 18th Division, after a night's work, were washing their clothes in a ditch along the road and hanging them out over the guns of their tanks amongst the scarred trees. They treated the civilian weekend traffic with complete indifference, as if it belonged to another planet.

The closer we came to the sea, the more brilliant the air became. Ditches widened into tidal mangrove swamps. Vast fields, converted into drainable lakes, produced pink mountains of salt. Further on, wagon-loads of shrimps lay raked out over the road in thick layers to dry, spreading the pungent smell of *nuoc mam* sauce everywhere. We had to pick our way around the heaps in first gear. Finally a glistening bay appeared, with wavelets breaking over rocks and wooden fishing boats dancing on turquoise water over their own shadows on the sand: Vungtau.

An old man was waiting for us on the veranda of his sea-shore house, and he welcomed us with sad affection. Tea arrived. During the ceremony of pouring and drinking, he kept speculating on the past. Had her father not been murdered, and had he been made prime minister instead of the inflexible Ngo Dinh Diem, South Vietnam would have had a better start. The Cao Dai and other religious sects would have rallied to him. Unfortunately, Diem had taken the contrary option of subduing the religious sects in battle, with the costly result that half of the sects' survivors had joined the Vietcong; so many missed chances. The frail old man himself had commanded the Cao Dai, army and he knew the emptiness of victories first hand. On the wall hung a lacquer painting of Vietnam in the form of a dragon. He unhooked it, reminiscing how different Vietnam could have been, and gave it to Kim Chi, for her protection in the year of the tiger. We almost had to kiss his hands before we could leave.

Over the beach we waded together, each lost in our own worlds. The South China Sea gives spiritual rather than physical relief, the old sea being almost too civilised and warm for bodily refreshment. Its ornamental waves roll in without force, and its water feels like old silk over the powdered sand and over the feet. From an invisible pagoda came the monotonous sounds of a gong.

I looked at her determined face. It showed total control, the eyes clear, the hair in flat curls on her cheeks, like a porcelain doll's. We spoke briefly and realistically. She was aware that Fate had built her up into a legend in which she had finally even begun to believe herself. It had all started in Hanoi, when her father used her to liven up his social functions. It ended a week ago at a party of the general of the third region with his staff and their ladies. The general had asked her to open the dance, a ridiculous *paso doble*, with him. The spotlight sought them out. And suddenly it struck her that she had reached the end of that road. She longed to reject the dominance of others over her life. 'My eyes have been opened to another way of life,' she said. 'But I belong to Vietnam. I will be content to sit in the shade on the farm, by the stream, reading books and your letters and listening to the pigs squeal.'

26

Farewell Vietnam

The longer I stayed, the less I could stomach Vietnam's pernicious lack of civilian prospects, and the more I began to welcome my recall to Europe, much as my predecessor Mike Corrie had done before. Can you blame the rats for leaving a ship that wants to sink? Some of my best efforts for the country had ended in disaster.

The State Energy Council had invited suggestions for savings on the country's fuel bill. Merely watching its members making their way to their chairs already filled me with apprehension. Some of the older political worthies had to be guided to their seats, others, in robes of silk, could just make it unaided. To keep it simple, I made only one suggestion: replace the imported fuel-oil for electricity generation, with local steam coal. Years back, the old coal mine of Nong Son in Quang Nam province, 50 miles up-river from the coast, had been closed when imported fuel oil had become cheaper than coal, a situation now reversed by oil price rises. Our mining engineers reckoned they could put the plant back in operation into a few months. An appreciative murmur ran through the assembly. The commotion kept growing, however, the geriatric smiles disappeared and everyone started to argue the vital point I had missed, how the mine could be militarily defended. It was all to be in vain, however. The enemy, who may well have listened with interest, acted first, in the way they knew best. Six weeks after our meeting, a North Vietnamese division brought the mine permanently under their control, so that nobody could exploit it: too many casualties; end of project.

My successor arrived. Tony Eyles was a sleek executive, gracious with notables and down-to-earth with staff. Reading every file from cover to cover, and coming back for more, he showed that prized attribute of a company executive, an entirely flexible view, which he could direct like a laser-beam, effortlessly, in forward or reverse or three dimensionally over any problem, without bringing the slightest personal conviction to the table. He paid for the gift with a certain greyness of expression, a lack of ability to inspire. In his own mind, he already saw many ways of improving results, now that oil supplies were plentiful again. Travelling by helicopter to war-ravaged outposts and the invariably smiling Shell dealers, he looked absentmindedly at them below, in the down-draft of the rotor blades, before winging back to Saigon. And yet, Eyles was no stranger to upheavals and guerilla war, having survived revolution and sequestration by terrorists in a previous appointment in Guatemala.

For the official re-opening of Nha Be, the Vice-President of the Republic of South Vietnam, Tran Van Huong, drew up with his escort of only two motorcycle outriders. An unassuming, quietly impressive lawyer, dressed for the occasion in a tan uniform to show that he appreciated the weight of military considerations. Our new installation manager, ex-colonel Phuoc, had organised formations of schoolchildren with teachers, singing national songs, and the inevitable bouquet offering by an adorable four-year-old. Labour representatives stood by in ranks. Phuoc did not bother to address Tony's questions on business. Instead, he proudly showed us his new dog patrol, consisting of four alsatians, held on leashes by their handlers, each dog gobbling in one meal the meat rations of an average Vietnamese family for a whole week. When Eyles approached to pat one, the trained dog attacked sharply, dragging his handler on the leash behind him. I did not blame Tony for feeling out of place, remembering my own reactions of a few years before.

We also paid a visit to the Singapore refinery, the fountain-head of our products. A scrap of paper thrown away on the spotless streets already meant a prison sentence in the city-state. At the airport barber's shop, long-haired foreign hippies were awaiting their turn for a regulation hair cut before being let in. But the local Indian population were freely allowed their extravagant religious festivals, as a safety valve, probably in return for supporting the boredom of industrial paradise for the rest of their productive lives. We found our road blocked by a Hindu procession. Young long-haired martyrs in loincloths carried unbelievably painful contraptions fastened by pins to their flesh. Eyes bulging, open mouthed and bleeding, they stumbled along, escorted by ecstatic women with *kohl*-smudged eyes. On the pavements, *fakirs* ran over burning coals. With resignation we left our car and walked, careful to avoid the coals, to the office.

One offshore island was entirely dedicated to our refinery, and our colleague's high-rise office dominated the city itself. The magnificent view through his plate-glass office wall included the whole main island, the sweep of Singapore bay, the shoreline dotted with freighters and junks, and other islands in the wide open ocean. We were his most profitable customer and he took an appropriate time to brief us on the latest developments. So many measures taken at the height of the energy crisis now had to be undone again. It was very tiresome, but it kept him quite extraordinarily busy. For my part, I never even hinted at Singapore's refusal to supply us at the height of the embargo, because recriminations and apologies only poison the atmosphere and slow down action. Nor did we indulge in moral arguments. They delivered oil to us. That Singapore refineries also delivered oil to Chinese tankers, whose owners paid cash and probably conveyed it directly to North Vietnam, did not break their hearts, nor was it my concern. China was obviously short of oil, the Soviet Vladivostok refineries were out of reach, and the US did not interdict supplies to Vietnam; *ergo* it was almost inevitable. If true however, it might be trading with the enemy on a grander scale than anything I had come across in Vietnam. Business in Asia, at least in the oil business, did not lend itself to moralising.

In Vietnam, the change brought by the monsoon was unsettling the weather. Saigon lay in the path of the high-sea monsoons, and suffered the whiplash of their tails. Afternoon rains fell in sheets, followed by unnaturally blue skies and gusts of wind that tried to rip the shutters off the windows.

After signing the hand-over documents, Eyles was in charge, making his first decisions. Like all his predecessors, he needed time to catch on to realities. Over the years, the personnel system had produced the right men at the right moments, Corrie to kick out French colonialism and lock the company into the American supply line, and me to downsize and Vietnamise it in the wake of American withdrawal. All of us would remember our initial enthusiasm and the tempering deceptions that followed. I had begun full of hope, by stretching our resources to take advantage of the ceasefire, to manage refugee settlement and rebuilding schemes, only later to recognise the need for retrenchment and withdrawal. Eyles too would soon recognise the task at hand.

On the night of my farewell reception, the rain came down in torrents. From the terrace, the garden was hidden behind an opaque curtain of noisy water. The steaming floodlights showed an overflowing swimming pool and a river where the path should have been. Most of the guests, whose car engines had not stalled in the submerged streets did not risk driving into the garden, with water cascading across the drive, and returned home to phone their apologies. Braver souls took off shoes, hitched up skirts and waded ashore under umbrellas over improvised gangways to the terrace. It became a noisy party instead of the usual fixed-smiles reception. I regretted the absence of Graham Martin, still unbent and dreaming of a military stalemate, cruising Washington in search of support, one honourable man set against the tide.

When they had all gone, Tony and I sagged in the deep chairs with glasses of brandy in our hands. Sao began to roll down the iron grill, as was his custom when he had had enough of our reflections. Iron shutters might also fall temporarily over Vietnam, we reflected idly. But I had been there long enough to know that if that happened it would only be a temporary phase. The resourcefulness, drive and individualism of the Vietnamese – what public speakers called their 'taste for freedom and free enterprise' – would be bound to prevail.

Next day, refreshed and having paid the servants and surrendered the keys, I became an 'ex-staff-on-transfer', meaning that I could hardly claim to exist at all in the eyes of my ex-colleagues. I considered my diminished condition philosophically, in a warm bath with an iced lemon drink, on my last night in town, and judged that I definitely needed the sailing voyage to bring me back to mankind.

At first light, I slipped out of Saigon aboard my newly-finished yacht *Western Horizons*, the only long-nosed barbarian in a boatload of chattering Chinese workmen from the shipyard, my transfer crew helping me to adjust the equipment. On the river, an escort of two river patrol boats with .50 machine guns insisted on joining us, on orders of Admiral Chonh, giving us more protection for the Rung Sat crossing than our 35,000-ton tankers got. I had not asked for the privilege, but felt the better for it. Overhead, monsoon clouds were hunting through the sky, while down at river level it remained flat calm. Later, a steady breeze sprang up which propelled us under sail until Saigon had become a mere line on the horizon behind us.

Passing Nha Be, a sampan with company staff circled *Horizons* for last snapshots and a shouted farewell. Thereafter, she sailed clear out of the troubled twentieth century into the timeless Rung Sat wasteland. Mangrove swamps and bamboo settlements mirroring in the stream slipped by without a sound. The city Chinese had never seen such silent nature. Dark, wild children, now and then visible among the stakes, gaped at the white sloop, restrained from aiming their arrows at us by our escorting sailors leaning nonchalantly against their machine-guns. By nightfall, even these trusted companions had to peel off, waving farewell and leaving us to face the open sea in the dark on our own.

A Navy lieutenant I had taken on board piloted us expertly by depth soundings over the changing shallows of the lightless estuary towards the Vung Tau naval base. There we moored under its guns. The

Chinese crew, exhausted by the experience, piled into a pair of ancient Renault taxis to return to Saigon. They had finished the boat to the best of their abilities, but frankly I was already glad to see the back of them, as sailing was a chapter in which they had no part.

The remainder of the night I stayed alone on board trying to catch some sleep, while arc-lights were shining through the port holes, rifles were fired and depth charges exploded around us to discourage enemy sappers. The next morning, a patrol boat's violent manoeuvring threw *Horizons* against her fenders and woke me. Then the mosquitoes started to bite. Soon after the arrival of my sailing crew, I found myself staring at the receding shoreline of Vietnam.

PART IV

Year of the Cat

27

Back in the Centre

Oh how secure Europe felt, sitting in a company jet, hopping over the North Sea from one Shell Central Office in London to its other half in the Hague in half an hour. Just the time to tick off a few memos or to talk shop. To me, Central Offices had all the safety and claustrophobia of the womb. When being moved, executives hardly noticed the change of scenery being moved, wrapped up with the same projects and the same experts, with few outside contacts: company drivers to speed them through London traffic in limousines, and at the other end limousines to deliver them home. No need for them to leave the closed circuit at all.

Yet to the bewilderment of these same executives, the outside world sometimes rattled their golden cage with public accusations and demonstrations, especially since the energy crisis. The struggle against the oil companies, 'agents of capitalism', was reaching its climax, and so was the Cold War in Europe.

Had we inadvertently engineered the oil scarcity for our own illegal profiteering purposes? The fire-bombing of our petrol stations and the lenient treatment of the perpetrators by the courts hinted at public sympathy for our accusers. In the past, we had been content to jog along as a moderately successful business, with a return on capital languishing at a modest 7 percent. When, courtesy of OPEC price rises, our return on capital more than doubled in 1973, and further increased to around 24 percent in 1974, it should have been no surprise that the public began to denounce our good fortune.

And what were we to do with the unexpected windfall of cash? To give it back to shareholders was not in Shell's nature. To our technology-driven executives, the answer came as a reflex: double the exploration and production investment in the North Sea, increase oil refining and chemical capacity, as well as embark on a new nuclear venture in the US. Coal, gas and metals divisions went on happy spending sprees too. So did research. We did not precisely endear ourselves to the great public, however, by thus flaunting our new wealth.

Serious complications also arose from our loss of ownership of the oil sources in the Middle East. It had diminished our control over the trade. In the old days, crude oil was produced under a concession system, which had a handful of companies pouring more than 50 percent of revenues into the wide pockets of a few un-democratic governments, ruling within dubious borders.

Now, however, after the nationalisation of our concessions, these local governments, like sorcerers' apprentices, had advanced to become traders of their oil in their own right. Almost inevitably, chaotic conditions came to prevail. The butcher, the baker, Saudi princes and Valery Giscard d'Estaing, President of France, were all jostling for position as new middlemen, anxious to take a cut and conclude their own government-to-government oil-for-weapons barter deals, thus fuelling the fire.

Opposite me in the corporate jet to Rotterdam, the oil trader, whom I shall call John, who had been with me at the Singapore meeting before the oil crisis, and whose opinions faithfully reflected those of other senior executives, was fiddling with his drink. Professionally, John was not too worried by the new arrangements in the Middle East, because the oil had to end up in the same refineries and markets of the established companies anyway, even if the preceding deals had become a bit more tortuous. No, to him it was the big picture that counted, and that had become really encouraging.

Before the oil shock, he argued, the free world had only some $150 billion available for investment each year. Presently, the creation of $100 billion extra in tax levied on the consumer and paid in higher prices to Middle Eastern governments, would lift that to previously unimaginable heights. This was a great boon, because those $100 billion had nowhere to go, except back into Western banks, which would have to channel them into Western investments, because the Arabs themselves could not spend it all at home. The new money flow to the West would lift Western capitalism to the extent that it would eventually win the Cold War. The oil companies and the banks had in effect become major actors in the Cold War. No wonder we had to endure some flak.

Personally, he suggested, I should thank my lucky stars for being back in the Centre again, in Europe where it was all happening. A great turn-around was occurring, a renaissance after the dark ages. He could feel it in his bones. (Was this the same man, I wondered, who had preached such pessimism in Singapore a year earlier?) Workaholics were back in fashion, he exulted. Our silent generation was getting belated recognition. In the fifties, we had enlisted in the armies, but we had also built the industrial complexes, the mindless suburbs and laid the basis for the addiction to hydrocarbons of all of civilised society. We had provided the income for the welfare state in our stubborn concern with defence and material production, paying exorbitant taxes, while behind our backs a smarter younger generation simply enjoyed the fruits. They were not going to fight because they already had everything for free. For them, the sixties were a roaring party of free love, pills, drugs and Woodstock festivals, while we moved awkwardly to the new music, not getting the message at all. We never believed the lyrics, we had no rich fathers. And we, the morons, stayed hooked on technical achievements, like Armstrong putting the first boot on the moon. Our material achievements had been temporarily eclipsed by the civil-rights movements in the US and the rolling wave of student revolts, from Amsterdam, through Paris and Peking, to Kent State University, the last of which, incidentally, sealed the fate of South Vietnam. Like good citizens everywhere, we could only shake our heads at the student disturbances on after-dinner TV, feeling a bit foolish for our preoccupation with physical wealth.

All that had now changed, John continued in full flow. The oil shock had reminded each and every one of us of the hard and brittle technical basis of our existence. Flower power was finished. The businessman in his grey suit had come back into his own, to enjoy recognition in late middle age. The tide had swung. Admittedly, there were still isolated outbreaks of euphoric mass movements, such as the red carnation revolution of Portugal, in which Lisbon thugs had taken over our Shell operating company. But this time we and our workers had kicked them out within days.

John helped himself to another drink from the primitive ice-box on the right-hand side of the plane and offered me some advice for working within the hierarchy. If I wanted to rise, I had to resist the natural tendency to take personal responsibility and to act, as we did in the operating companies. At the Centre, you merely had to position yourself on global issues, avoiding commitment and errors at all cost. Errors are made by individuals in the heat of their enthusiasm. So the recipe at the Centre was for cool consensus. Supreme responsibility had to be diffuse. All advice, therefore, had to be offered in grey language, with plenty of conditional sentences, so that the right decision could emerge without offending any of the originators or recipients. Decisions were built up incrementally at each level for ratification by the top. The sole aim of the 3000-man operation at the Centre was to keep our directors impeccably informed, flexible and relaxed throughout, providing them with the means to strike when the moment was ripe.

Personal engagement was for underlings in operating companies, still having to prove themselves. Massive organisations, like ours, OPEC or the Catholic Church needed gradual adaptation to circumstances more than flair in seizing opportunities in real time. Nobody could beat such big organisations with their central brain, inching forward, like a blind man tapping obstacles gently with a white stick before taking a step. It all made my head spin.

The captain stuck his face around the door to tell us that we were already on the descent to Rotterdam airport, a business airport nearer to the Hague and much faster for transit than Schiphol, Amsterdam. And what would my new job consist of, John kept probing. I had to shrug in reply. As far as I knew, the job had a title, a prefix and a grade, some routine, but hardly a fixed content. I could contribute whatever was needed. Perhaps many jobs at the Centre were like that, I lamely suggested. 'Splendid!' he roared. 'Detailed job descriptions are only for fixing salary scales!'

We watched with a mixture of pride and awe as the plane made its approach over the greatest concentration of oil refining and storage in the world. Man-made islands of geometric design, filled with tanks, pipelines and distilling columns, protected by stone dykes against the water. Little pollution anywhere. Toy super-tankers below us moving in radar-controlled lines to and from Rotterdam harbour. At the business-like airport terminal, we were so quickly processed that within five minutes of touchdown we sat in the fast lane of the motorway to the Hague. The driver handed me a brown envelope with messages from the office and letters from Vietnam.

28

Peaceful Europe

One bright morning in early January 1975, I was walking through the frozen park to the Royal Dutch Shell office in the Hague, the stately office Henri Deterding built well outside the town, but now almost part of it. Wags called it the 'mausoleum' for its mournful entrance hall with the names of employees fallen in two world wars on the walls, and the always-fresh flowers placed there in their loving memory.

Climbing the carpeted marble stairs with the polished brass handrails to the Chairman's first-floor office, I tried to clear my mind of lingering anxiety over Vietnam. The subdued light falling through the stained-glass windows like in a Gothic cathedral did nothing to lift my mood, however. That morning, the radio had announced the fall of the provincial capital Phuoc Binh. A few weeks earlier, in Hanoi, the Soviet chief of staff, General Kulikov, had approved the attack as a last test of American will to help their allies, and if no American reactions were forthcoming, he had agreed for the final assault on the highlands to be launched soon after. I could not know this, and did not want to speculate. Having left Vietnam, I lulled myself with the thought that Generals Phu and Truong were excellent commanders with excellent troops, who would manage things as always before. The meeting with Gerry Wagner now claimed my full attention.

The oil shock had sharpened public awareness of our companies. As a result, the Chairman's own public profile had ballooned from that of a potentially boring company boss, when I first knew him, to that of an overpowering Godfather figure, selling oil supplies to nations at prices they could not refuse. That not altogether benevolent image change had to be managed by ordinary executives, to whom, as to the proverbial butler, the Chairman was rather like the rest of us, dependent on fellow workers to compensate for weaknesses at every turn, although of course he remained an undisputed first among equals.

Contrary to public fantasy, the Chairman could often be just sitting at his desk, playing with a pen-knife and staring out of the window. Most of the creative thinking was done by junior executives and submitted to him after the wrinkles had been ironed out. But he alone could give the go-ahead and massage the egos of the supervisory board, or meet visiting heads of state, and his face alone had come to represent the company in public, although his pronouncements seldom deviated from the written briefings. His TV interviews were deliberately flat. The articles that appeared in the press from his hand were written for him. The decisions were committee decisions.

Nevertheless, his overriding personal ambition was no less than to unlock the international business potential for the good of the world. If it meant taking on the Hydra of socialist doctrine at the grass-roots in word, print or electronic image, so be it. Actually, he had no choice; the fight for the control of the company was put to him. Had he submitted to the current spate of public proposals for workers committees, staff councils, dismemberment and of restrictive codes of conduct elaborated by the United Nations and other high councils against the very existence of multinational businesses like ours, he might as well have handed the office keys to a Kremlin *kommissar*. At least that was the way he saw it. It was war in another guise. To fight it, he needed staff to do the legwork, and that was where I came in, as a member of an informal working-group.

The ironic background was that Group profits had just reached the never-before-attained level of $3 billion, five times higher than the level achieved in 1972. The price rise had increased the value of our 1974 oil stocks by $2.5 billion, in addition to making many of our lame-duck production ventures suddenly highly profitable. In normal times, this should have been good news not just for shareholders but for the world at large, he claimed. However, public anger at such outstanding profitability achieved in a crisis which hurt the rest of the community was a grave concern, he conceded. The public at large felt cheated. Why had elected governments not prevented the price increases? Why were these large multinationals, already arranging large chunks of peoples' lives, now making off with vast wealth to invest according to their own judgement, without being held accountable for the overall social effects?

The public had taken acute fright at our sheer size. We appeared threatening indeed, like the legendary white whale, Moby Dick, surging ahead with barnacles on his hide, broken harpoons sticking in his fat, but with his jaws intact. While not an inaccurate picture, this was an uncharacteristic use of imagery for the bland Wagner. But getting into the theme, I argued that we could ignore most of the media harpoons because the majority of attacks were based on outdated opinion. We had to be positive, and argue on behalf of the future and the favourable changes that were taking place. We had to trust that people would discover for themselves that our results were a good thing, and to their benefit because the free market was finally being allowed to give the right signals.

Public opinion lagged years behind, I opined, now in my stride. Even as we spoke, so soon after the oil crisis, 90 percent of Americans continued to believe that all oil came from Texas, whereas every statistic showed that more than half was imported. We could only try to hasten the inevitable recognition that Americans too were dependent on the global market, from which they could not isolate themselves.

Wagner had a personal reason to warm to this part of the theme. In America, Senator Henry Jackson had been hammering on the 'obscene' profits of the American oil companies while Senator Frank Church was repeating *ad nauseam* that the lifeblood of industrial society cannot be left to such companies. Not surprisingly, our executives began to feel like an endangered species in trying to point out that you could not take the world oil reserves out of Arab hands, nor regulate the prices they charged. Such new realities took time to sink in, and meanwhile each time our Chairman went to board meetings in Houston, he ran the personal risk of arrest. In the topsy-turvy world of legal America, when the State Department asked him to discuss Middle East oil with US competitors, within the framework of the OECD, the anti-trust authorities threatened him with multi-million dollar fines against such compliance. And he simply hated travelling with clouds of lawyers for protection.

During the meeting with Wagner, my eye had been wandering to a painting on the wall, of a peasant shovelling snow on a country road. Not a purposeful worker as Van Gogh would have created, but just an aimless end-of-nineteenth century middle-ground figure, embarked on an endless task. After a while, both of us rose and looked at it from up close with the light at our back. He clearly liked the innocent painting, but I was less sure. As far as the Chairman was concerned the content of my new appointment was settled. He advised me to enjoy myself, by representing him as a sort of expendable first line of defence in public hearings, debates and interviews to which I would be automatically nominated, urging me smilingly to usurp his authority a little, to sharpen my teeth on a few left-wing seminars, to get the hang of the thing.

My day-to-day work was definitely on a more modest level. I joined a department in the Hague as a Vice-President (unusual title in the

Centre because of its hint at operational responsibility). The department had the high-sounding mandate to guide our national operating companies in a free-trading Europe without internal borders. That concept, however, was at least 20 years ahead of its time and therefore unworkable, as I soon realised when I met the compartmentalised world of what passed for the common market. The European Commission itself was still heavily subsidising state-owned companies in government-preferred sectors.

I therefore made it my practical job, as part of an industry effort, to assist the Brussels Commission in the establishment of a common European energy policy. We wanted to make it a minimalist framework, in which civil servants from nine governments and oil companies could work for the first time together, with, rather than against, market forces. We needed more light on the workings of the market and a better exchange of information, because the need for better intergovernmental and industry co-ordination in the next energy crisis was all too evident. Political tolerance of free markets, however, still lagged way behind and I had to argue hard in discussions, sometimes even inside our company and in my own mind.

Our sedate office still breathed outdated fashion, and showed it. There was, for instance, this arrogant concept that in a rich society true art does not need to find a buyer. The state would always provide. The walls therefore dripped with mediocre works by state-supported artists, obtained on the cheap by office services and appreciated by nobody. Most senior executives, however, worked smoothly together, knowing each other intimately from years of overseas operations. In the corridors, they could convey to each other, with one look from their well-worn faces, without slowing their step, how the European business of oil, gas and chemicals was faring. But in true Central Office tradition, they did not run any operations themselves. It was the national operating companies which still ran the refineries, the oil and gas fields and the marketing facilities.

On one occasion, our team was flying to Paris for a budget meeting with the ailing French operating company. The French Chief Executive of Shell Française was a top-of-the-line *polytechnicien*, ex-resistance paratrooper with a Legion d'Honneur, well connected in the best Gaullist tradition. His lieutenants jumped to attention to squash any of our timid suggestions for change. Everyone knew that 5000 German workers shifted the same amount of oil as 10,000 Frenchmen, but until the energy crisis productivity had not mattered, as long as the French state assured profitability. For years, our Chief Executive had been working hand-in-glove with the French Energy Minister, another *polytechnicien*, for the glory of France. Thus we had been obliged to invest in prestige projects, like building the world's largest super-tanker in

France. After its launch by the French Prime Minister and one single voyage, the tanker had just made it to a Norwegian fjord to gather rust.

The 1973 oil shock had knocked such cosy relations between industry and state a little out of kilter, but few of us were able as yet to face the consequences. In particular, we dared not challenge our chief executive, and we approved his expansionary budget for the loss-making company because the pain of cutting down activities and staff numbers could not be imposed by a gaggle of interfering foreign executives on a loyal Frenchman who of course knew best.

Similarly in Sweden, we conformed to the most restrictive rules on private enterprise, with high taxes and worker co-determination to the extent that an office driver carried almost as much weight as the company president. In Belgium, success was recognised to be impossible without a strong stomach for the most Burgundian business lunches of Europe. In Finland, the sauna replaced the boardroom for creating business consensus. In Greece, government's arbitrary lying almost obliged you to do the same. Not to forget oil-rich, isolated Norway, where the national oil company was a protected species and where the legislature took a well-deserved six month's holiday. Faced with such stubborn national heritages, hardly shaken by cross-border competition, the Centre had no alternative but to compromise. Although in 1975 some of those cobwebs were being blown away, the continent seemed more fragmented than when its tribes had been held together through faith and the marriages of kings, with Latin as the common language.

Meanwhile, distracting news of actual doom came through letters and the news. A string of sudden defeats had broken the Vietnamese front. At Ban Me Thuot, the North Vietnamese, emerging from their Cambodian sanctuaries with a five-to-one local advantage, had finally crushed General Phu's luckless 23rd Division. But I was still far from imagining that President Thieu could be so ill-advised as to order an improvised withdrawal from the highlands, which would turn it into the opening disaster of the last campaign. Nor could I believe that brave General Phu and his simple-minded troops, whom I had admired at Pleiku, would be ordered to surrender that city, and never in my wildest nightmares that my friend Phu was to shoot himself a few weeks later.

The news from Vietnam was deeply shocking. From Quang Tri to Quang Nam the South Vietnamese army was crumbling. The élite troops which had defended the Northern region with such confidence, and their commander, General Truong, who had explained his military situation to me with such candid resignation, had all been routed. Their hope was lost and their will broken. Too late they realised that their powerful patrons, the USA, had accepted the conditions for their defeat long before, by forbidding actions against the sanctuaries, by switching off supplies while the Russians kept feeding their own clients. Cambodia's fall seemed near once again, and a whole generation of Vietnamese and Cambodian friends for whose fate I felt answerable, was heading for the deep-freeze. I could hear their voices in the night.

Letters from Vietnam showed the twilight quality of life in Saigon. They described the strangely normal behaviour of neighbours and acquaintances, and the mounting anxieties behind closed oriental faces. They spoke of middle-class people keeping their options open, to flee or not to flee, hidden in themselves, despite endless probing from others about their intentions. Kim Chi casually wrote that she was selling her valuables at knocked-down prices and borrowing millions from her Chinese money-lender at an interest rate of 30 percent per month and judging it fair. Ignoring my pressing advice, she was still working on her farm without a hint that she was ever to consider leaving.

29

A Chinese Encounter

In Europe, the death throes of South Vietnam counted for nothing. The April fields just a few hundred yards from my office were ablaze with red and yellow tulips, and gaudy spinnakers were visible on the inland lakes. My colleagues were full of optimism. In their view, the oil shock had been a salutary bump against the resource limits of the planet, more effective than a won war at bringing it back to reason, and to a better appreciation of our high technology. OPEC had temporarily retreated with its tail between its legs.

Although inflation and unemployment were still high, this was the turning-point. Industry return on investment, in decline since the 1950s, began to pick up once more, under the incentive of making everything, from housing to transport, more energy-efficient. Every sector of industry had received its salutary jolt from increased oil prices. And the youngsters of Silicon Valley, who had so skilfully avoided the Vietnam draft, now showed equal skill in showing how much more could be achieved with less, making themselves overnight millionaires in the process.

The Soviets had only just begun to grasp what had hit them, how the economic and information technology revolution was leaving them high and dry; how the hated multinationals were re-investing in the Third World with the active encouragement of its dispossessed populations and, from the inside, undermining the unproductive Soviet police regimes created at such great expense. Meanwhile, the Soviet wastage of artificially cheap oil and gas at home and in their satellites was spinning out of control, eroding the export capacity of their best hard-currency earner. This made them unable to profit from

OPEC price increases. Just to maintain exports at current levels, oil reserves would have to double, but preventing their decrease alone already stretched their resources to the limit. If Soviet power depended on oil and gas, its decline was clearly on the cards.

The Chinese managed their oil interests quite differently. Coming out of the Cultural Revolution with far lower levels of production, technical knowledge and infrastructure, they had the practical sense to curb ideology in the economic sphere and to catch up with the free world through business alliances with some carefully selected multi-nationals. Their indifference to the colour of the cat who catches the mice was well known. Less known was the fact that the cat's colours were to be the red and yellow of Shell. We had been expelled from Communist China in 1949, and were somewhat surprised when a large delegation of politicians, scientists and technicians from the People's Republic of China, under their Minister for Oil, suddenly appeared on our doorstep in the Hague with the sole purpose of learning our methods and involving us in joint-ventures. In one of the Hague's many Chinese restaurants, the President of Peking University gave a hushed audience of Shell executives his indelible first-hand account of how the Cultural Revolution had destroyed Chinese research and degraded its practitioners. But all that was to come a few years later.

In April 1975, the first signs of forthcoming change in Chinese attitudes came only by hints and smoke-signals. One came from an old companion of Mao's Long March, standing in the glass side-room of a pre-war Dutch country house which had been converted into the Chinese embassy. I found him keeping his distance from the excited buzz of Western businessmen and Chinese aides who were getting a first glimpse of each other on the occasion of a national feast. Still in Mao uniform, he was accepting green tea in porcelain cups from a very young Chinese girl in Western dress. Such personal servants were a traditional tribute to rank and age. I was curious to learn if he had any influence left in South Vietnam while it was being overrun. He was, however, only interested in warning us to exclude Vietnam (of whatever political colour) from our plans for exploration in the South China Sea, as his colleagues had already hinted by their occupation of the Paracelles.

When I asked about North Vietnamese intentions after their inevitable victory, he lowered his tone. The Vietnamese 'dogs', he claimed, had rejected Chinese advice, and had even dared to purge their party of all friends of China. They had now sold themselves entirely to Moscow and the senile Brezhnev. He was sure that a lot of dominos would still have to fall, before the Russians, in their obstinacy, would realise that they had little to show for their billions of dollars of military investment. All over Africa, Russian advisors had already been expelled from Algeria, Ghana, Sudan, Congo and Egypt. Military victory in Vietnam, he predicted, a tragedy for Vietnam's long-term prospects, would once more go to Russian heads and make them pour more billions into military ventures in Somalia, Ethiopia, Angola, Madagascar, Mozambique and South Yemen. But finally, Russia would overreach and bankrupt itself.

Used as I was to the condescending tone of Chinese when talking about other nations, I was surprised that his ideas coincided so closely with ultra-conservative opinion in the West. On a personal level, however, he was clearly in no position to do me any favours in Saigon. Besides, in his world no amicable relations with foreign devils existed anyway. My marginal usefulness to him did not go beyond a discussion of oil exploration prospects in the South China Sea.

This posed an awkward personal dilemma. So far I had been able to tell myself that all my private responsibilities henceforward lay in Europe, and that I had none left in Vietnam. However, in those strange, high-strung days, people in Vietnam still seemed to be able to put life-and-death questions to me casually over the telephone, about their escape plans, trusting, apparently, that as of old I could settle such questions with a flick of the hand. I could not explain to them, and they would not have understood, that in my present position I lacked the means to help them. I was now a cog in a machine. My salary and elegant house were essentially modest.

Vietnam, however, is a bewitching country which keeps those who have ever lived there in its thrall. Against all reasoning, an inner feeling grew that I could not be who I pretended without helping in practice some Vietnamese friends to escape the Communist menace; at least to try and extract those who now seemed unable to help themselves.

I therefore took no notice of the well-meaning protests from the hierarchy, but paid my respects, took my leave, cleared my desk, locked the house and drove my brand new sports car through a late-April blizzard to Brussels airport for the flight to Saigon. As the wipers cleared the snow off the windscreen, the radio was reporting that the advance on Saigon had been halted, pending the re-groupment of Northern military units for the final attack. I counted on that interval to allow me a safe in and out.

30

My Return
Ticket

From Bangkok, where most travellers disembarked, onwards to Saigon, all my co-passengers seemed certifiably insane. Many well-dressed French-speaking Vietnamese men and women of all ages had taken single tickets to Saigon, like moths attracted to a flame. Apparently, some believed in the existence of a 'third force' of intellectuals who could help build Communism with a human face. Air Vietnam stewardesses went around with wads of Kleenex for the women to keep wiping their tears. Blank-faced young men, savagely drinking orange juice, queued up for the toilets. Everyone seemed drawn to their families, hoping to redeem themselves by heroic example.

My claim to rationality consisted of a safe return ticket in my pocket, but colleagues had questioned my sanity too. Beside me, an old medical doctor was going on about his sacred duty to join his family in Saigon, and perhaps soon his ancestors, in view of his advanced age. He came sadly prepared for all eventualities, however, having sown gold taels into the lining of his jacket.

When the door of our wretched little world opened to the damp smell of defeat at the bustling Tan Son Nhut airport, nobody wanted to be the first to descend the ladder into the cauldron below. We felt deflated and useless. In the arrivals hall, customs officers with rubber stamps went about their timeless duties as always, with remarkable aplomb, oblivious of the frenzied families clutching at the new arrivals. A stunning ground hostess in white, with a black band of mourning around her arm, came up to me begging to take her out of the country as a servant. Western men were accosted by respectable Vietnamese women all over town.

Saigon still sported the appearances of its bad old days. No way the soldiery could change its cocky behaviour, even in defeat, or make the modish students drive their scooters any less idiotically, or the market women temper their tongues. Girls still flaunted their bodies. But at the same time, life had lost all meaning; money too. The markets still dealt in piastres from force of habit, but small paper notes lay scattered in the streets, with only urchins bothering to pick up the devalued currency.

I checked my luggage with an overwrought receptionist of the Caravelle Hotel and took an old Renault taxi, with plastic seats and whirring fans, directly to Phan Thanh Gian Street. When the garden doors opened, a servant girl and one emaciated alsatian just stood gaping at me. I burst in and found Kim Chi, smaller than I remembered, facing a window in the long reception hall, without make-up, her hair tied back in a tail. It had grey strands amongst the gleaming black. Her face was now truly reduced to a pharaonic skull, with only the eyes burning with stubborn fire. She could still not accept defeat and had rejected all pleas for her evacuation and all other offers of help. To my horror, she was again living in a chivalrous world of her own, refusing to face the fact that she would be the first to be arrested, humiliated and probably killed, after the take-over.

Since the fall of Ban Me Thuot and the botched withdrawal of General Phu from Pleiku, the hopelessness of further resistance had become apparent to the lowest soldier. When the final attack came, therefore, the élite divisions had rapidly disintegrated, like Napoleon's Imperial Guard at Waterloo, like élite divisions always do when they realise the overall hopelessness of a position. Their generals, with their heads in the clouds of honour and glory, are usually the last to anticipate the collapse of their splendid formations, who braved death at their command only yesterday but who are now running to their wives at the first whisper of an enemy approach. Kim Chi, in spite of her earthy common sense, still belonged to that out-of-touch caste of warlords and generals. She was a pure Northerner by birth and of the strictest old honour tradition as well. Yet I heard her being informed in gruesome detail of the disastrous loss of the first region by her own cousin, General Thi, in an agonising late-night telephone conversation. He had been in command of the best troops of South Vietnam, but had not been able to put up a fight.

Bewildered by orders and counter-orders from President Thieu, alternately to defend and to withdraw from Hue and Da Nang, the General had finally set himself to make a stand to the death. But when he found that his communications had been cut, and that he commanded nobody and nothing any longer, not even a launch for a withdrawal to a navy vessel at sea, he had bolted too. He had to swim to a vessel, where he found his boss, the famous General Truong, true hero of many successful battles, out of his mind, anxiously pacing the deck, trying to marshal no longer existing troops by radio, with the ship already sailing in the opposite direction. The rapidity of the collapse was truly breath-taking. At their arrival in Vungtau, with other stragglers, President Thieu, in an attempt at damage limitation, had ordered the famous Truong into isolation at a military hospital, but had Thi arrested and referred to court-marshal as a scapegoat for his own strategic failure. Then the President suddenly abdicated and fled the country himself. Thi was phoning her from the detention camp to unburden his conscience to someone from the family.

In spite of all these defeats, Kim Chi could not empty her head of romantic chivalrous notions. She now rejected my offer of evacuation out of hand. Instead, she chose to believe General Toan, the commander of the last troops around Saigon, who assured her, in another ghastly telephone conversation, that he would hold the perimeter around Saigon, if only to restore the honour of the ARVN. And indeed he was as good as his word, succeeding in imposing his will on his troops for a last stand, when all others had fled. That particular battle was still raging as we spoke.

Nhung, my ex-secretary, had married an American official. The couple could now leave together, and we celebrated their honeymoon departure to the US with lukewarm champagne. And then, although the reappearance of his predecessor cannot have been all that welcome, Tony agreed to review his staff evacuation plan with me. Most expatriate staff were already leaving by commercial airlines. The evacuation of endangered local personnel with their families from a war-zone was also normal practice in Shell, but not on the scale needed here. He had only been involved in a small exercise in Latin America. The volume of advice now spewing forth over the telex wires from London almost prevented him from lifting his head to the size of the problem. Some 20 families had to be on the North Vietnamese death-list. These Shell managers were leaders in their communities, and up till now the communists had always picked up and shot such individuals as soon as they found them. They would obviously have to leave. Others, under less of a threat, would have to make their own choice. A small tanker was standing by for them in the Saigon River. No other company was even remotely going to the same lengths. American banks simply abandoned their Vietnamese personnel, having no tradition or apparent pride in these matters. Even the American embassy and the CIA, perhaps believing for too long in a negotiated exit, and although trying hard to get vulnerable Vietnamese out, finished leaving many behind in the turmoil. Moreover, they forgot to delete the names and qualifications of a million

South Vietnamese (military and civilian) 'collaborators' from the abandoned computer files.

I argued desperately with Eyles for one of us to stay through the take-over of Saigon, in a safe refuge, like the French embassy or the Grall hospital, to be able to represent our interests afterwards with the new government. It would have made little difference. In the end, Eyles flew out on one of the last helicopters, leaving a wizened old Vietnamese accountant, Mr Tao, in nominal charge of the company. After the North Vietnamese marched in, they would get rid, in rapid order, of their own Southern shadow government, the GRP, of the Buddhist *bonzes* who had courageously opposed Thieu, of any remaining 'third force' intellectuals and of our hapless accountant, Tao. Our entire investment, like that of all American companies, would be taken over without compensation, although a claim would be lodged against the government which will undoubtedly lie dormant for many years to come.

Nobody seemed to sleep in those feverish last days of Saigon. I kept phoning the Shell outposts in the North, where district managers were leaving through jungle, over congested roads, or by sea. The South was not under attack, but the district manager in Can Tho was preparing a boat for the evacuation of his own family, as well as for the disorganised American consular staff. Together they had to run the gauntlet of Vietcong and disaffected ARVN and Navy units everywhere. As I phoned, I got the feeling of the circle around us contracting by the hour. The telephone kept operating for a short while after the fall of territories, then it would fall silent. In the end, I flew back heartbroken, having achieved little, a week before the Communist tanks rolled into downtown Saigon.

*   *   *

Helplessly we watched in our homes the helicopter evacuation from the screaming turmoil of Saigon's rooftops live on TV. It seemed the world had turned into one big *voyeur*'s eye, observing in excruciating detail the battle-wary aircraft-carriers ploughing the waves off Vung Tau, turning away overloaded refugee boats with women and children, often zooming in on exhausted dignitaries, alighting from helicopters, dignitaries I had known under different circumstances. They stumbled onto the deck in an endless stream. Finally frail old Ambassador Graham Martin himself appeared, clutching an American flag from his embassy, saluted and supported by freshly-shaven admirals before being bundled away, off camera. Once in a while, the TV eye would take a little time to pan over the abandoned Vietnamese, the hopeless ones.

Epilogue

After the fall of Saigon, a tidal wave of refugees overwhelmed East Asia, spreading to Europe and the US. Of course, many of my friends and colleagues were amongst them, and two million 'boat people' who escaped Vietnam in later years.

Tran Ngoc Giu, our influential and canny personnel manager, had to flee his country for the second time following his earlier retreat from Hanoi after the French debacle in 1954. He was one of the last to leave Saigon, and eventually found his way to Canada, where he continued to work for Shell. After a number of years he retired to Montreal, Quebec, a patriarch surrounded by his family.

Ex-colonel Le Van Phuoc, our pugnacious Danang district manager, who had such an ingenious hold over the military high command of the Northern region, moved to Paris. Like many other Vietnamese managers, he found employment in Shell Française and settled in the large Vietnamese community in France. He and his wife operated a Shell service station on the Paris ring-road with characteristic boundless energy. As a result, he now navigates a giant Mercedes through the impenetrable Paris traffic.

Mike Precious, our wise and laid-back English marketing director, also moved to Paris into a senior management role in Shell Française. Sadly, he died shortly afterwards.

Mike Corrie, my predecessor in Saigon, left Shell after it became clear that the company could not accommodate his entrepreneurial flair. He became an American citizen, and decided to make 'some real money' with an international oil trader in New York.

James Eyles, my successor, spent much of his time after Vietnam helping to resettle the scores of Shell Vietnam refugees who fled the country. It was a daunting and depressing task, and he was glad of his next assignment, running Shell operations in Latin America and the Caribbean, from where he eventually retired.

Pham Kim Ngoc, the South Vietnamese Minister of the Economy, who flamboyantly graced many a dinner in my house packing a pistol in his back pocket, and who was my main intermediary with the government, became a successful banker in Virginia.

Nguyen Thi Nhung, my highly effective secretary, whose marriage to an American official I attended during my last trip to Saigon, now lives in Singapore with her husband. Together they travel extensively in Asia, and also maintain an elegant house in what is now Ho Chi Minh City. I don't know if she still plays *mah-jong*.

Trung, the operations manager, who resigned in frustration when his efforts to halt the oil thefts at Nha Be failed, simply disappeared. I failed to trace him, and sometimes wonder about his fate and that of his girlfriend, our telephone operator.

Ted Serong, the ex-commander of the Australian brigade and military guru to President Thieu, who expressed his sensible views of the war to no avail, went back to Australia and his roots, still writing and corresponding with professional friends across the globe.

Elsworth Bunker, the ancient and imposing US Ambassador in Saigon, retired with honour and died in 1984, ninety years old and satisfied to the last with his major role in the 'just war'.

Graham Martin, his charismatic successor in Saigon, had a troubled time after his return to the US. America's failure in the war deeply affected him, and his reputation suffered under the onslaught from his former underlings. His health declined, and he died in 1990.

Tom Polgar, the CIA station chief, did not get the promotion to a top job within the agency that his predecessors had received as a matter of course following their tour in Vietnam. He soldiered on with the agency, but retired before long, a victim, like so many others, of his country's defeat.

Charles Whitehouse, US Ambassador to Laos, also had a curtailed career, and faded into retirement after his South East Asia posting.

V.E. ('Vee') Vizard, my enigmatic superior at Shell Centre, retired peacefully in England.

Gerry Wagner, after stepping down from his top post at Shell in 1977, was instrumental in helping the Dutch government to transform the Dutch economy from a social democratic to a free market liberal one. He lives in Wassenaar, a leafy suburb of the Hague.

And Kim Chi. She managed to escape on her own from Saigon by the very last commercial flight. Air France, bless them, ran mercy flights to the end, right alongside the chaotic military traffic. The Saigon Air France manager had accepted her valueless piastres with a straight face in return for a priceless ticket to Paris. She only carried a suitcase, a diplomatic passport of the defunct Republic of South Vietnam and a jewellery box. Eventually she moved to be with her family in the large Vietnamese community in Orange County, Los Angeles, where she could readily imagine herself in Vietnam. She still has her preference for driving around in a large old Cadillac.

And what of Vietnam itself? It continues to be the enchanting land of pagodas, wide placid rivers, mysterious villages, blue mountained horizons and beaches washed by the emerald sea. Its 80 million souls – amongst the poorest populations in East Asia – now live in peace. But better times continue to elude them.